HOME CARE IN EUROPE

This study was commissioned by the European Association of Organizations for Home Care and Help at Home and funded by the Dutch Foundation for Research and Development of Community Health Care (*Stichting Onderzoek en Ontwikkeling Maatschappelijke Gezondheidszorg: STOOM*).

Home Care in Europe

A country-specific guide to its organization and financing

edited by
JACK B.F. HUTTEN
ADA KERKSTRA
Netherlands Institute of Primary Health Care (NIVEL)

© Jack B.F. Hutten and Ada Kerkstra 1996

Published by
Arena
Ashgate Publishing Limited
Gower House
Croft Road
Aldershot
Hants GU11 3HR
England

Ashgate Publishing Company
Old Post Road
Brookfield
Vermont 05036
USA

British Library Cataloguing in Publication Data

Home Care in Europe: Country-specific Guide
to its Organization and Financing
  I. Hutten, Jack B.F. II. Kerkstra, Ada
  362.14094
ISBN 1 85742 336 4

Library of Congress Catalog Card Number: 95-83049

Printed and bound in Great Britain by
Hartnolls Limited, Bodmin, Cornwall

Contents

Preface

This book gives a systematic overview of the organization and financing of home care in the fifteen countries of the European Union.

This study was commissioned from the *NIVEL* foundation in Utrecht (the Netherlands) by the *European Association of Organizations for Home Care and Help at Home* in Brussels (Belgium). The Dutch foundation for Research and Development of Community Health Care (*Stichting Onderzoek en Ontwikkeling Maatschappelijke Gezondheidszorg: STOOM*) funded the project.

The authors would like to express their gratitude to all those who participated in this study. We would also like to thank Mrs Brigit Sluijk and Mrs Bernadette Kamphuys for the wordprocessing and lay-out, and Mr Paul van der Heijden for his help with the literature search.

Jack B.F. Hutten
Ada Kerkstra

A cross-national comparison on home care in Europe
Summary of the findings

Ada Kerkstra & Jack B.F. Hutten

The European Association of Organizations for Home Care and Help at Home has commissioned the Netherlands Institute of Primary Health Care (NIVEL) to carry out an international comparative study on home care in the member states of the European Union. The purpose of this study is to provide a systematic overview of the way home care is organized and funded in the fifteen countries. In the study, home care has been restricted to nursing care at home and home help services.

In this chapter firstly, the background and the methods of the study are described. Secondly, a cross national comparison is made on the main trends in the financing and organization of home care in the European Union based on the data collected in the separate countries. Finally, some problems in home care that arise in many countries are discussed. In the cross-national comparison, the situation of home care in each country is generalized, neglecting all kinds of variations within a country, despite the fact that in some countries the differences between regions are very large. In chapters 1 to 15, however, a detailed description of the organization and financing of home care in each separate country is given.

Ada Kerkstra & Jack B.F. Hutten

1   Background and research questions

Information on home care in the member states is needed because of a number of important developments in Europe.

The Unification of Europe. The Treaty of Maastricht in 1992 was an important step towards a greater integration of the countries within the European Union (EU). The Union which started as a purely economic organization called the European Economic Community (EEC), now also finds itself in a process of mutual co-operation and integration of policies in other areas such as education, culture, social security and health care. Consequently, information about the present situation in home care services is required to improve communication and co-operation among home care organizations as well as among policy makers at European Union level. In addition, the increasing integration of the member states is also reflected in the extended opportunities for nurses to work in other countries (free movement of people within Europe). Although there are EU guidelines concerning the education and training of nurses, it is also important for a country to know the organizational structure in which the foreign nurse actually worked in her/his own country, which job she/he did and how she/he was paid.

Increasing demand. Nearly all countries of the European Union are being confronted with an steady increase of the percentage of the elderly in their populations. The proportion of people over 80, in particular, is increasing rapidly [1,2]. This leads to a rise in the demand for professional home care which is enforced by the fact that the role of informal carers, such as family members and friends, is decreasing in most of the countries. Smaller families, a growth in women's employment and an increasing number of elderly single people are the main causes of this development [3].

Policy of substitution. A second common problem is the development of health care expenditure. Owing to an increase of the costs of health care, governmental policies are increasingly focused on home care instead of institutional care (both residential care for the elderly, and hospital care for the sick). The aim is to let the elderly stay in their own homes as long as possible and to limit the length of stay in hospitals [3,4].

The changing nature of home care. Besides a quantitative growth of the demand for home care, there are also important changes in the content of the care provided. Because of epidemiological developments, the policy to substitute home care for hospital care and the increase in opportunities to provide technically advanced medical treatments at home, the nature and complexity of the home care is changing.

Definition of home care
There are, of course, differences among the countries in the exact definition of home care. When these different national concepts are used as a starting point for research, it is scarcely possible to provide a systematic overview and international comparison. Accordingly, we had to use our own definition and restrictions. Home care is restricted to the care provided at home by professional home nursing organizations and home help services. Other professionals providing home care like general practitioners, occupational therapists, physiotherapists, etc. are beyond the scope of this study. The role of the general practitioner will only be mentioned when his/her role is relevant with regard to the funding of home nursing.

As a result, the study concerns two disciplines: home nursing and home help services. Home nursing services include rehabilitative, supportive, promotive or preventive and technical nursing care. The emphasis is mainly on the nursing of sick people at home. Other possible community nursing activities are not included, e.g. preventive mother and child health care, psychiatric care, midwifery, school health nursing and occupational nursing. This means that for instance in the United Kingdom only district nursing is considered. Home help services are defined as housework, such as shopping, cooking, cleaning, and administrative 'paperwork' (filling in forms, paying bills). Activities such as socializing or going for a walk and the delivery of personal care (i.e. help with bathing and dressing) are also considered as part of home help services. However, organizations exclusively concerned with one aspect, such as meals-on-wheels or gardening services, are excluded.

For an overview on two specific subjects in home care, i.e. experiments on 'hospital care at home' and rehabilitation technology in home care in Europe, we refer the reader to two recent other studies [7,8].

The main purpose of this research is to provide a systematic overview of the organization and financing of home care in the European Union. In order to structure the study, the following research questions were formulated.

1. How are home nursing and home help services organized in the fifteen member states of the European Union?
   a. What organizations provided these kinds of services?

3

b. What kind of tasks are performed by the home nursing and home help services?

c. What are the relations between home nursing and home help services in the provision of home care?

2. How are the home care provided by home nursing and home help services funded in the fifteen member states of the European Union?
   a. What is the financial contribution of the central government, local authorities, insurance companies and clients/patients themselves?
   b. Do home care organizations have to meet special conditions in order to be funded?
   c. How are the clients/patients insured for the costs of home care? Are special conditions and/or co-payment required?

3. Are there specific problems and recent developments with the organization and financing of home nursing and home help services?

2   Methods

Following earlier research in this field [5], three complementary research methods were used in this project:
- desk research;
- a comprehensive postal questionnaire to experts on home nursing and home help services in each country;
- interviews with experts in nine countries for additional information.

Research commenced with an investigation of the literature that was available in the files of NIVEL, the Utrecht University and the international database medline. This largely provided a general description of the health care system in each country. Broadly speaking, there were only a limited number of references to our research topic. Special attention was paid to two studies on home care in different countries. First, Verheij and Kerkstra [5] studied the home nursing in nine countries. This study included the following member states of the EU: Belgium, (West)-Germany, Finland, France, the Netherlands and the United Kingdom. Secondly, the book 'Home care for older people in Europe' edited by Jamieson [6] provided extended descriptions of the way home help services for the elderly were organized and financed in seven countries of the EU: Belgium, Denmark, (West)-Germany,

4

France, Italy, the Netherlands and the United Kingdom. This means that there was no specific information on home care available for Austria, Greece, Ireland, Luxembourg, Portugal, Spain and Sweden. Information from the other countries also needed to be updated because major changes had recently occurred.

Experts on home nursing and/or home help services were contacted in all countries. Preference was given to people engaged in research into home care or involved in home care policy, both at the governmental or professional level, because it was important that they were able to provide a national overview. The experts were identified by means of:

- personal contacts of NIVEL: e.g. from earlier research in this field and participation in conferences about this subject;
- contributions to the literature on home care: e.g. participants in the studies of Nijkamp et al., Jamieson, and Verheij and Kerkstra [4,5,6];
- members of the European Association of Organizations for Home Care and Help at Home.

Potential experts received a letter asking them to participate or asking whether they knew others who were able to provide the information required. The first objective was to find one expert on home nursing services and one expert on home help services in each country. However, in some countries one expert for both kind of services was sufficient, and in other countries more experts were required. A complete list of all participants is given in Appendix 1.

The questionnaires, in English, were sent to all experts. There were separate questionnaires for home nursing and home help services. The questionnaires were in two parts. Part one contained questions on the organization of home nursing or home help services. Topics discussed were the organizational structure, the type of nurse or home help working in home care, the patients or clients, and the way services were provided. Part two contained questions on the financial aspects, e.g. the funding of the home care organizations, the salaries of the nurses and home helps, the insurance system and (co)-payments by patients or clients.

To allow comparison of the information from the fifteen countries, one reference date was chosen -the end of december 1993- unless important changes had taken place in 1994. When quantitative information was required, concrete and the *most recent* figures based on official statistics or research results were preferred. However, if such published information was not available in the country, participants were asked to make their own estimate for 1993.

In addition, experts in Austria, Denmark, Finland, France, Germany, Italy, Luxembourg, Sweden and the United Kingdom were visited personally by one of the researchers to collect additional information, e.g. about recent developments.

After all information had been collected, a draft chapter of home care in each country was written and returned to the national experts for correction and additions.

It is important to note that there are differences among countries in the type and amount of information. In some countries, it was hard to get data at a national level. Because there are large differences within the country and for a lack of organizations or institutions collecting statistical data on home care.

3   Home care from a cross-national perspective

Nowadays, all fifteen member states of the European Union have organizations for home nursing as well as for home help services, although in Greece and Italy the organization of home care is still in its infancy. In many parts of these countries there are no home nursing or home help services available. In all countries home nursing is part of the health care system, whereas home help services in most countries are part of the social services. In Sweden, since 1992, as part of the reform of the health care system, home nursing will no longer belong to primary health care but to the social services. In some regions of Italy home nursing care is also provided within the social services. Consequently, home nursing and home help services are financed in a different way.

3.1   The financing of home care

Funding of home nursing organizations
In all countries studied, home nursing organizations were usually non-profit. In some countries, however, cost-containment measures include the introduction of competitive elements in the health care system. This may mean the advent of a for-profit sector in home nursing too.

Two funding models for home nursing organizations can be distinguished.

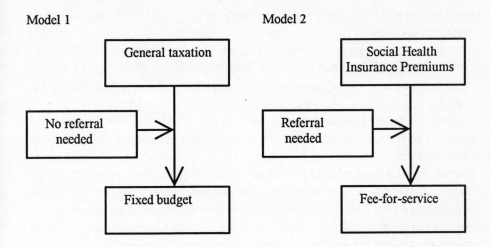

Figure 1
Two models of funding home nursing organizations in the European Union

In the first model, home nursing is mainly financed from general taxation. The home nursing organizations receive a fixed budget from the central government or local authorities. The budget generally depends on the number of inhabitants or of the elderly in the catchment area or on the number of staff. In this model, patients have direct access to the home nursing organization, that means that no referral of a doctor is needed. This is the main model in Denmark, Ireland, Italy, Portugal, Spain, Sweden and the United Kingdom.

However, the funding system in the United Kingdom is undergoing a significant change. In the old system, model 1 is applied, i.e. the District Health Authorities receive a fixed budget based on the number of inhabitants and the demography of the population. In the new system, the funding of the new Community Trusts is based on the services that they deliver to patients. This means a shift from fixed budget funding to a fee-for-service reimbursement. At present both systems co-exist.

In the second model home nursing is largely financed through a social health insurance scheme. In these countries the premiums for this compulsory schemes are paid by employees and/or employers. In this model home nursing organizations are reimbursed on a fee-for-service basis. To receive reimbursement, a medical referral is required. This is the main model in Austria, Belgium, France, Germany and Luxembourg.

There are various types of reimbursement on a fee-for-service basis. In the most simple type, reimbursement takes place on the basis of a list of nursing activities (nomenclature) and states the price of these activities. This price can be reimbursed to the home nursing organization or to the patient. This method is part of the reimbursement system in Austria, Belgium, Luxembourg and France. In these countries mainly technical nursing procedures are reimbursed and hardly any preventive or psychosocial activities. Especially in Austria and in Luxembourg only technical nursing procedures prescribed by a doctor are reimbursed. In these countries, more basic nursing care like bathing and help with getting out of bed is not reimbursed and has to be paid by the patients themselves. However in Luxembourg, people living at home who need care receive as partly compensation a monthly government allocation and in Austria, since 1993, everyone who is in need for home care for more than six month can apply for an attendance allowance (*Pflegegeld*) by the municipality.

Reimbursement can also take place, based on the number of home visits. Here a distinction can be made between various types of home visits according to the type of care that is delivered during these visits. This is the case in Germany, where a distinction is made between *Grundpflege*, which involves mainly personal hygiene care, and *Behandlungspflege*, concerning technical nursing procedures as a support for medical treatment. However in 1995 in Germany the funding system is changed. Patients are categorized in three levels of need for nursing. The home nursing organization receives a reimbursement per patient per month according to the level of care dependency of the patient. There is a maximum allowance for each category. Furthermore, it is also possible to provide a budget to the patient him/herself, allowing him/her to buy his own home care.

A third type of fee-for-service reimbursement is based on the number of days of care. This is part of the system in Belgium as far as heavily or moderately dependent patients are concerned. The amount reimbursed varies with the level of care dependency of the patient.

In France, a special form of the fixed budget method exists in addition to the fee-for-service system. Here the organization is authorized by the Health Insurance funds to care for a fixed number of patients under two schemes: 'Hospitalization at home', under this scheme most patients are discharged from hospitals, and 'Elderly care at home'. Patient's reimbursement is about three times as high for 'Hospitalization at home'.

Finally, in Finland, Greece and the Netherlands a mixture of the two models is used. Home nursing in Finland is funded from general taxation and the health centres which provide nursing care receive a yearly fixed budget from the municipalities, but patients have to be referred by a general practitioner. In Greece no referral of a doctor is needed, but only the home nursing organizations of the National Health Services and the Hellenic Red Cross receive a fixed budget; private organizations are reimbursed on a fee-for-service basis. In the Netherlands, home nursing is financed by a compulsory social health insurance scheme, but the home nursing organizations receive a 'fixed' budget based on the number of personnel, and no referral from a doctor is needed to receive home nursing care. However, in the near future the funding system will be changed i.e. the budget will be based on the number of hours of care provided.

Funding of the home help organizations
With the exception of Greece, organizations for home help services in all countries are to some extent funded or subsidized by the central government (sometimes as part of public insurance), local authorities, based on central or local taxation, or by both (table 1).

Table 1
Funding of home help organizations in the European Union *

Local authorities	Central government	Insurance
Austria	Belgium	France (partly)
Denmark (partly)	Denmark (partly)	Germany (partly)
Finland (partly)	Finland (partly)	Spain
France (partly)	Luxembourg (partly)	
Germany (partly)	Ireland	
Luxembourg (partly)	Italy	
Sweden (partly)	Portugal	
United Kingdom	The Netherlands	
	Sweden (partly)	

---

*   In Greece home help services are not funded by the authorities or insurance schemes

In the Scandinavian countries, Denmark, Finland and Sweden, the home help services are financed through local and national taxation. In Sweden home help is mainly financed through local taxation (75%), the contribution of the central government is 17%, whereas in Finland 46% is financed through state subsidies and 46% through municipal taxes. The municipalities or local communities are responsible for the services and in the three countries they have some freedom to allocate budgets. In Austria home help services are subsidized by the province and municipality. In France, home help services for the elderly with low incomes is financed by the *départements* (30% of the budget) whereas services to clients with a higher income are reimbursed by private insurance companies (45% of the budget). In Germany, only home help provided by *Sozialstationen* in addition to nursing care is reimbursed by the public health insurance companies (Health Insurance fund). Other services, including the services provided by the *Mobilen Sozialen Hilfsdienste* receive some budget from the local authorities based on the number of staff and the number of hours of service provision. Home help services in Luxembourg are financed by the Ministry of the Family (40-50%) and by the municipality (not more than 20%). In the former United Kingdom system, the local authorities were responsible for home help services. They received funding by general taxation. The new system largely involves local authorities buying blocks of home help from independent agencies. The number of hours bought and provided varies enormously across the country. It is estimated that in this transition period some 50% of home help agencies are exclusively for-profit while the remainder are voluntary or still run by local authorities.

Home help services in Belgium, Ireland, Italy, the Netherlands and Portugal are funded by the central government by central taxation. In Belgium, this involves 75% of the costs of home help services and the subsidy is based on the number of clients, home helps and cleaners. The number of hours of home help that can be reimbursed is fixed per organization. Public funding of the home help services in Ireland takes the form of a fixed budget which is negotiated from year to year, based on assumptions about the number of home help organizers, the estimated number of clients served and historical criteria such as the given pay rates for a particular Health Board. These latter vary greatly for home helps and to a lesser extent for home help organizers. The social services of the local authorities in Italy are for about 50% financed through general tax revenues. The state contribution is distributed among the local authorities by the regions. The amount of subsidies is based on the number of potential users, the actual users, the available personnel and the functions of the social services. In some regions, local authorities contract out the home help services to private organizations, the social co-operatives. These private organizations are reimbursed on the number of hours that home help is delivered and receive no structural funding. In the Netherlands, since 1 January 1989, about 90% of the costs of home help services have been financed by a system of public insurance based on the General Act on Exceptional Medical Expenses (AWBZ). The premiums are collected through taxes by the central government. The organizations receive a fixed budget based upon the number of inhabitants in the catchment area and the age distribution of inhabitants. In Portugal, the Ministry of Employment and Social Security provides a financial contribution to public as well as private non-profit home help organizations. The budget of each organization is based on the number of clients and types of services provided.

As part of the social services in Spain, the costs of home help services are covered by public insurance. For instance, in the zone of influence of *INSERSO*, about 90% home help services are funded by social welfare administration and the allocated budget is based on the number of hours of care delivered.

Finally, in Greece the home help services delivered by the Hellenic Red Cross and the Orthodox Church are funded by their own resources and from voluntary contributions. The costs of home help from private organizations have to be paid by the clients themselves.

Co-payments by the clients
In the majority of the member states there is no co-payment for home nursing, that is home nursing services are usually free of charge or are reimbursed by the patients' health insurance. Table 2 shows that in Denmark, Germany, Ireland, Portugal, Spain and the United Kingdom patients do not have to pay for home nursing. In Belgium and the Netherlands only small membership fees have to be paid to the home nursing organization. The membership fee in the Netherlands is about NLG 50 a year per family and in Belgium the membership fee of the White/Yellow Cross varies between BEF 500 and 1000 per family per year. Furthermore, in Belgium and France co-payment depends on the type of insurance of the patient. However, in these countries most people are additionally insured and therefore do not have to pay.

Table 2
Co-payment for home nursing in the European Union

No co-payment required	Sometimes co-payment required	Co-payment required
Denmark	Austria	Belgium
Germany	(dependent on type of care)	(membership fee)
Ireland	France	Finland
Portugal	(dependent on insurance)	Greece
Spain	Italy (dependent	Netherlands
United Kingdom	on type of organization)	(membership fee)
	Luxembourg	Sweden
	(dependent on type of care)	

As mentioned before, in Austria and Luxembourg co-payment is required for general basic nursing care, but not for technical nursing care prescribed by a doctor. In Italy it depends on the type of organization, whether or not co-payment is required. Home nursing provided by the local health units of the National Health Services is free of charges, whereas for home nursing provided by the social services of the communities and by private organizations, co-payment is required. The level of co-payment is income-related and varies between the communities because the amount is determined by the local authorities. In some communities no co-payment is required.

Finland, Greece and Sweden are the only countries where all patients have to pay fees themselves. For occasional nursing care in Finland, a fee of FIM 30 per visit by a nurse is charged. Concerning a longer episode of care, all patients have to pay a percentage of the costs themselves. The level of co-payment depends on monthly income and the size of the family and varied, in 1994, from 11 to 35%. In Greece for all nursing services at home an co-payment of about 20% of the costs is required. With regard to co-payment in Sweden a distinction must be made between home nursing care provided by county councils (health care) and by the municipalities (social services). In the first situation, patient's fees for home nursing care are a part of a general co-payment scheme for primary health care (with a maximum amount of SEK 1,600 a year in 1994). However, this also includes other kinds of primary health care such as dental care and pharmaceutics. The exact amount charged per home nursing visit can differ between the regions. It is estimated that the average is about SEK 50. The fees are not income-related. The municipalities providing home care can operate different co-payment schemes for home nursing activities. Sometimes they are included in the total home care fees (including also home help) and it is also possible that the municipalities include the fees in the health care payment system which is mentioned above.

In contrast to home nursing, in most countries co-payment for home help services is required, mostly related to the income of the family and sometimes also to the composition of the household (table 3).

Table 3
Co-payment for home help services in the European Union

Country	co-payment	average % of total costs
Austria	yes, dependent on income	13
Belgium	yes, dependent on income and household composition	20
Denmark	no	
France	not below a certain income, otherwise dependent on old age insurance	
Finland	yes, dependent on income and household composition	11-35
Germany	not for home help in addition to home nursing, otherwise yes	10 *(Sozialstationen)* 20 (other)
Greece	yes, for private organizations full amount of costs	20
Ireland	yes, dependent on the Health Board	10
Italy	yes, dependent on the means of the family	50
Luxembourg	yes, dependent on income	30
The Netherlands	yes, dependent on income and household composition	10
Portugal	yes, dependent on income	n.a.
Spain	yes, dependent on income	10
Sweden	yes, dependent on income and hours of care	n.a.
United Kingdom	yes, different systems	20

Denmark is the only country in which the home help services are usually free of charge, there is only some co-payment for acute home help of non-permanent character (usually for younger persons after accidents), and for additional services like gardening.

In the United Kingdom the arrangements about co-payments vary among the local authorities because there are no national guidelines. In some municipalities each client pays the same amount regardless of the means available, in other municipalities payment is according to income or to the means available, while in yet other municipalities no co-payment is required. In Ireland the amount of co-payment varies among the Health Boards and is also influenced by the negotiating abilities of the clients.

In Germany clients have to pay for the home help services of the *Mobilen sozialen Hilfstdienste* and if the home help is not in addition to home nursing. And in Greece co-payments (for the full costs) are only required by private organizations, not for the services of the Red Cross and the Orthodox Church.

Finally, Table 3 shows that if co-payment is required, the co-payments contribute 10 to 20% of the budget for home help services in the countries. Only in Luxembourg is this contribution about 30% and Italy even about 50%.

3.2 The organization of home care

Organizational structure of home nursing
As mentioned before, in all fifteen member states of the European Union home nursing is part of the health care system. Only in Sweden, since 1992, as part of the reform of the health care system, home nursing will no longer belong to primary health care, but to the social services. Although home nursing belongs to health care in the European Union, there are large differences between the member states both in terms of the history of home nursing and the way it is organized. In Belgium, the United Kingdom, Denmark, Finland, Ireland and the Netherlands home nursing already has a long tradition and has been developed many years ago, whereas in some other countries like Austria, Italy, Spain, Greece, Luxembourg and Portugal home nursing only developed in the last fifteen years or is still being developed. In some countries home nursing has a religious background. For example in (West-) Germany; this can still be seen in the system of umbrella organizations each with its own religious affiliation. But in e.g. home nursing

14

became the responsibility of the local government at a relatively early stage. France, Spain, Italy and especially Greece do not yet have home nursing in every region of the country.

Related to the differences in financing of home nursing, there are also differences in the organizational structure of home nursing between the member states. The countries differ e.g. with respect to the number of different organizations that provide home nursing (Table 4).

Table 4
Organizational structure of home nursing in the European Union

Mainly one type of organization	Mainly two types of organizations	Three or more types of organizations
Denmark	Belgium	Austria
Finland	France	Greece
Ireland	Germany	Italy
The Netherlands	Luxembourg	
Portugal	Spain	
Sweden		
United Kingdom		

In seven countries, Denmark, Finland, Ireland, the Netherlands, Portugal, Sweden and the United Kingdom, home nursing is provided by mainly one type of organization. As mentioned before, in all of these countries the community nursing organizations receive a fixed budget, although the Netherlands and the United Kingdom are in a transition period towards a fee-for-service funding. In Denmark home nursing is provided by the municipalities (the local communities) by the same department as home help services. At national level the association of communities negotiates with the nurses' association about general guidelines for the relationship between the number of head nurses, nurses and assistant nurse at community level. In Finland health care is also mainly the responsibility of the municipalities. The actual home care is provided from health centres. The local authorities appoint a health board which put a health manager in charge of the health centre. In Ireland home nursing is provided by public health nurses employed by statutory Health Boards, which operate in eight geographical areas. In the Netherlands home nurses are employed by the so-called Regional Cross

Associations or Home Care Organizations. The Cross Associations are members of the umbrella organization The National Association for Home Care which determines policy on the national level. In Portugal the National Health Service covers the whole country with a network of health centres. Home nursing is provided by nurses employed by the health centres. In Sweden the county councils were responsible for home nursing. The care was mostly delivered from primary health care centres. However, The Care of the Elderly reform in 1992 moved the responsibility for the care for the elderly, including home nursing, towards the municipalities. At the end of 1994, in about 50% of the counties home nursing has already been delegated to the municipalities, and this reform process is still going on. As a consequence of this reform, home nursing becomes a part of social services and will belong to the same organization as the home help services. Finally, in the United Kingdom home nursing is also part of the National Health Service and is provided by the community unit of the District Health Authorities or since the reform of the National Health Services in 1990 by the Community Trusts.

In three countries, Belgium, France and Germany, home nursing is provided by mainly two types of organizations. As we have seen before the home nursing organizations in these countries are reimbursed on a fee-for-service basis. In Belgium the largest organization is the White/Yellow Cross which covers the whole country and performs about 50% of all home nursing activities. The much smaller organization is Solidarity for the Family, which provides both home nursing and home help services. Besides these two organizations an increasing number of independent nurses are working in private practices. It is estimated that about 40% of the market is covered by independent nurses. In France the majority of home nursing activities is provided by private non-profit organizations. About one third is delivered by the municipalities. And in addition, there is a large number of independent nurses. In many cases independent nurses are hired by home nursing organizations. And in Germany home nursing is provided by the so-called *Gemeindekrankenpflegestationen* and increasingly by the so-called *Sozialstationen* which also provide home help services. The total of all those non-profit organizations is called the *Freie Wohlfartspflege*. Though the market of home nursing is dominated by non-profit organizations, in recent years a growing number of nurses have decided to work freelance or have developed for-profit nursing organizations, especially in the urban areas. For instance, in Hamburg, 60% of home nursing is delivered by for-profit providers.

Finally, in five countries - Austria, Greece, Italy, Luxembourg and Spain - home nursing is provided by three or more different organizations. Those are also the countries in which home nursing was only developed recently or still has to be developed in some parts of the country. Nowadays professional home nursing exists nearly everywhere in Austria. In most provinces of Austria four or more types of organizations provide home nursing. Some of them provide home help services as well. Home nursing care is provided mainly by independent charity associations but also by organizations which are set up by political parties and by self-organized groups in private business. There are, however large differences between the provinces in the way home nursing is organized. In many parts of Greece home nursing services still do not exist. In some regions home nursing is provided through the National Health Services by nurses from the hospitals, in the big cities home nursing is mostly delivered by for-profit private organizations or by the non-profit Hellenic Red Cross. A main problem in the description of home nursing in Italy is the lack of a general terminology about what kind of services should be provided. For example there is still a discussion whether home care for the chronically ill is a matter of the health care service or of the social services. Officially, home nursing services are part of the National Health Service, but they are not yet extended to the entire country. However in many places home nursing is still organized by the social services of the municipalities. Besides, there are an increasing number of private organizations providing home nursing. In the smallest member state of the European Union Luxembourg the two largest organizations for home nursing are *Hellef Doheem* and the *Croix-Rouge*. In addition there are four smaller organizations, two of them are non-profit organizations that also provide home help services. All those six organizations cover together the whole country. Finally, home nursing is provided within the Spanish primary health care system, which now covers approximately 65% of the total Spanish population. Between the communities large differences exist in the types of home nursing provided. Home nursing has still to be developed in the more rural parts of the country.

Manpower. In eleven countries there are at least two levels of expertise in home nursing. In general, the length of the basic training for the first expert level nurses varies between three and four years. The length of education of the second expert level nurses varies between one and three years. So, there is a lot of variety. A second level home nurse from the Netherlands, for example, has had three times as much training as a second level home nurse

17

in France. In the remaining four countries, i.e. Italy, Luxembourg, Portugal and Spain, only registered or first level nurses are employed in home care. Maybe, this is due to the fact that home nursing in these countries only recently started. An other reason is that, for example in Portugal, the tasks of home nurses are strictly limited to technical nursing procedures, health education, psychosocial care and support of informal carers. Personal hygiene care like bathing is not a nurse's task.

In all countries, lower level nurses are always more involved with personal hygiene care and uncomplicated technical nursing than those with higher level qualifications. The most highly differentiated system is used in United Kingdom: the clinical grading structure for nursing staff, which was introduced in 1988, has nine grades. Each grade has its own task profile and required qualification and experience. In Belgium, on the contrary, there is no task differentiation between first and second level nurses in home care; both types of nurses have the same legal competence.

Unfortunately it is not possible to make a cross-national comparison on nurse: population ratios, because only organization-specific information about the number of nurses is available for most countries; for other countries this information is only available for particular regions.

However hazardous, it was still considered useful to look at the way in which levels of expertise relate to each other. Table 5 gives the ratios between level of expertise in home nursing in the fifteen countries.

Table 5
Ratios between levels of expertise of home nurses (FTEs)
in the European Union

Country

Austria
qualified nurse: geriatric aid: assistant nurse   n.a.
Belgium (White/Yellow Cross, liberals excluded)
graduate nurse : brevetted : hospital assistant nurse   1 : 1.1 : 0.1
Denmark
home nurse : assistant nurse   n.a.
Finland
public health nurse : registered nurse : practical nurse   1 : 0.3 : 0.3
France
salaried and independent nurse : auxiliary   1 : 0.9
Germany (*Sozialstationen*)
(community) nurses : geriatric aid : auxiliary   1 : 0.2 : 0.1
Greece
visiting nurse + health visitor : assistant : auxiliary   1 : 1.9 : 17.8
Ireland
public health nurse : enrolled : home care attendant   1 : .07 : .07
Italy
registered nurse : -   1 : 0
Luxembourg
registered nurse : -   1 : 0
The Netherlands (Cross- and Home Care Organizations)
community nurse : general nurse : auxiliary   1 : 0.1 : .04
Portugal
registered + public health nurses : -   1 : 0
Spain
registered nurses : -   1 : 0
Sweden
registered nurse : home care assistant   1 : 4.4
United Kingdom
district nurses : RGN : enrolled nurse : auxiliary   1 : 0.2 : 0.3 : 0.4

The ratio's dependent of course on the definition of first and lower levels in each country and the figures should be considered with much caution, but it is legitimate to state that Greece, Belgium and France have a high number of lower level nurses compared to the other countries. Special attention must also be given to the fact that the figures of Greece are based on estimates and the severe shortage of qualified nurses. In Sweden the home care assistants include nursing assistants and qualified home helps. No differentiation is made between these two types of professionals, because their actual tasks look more and more alike. However, one has to keep in mind that about 80% of their working time are spent on home help activities instead of home nursing care. Comparison with the figures of the study of Verheij and Kerkstra [5] showed that, during the last few years, the relative number of lower level nurses in the Netherlands and the United Kingdom has increased; while in Belgium the number of second level nurses has decreased in relative terms.

Provision of services. In all countries it is largely the elderly who receive nursing care at home. They form the largest client population for home nurses. When patients need nursing care at home, they have no choice in almost all cases as to which home nursing organization they can approach because there is only one home nursing organization in their region or because, like in Austria, the health insurance company of the patient has a contract with a particular home nursing organization. Belgium is the only exception: recently the opportunity to choose between home nursing care delivered by formal organizations like the White/Yellow Cross and home care by independent nurses has increased considerably.

As mentioned before, in some countries a medical referral is required for nursing care at home; while in other countries patients can contact the home nursing organizations themselves. In Denmark, Greece, Ireland, Italy, the Netherlands, Portugal, Spain, Sweden and the United Kingdom no medical referral is needed. In Austria and Luxembourg, a formal referral is only needed for (complicated) technical nursing, necessary for reimbursement, and not for other types of nursing care. In France and Germany, a physician's prescription is needed for all types of care eligible for reimbursement. In Belgium this is true with the exception of hygiene care.

As a consequence, countries also differ in respect of who makes the assessment of the patients' need (Table 6).

Table 6
Professionals who are making the assessment of patients' need
for home nursing in the European Union

Qualified home nurse	Qualified home nurse and/or physician	Physician
Austria	Belgium	France
Denmark	Finland	Germany
Ireland	Greece	
The Netherlands (partly)	Italy	
Sweden (partly)	Luxembourg	
United Kingdom	Portugal	
	Spain	

In Austria, Denmark, Ireland and United Kingdom, the assessment is made by the first level nurse who is also going to provide the care or have it provided by a lower level nurse. In the Netherlands, within the process of integration of the home help services, most home care organizations plan to combine assessment of patient need for home help and nursing care. There is a debate about who pays the assessment visits: a first level nurse who also provides care, a manager of the home help services or a special assessment team. The fact is that the health insurance companies demand more standardized and objective methods of assessment and support solutions, including special assessment teams, more or less outside the care-giving organization. At this moment therefore, who pays the assessment visits depends on the organization. Within the Swedish home nursing system, two different methods exist. When the nursing care is the responsibility of the county councils, the assessment is made by a registered nurse working in a primary health care centre, but when the care is provided by the municipalities, the assessment is the responsibility of the home help administrator of the social service department. The decision is made within the frame work of the Social Services Act. The home help administrator mostly assesses the total need for home care: both home nursing and home help needs.

In Finland, Greece, Italy, Luxembourg, Portugal and Spain frequently the assessment is carried out by a nurse together with/or by a physician, (sometimes) depending on the patient's need. In Belgium, patients have a prescription from their general practitioner, which is necessary for reimbursement of all nursing activities except ADL-assistance. After a referral by a doctor, a first or second level nurse pays an assessment visit to decide whether it concerns a dependent, a very dependent or an independent patient. A standardized form (*De aangepaste KATZ-schaal*) is used to determine the patient's degree of care dependency. This assessment of dependency determines for how the care will be financed. And finally, in Germany and France the assessment is always done by a doctor, who prescribes the nursing care.

In summary, there is a tendency that in the countries where a prescription of a doctor is needed, home nurses are less autonomous in the assessment of the need for nursing care and the decision about the provided care compared with home nurses in countries where no medical referral is required.

Organizational structure of home help services
All fifteen member states of the European Union have organizations for home help services as well, although in Greece and Italy the organization of these services is still in development. In some parts of those countries there are no home help services available.

Home help services are not a part of the health care system in most countries but belong to the social services and are organized by and the responsibility of the local authorities, ie. the municipalities.

Table 7 shows that this is the case in Denmark, Finland, Luxembourg, Spain, Sweden and the United Kingdom, whereas in Austria the provinces are responsible for the home help services. Belgium, France, Italy and Portugal have a mixture of home help organizations organized by the municipalities and private organizations. Ireland, Germany and the Netherlands are the only three countries in which home help services are part of the health care system. However, in Germany, this only involves home help services in addition to home nursing delivered by the *Sozialstationen* or *Haus- und Familiepflegestationen*. Home help and additional services for the elderly provided by the *Mobilen sozialen Hilfsdienste* like meals-on-wheels and cleaning services are not part of the health care system. In Ireland, home help services are provided directly by the Health Boards or by voluntary organizations funded by a Health Board. Finally, in Greece home help services are provided by a mixture of private organizations, non-profit organizations like the Hellenic Red Cross and Greek Orthodox Church and

22

voluntary organizations.

Table 7
Organizational structure of home help services
in the European Union *

Social services Municipalities	Social services Municipalities and private organizations	Health care system
Austria	Belgium	Ireland
Denmark	France	Germany (partly)
Finland	Italy	the Netherlands
Luxembourg	Portugal	
Spain		
Sweden		
United Kingdom		

Manpower. In all countries direct help to the clients is provided by home helps. In most countries these home helps do not have formal training, but a few short courses and a 'training on the job'. Only in Belgium, Germany, Italy, Sweden and about 65% of the home helps in Finland and about 20% of the home helps in the Netherlands do have specific training varying from six months to three years in duration. In Denmark, only recently a one year education programme for home helps was introduced.

There are large differences among EU countries in the availability of home help manpower (table 8).

---

* Home help services in Greece are provided by voluntary non-profit organizations and private agencies. They are not a part of the public health care or social security scheme

Table 8
Number of inhabitants per one FTE home help in the European Union *

Country	Inhabitants per home help (FTE)
Austria (Vienna)	749
Belgium (Flanders)	448
Denmark	161
Finland	528
France	1,410
Ireland	1,165
Italy (Genoa) **	5,690
Luxembourg	6,400
The Netherlands	496
Spain	5,055
Sweden	111
United Kingdom	1,100

Table 8 shows that, in terms of the number of inhabitants, the density of home helps is the highest in Denmark, Finland, Belgium, Sweden and the Netherlands, whereas in Italy, Luxembourg and Spain relatively few home helps are available. A possible explanation for these differences is that in Italy (Genoa), Luxembourg and Spain, home help services only developed during the last ten years and that people in those countries make considerable use of informal care.

Provision of services. Most clients of the home help services are the elderly, many of them living alone. In some countries, like Germany, the Netherlands, Finland and Luxembourg home help was originally aimed at assistance to families with young children in case of the illness or hospitalization of the mother, but gradually emphasis has shifted to helping elderly people. Only in

---

* These figures were not available for Germany, Greece and Portugal.

** The figure of Genoa is not representative for the whole country: the national figure is higher.

Finland 35% of the clients are under 65 years of age. Especially, families with young children use home help care, for instance when children are ill and parents have to go to work.

In most countries, there is only one home help organization in a region. Consequently, people do not have a choice what organization they should approach when they need home help. Only in Belgium, there are in some cases more organizations in one region. And of course, people are always free to arrange private help for household tasks, but this solution might be more expensive.

In none of the countries, a referral from an other professional care provider is required for home help services. So, the clients may contact the organizations themselves.

Table 9
First contact with home help services initiated by: *

Client (> 70%)	Client or care provider	Care-providers (> 70%)
Italy	Austria	France
Luxembourg	Belgium	Ireland
The Netherlands	Greece	United Kingdom
Spain	Portugal	
Sweden		

As table 9 shows, in Italy, Luxembourg, the Netherlands, Spain and Sweden most of the clients or their families contact the organizations themselves; whereas in France, Ireland and the United Kingdom, the majority of the clients are referred by other professional care-providers, like general practitioners, hospitals and home nurses. In Belgium, Greece and Portugal about half of the clients contact the organizations themselves, the others are referred.

In all countries, except in Sweden, the assessment of the need for home help is made by a professional (home care organizer), who is not involved in direct home help care. In nearly all countries this professional is a social

---

* No data were available on this subject for Denmark, Finland and Germany

worker, but exceptions are made in integrated organizations for home help services and home nursing; in that case the assessment is sometimes made together with a nurse or by a nurse. In Sweden the assessment is made by home help administrators of the local social services. They are also involved in the actual care providing process; mostly in counselling and advice, both to the client as well as to the family members. In most countries, the home care organizer also decides about the amount and type of home help care to be provided. Belgium, Ireland and Italy are exceptions in this respect. For example, in Belgium the decision about the type of home help care to be provided and the period of time is made by the service managers or special committees of the organizations. In Ireland normally the home help organizer and the public health nurse decide jointly what care needs to be provided and in some communities in Italy the decision is made by a special team consisting of the social worker, a nurse and home helps.

The next step is the actual provision of the care to the clients by home helps. Table 10 gives an overview of the different tasks performed by the home helps in the fifteen countries.

Table 10
Tasks performed by home helps in of the European Union

country	homemaking activities	personal care	general support	stimulating informal care	moral support
Belgium	x	x	x	x	x
Greece	x	x	x	x	x
Ireland	x	x	x	x	x
Luxembourg	x	x	x	x	x
The Netherlands	x	x	x	x	x
Denmark	x	x	x	x	x
Austria	x	x	x		x
France	x		x	x	x
Portugal	x	x	x	x	
Italy	x	x	x		
Spain	x	x	x		
United Kingdom	x	x	x		
Sweden	x	x	x		
Germany	x	x	x		
Finland	x	x			x

The main tasks of home helps can be described as homemaking activities (preparing meals, washing dishes, cleaning, doing the laundry etc.), hygiene and other personal care (bathing, ADL-help), general and family support (shopping, going for a walk with the client, administrative support), stimulating informal care (ie. help from family members, neighbours or friends) and moral support with psychosocial problems (counselling and advice). As we can see in Table 10, all these tasks are performed by home helps in Belgium, Greece, Ireland, Luxembourg and the Netherlands. Furthermore, France is the only country in which home helps are not allowed to provide personal care. In addition, though frequent, family support, stimulating informal care and moral support are not officially part of the home help's job in France. Sweden is the only country in which home helps, home care assistants, also perform routine technical nursing procedures (e.g. injections, dressings). In all countries home helps spend most of their time on housework.

3.3   Relations between home nursing and home help services

The growth in the number of the elderly induces a greater need for home help and home nursing services. Consequently, in many countries policy makers recognize the advantages not only of co-operation, but also merging the two services into one organization.

Within Europe there seems to be a tendency towards integrating home nursing and home help services. Table 11 shows that in Denmark and Ireland both services are part of the same organization. In Denmark the services are organized by the municipalities and in Ireland the two services are broadly under the community care programme of the Health Boards, but their relationship is not uniform in all regions. In Austria, Finland, France, Germany, the Netherlands and Sweden both services are often integrated. In Germany the two services are integrated in the *Sozialstationen* and are provided from the same location, improving possibilities of contact between different professions. The number of integrated *Sozialstationen* is still increasing. In the Netherlands, the umbrella organizations for community nursing and for home help services merged in 1990. At this moment this integration is taking place at the regional level. About 50% of the home nursing organizations have already merged with organizations for home help services. It is hoped that the integration will increase the efficiency in home

Table 11
Level of integration of home nursing and home help services in the same organization in the European Union

Part of the same organizations	In many organizations	In some organization
Denmark	Austria	Belgium
Ireland	Finland	Greece
	France	Italy
	Germany	Luxembourg
	The Netherlands	United Kingdom
	Sweden	Spain
		Portugal

care and will avoid unnecessary overlap between home nursing and home help services. As already mentioned, the Swedish act on 'The Care of the Elderly reform' in 1992 moved the responsibility for the care for the elderly, including home nursing, towards the municipalities. At the end of 1994, in about 50% of the counties home nursing has already been delegated to the municipalities, and this reform process is still going on. As a consequence of this reform, home nursing becomes a part of social services and will belong to the same organization as the home help services. In some regions home nurse and home helps work already together in a team. They discuss mutual patients and are more able to tune their tasks.

Belgium, Greece and Luxembourg have some organizations for both types of services. In addition, in Belgium multi-disciplinary co-operation initiatives are subsidized on the condition that general practitioners, community nurses, home helps, social workers as well as three other professions take part in them. In the private sector of the United Kingdom there are organizations which provide both home nursing and home help services. Furthermore, one of the major conditions for the new approach in home care in the public health system is an extended co-operation between home nursing and home help services ie. consultation between social services and health agencies is required. Finally, in Portugal and Spain too, developments are taking place towards more intensive co-operation between the two disciplines. Integration of the two services has recently been established in a few places, sometimes as an experiment.

3.4   Reported problems

Finally, attention is paid to some problems in home care that seem to obtain in many countries.

First, *waiting lists* for home help services are common in most countries. In Denmark, Finland, Germany, Luxembourg, Sweden and the United Kingdom no waiting lists are reported. According to the experts, the waiting lists are caused by *budget problems*, i.e. the budgets are too low, while the demand for home help services is increasing. The lack of sufficient resources is, according the experts in many countries, due to the fact the home help services have a low priority in policy. In some countries it was also reported that it was difficult to target the available resources to the right people: those who really need home help.

In many countries there is a *shortage of home helps* which is related to the first problem. Experts claim the profession is considered unattractive, because it has low status, it is poorly paid and the training is considered to be inadequate.

A shortage of qualified home nurses was reported in Austria, Denmark, France, Ireland, Greece, Italy, Portugal and Luxembourg. In some countries the experts reported that hospital nurses were better paid than home nurses and that equal payment would help. An increasing number of part-timers was also reported to be a reason for staff shortage, as well as the fact that nurses remain in the profession only a short time.

In a number of countries, Austria, France, Greece, Ireland, Italy, Portugal, Spain, large differences obtain among the regions in the supply of the home care. Consequently, the accessibility of the services is not the same for people who need home nursing or home help services. In many parts of Greece, Italy and Spain, there are no home care services. This means that within the policy of substitution of home care for hospital care, patients have to stay in the hospital too long or have to rely solely on the informal care of their families.

Finally, with regard to the *co-ordination of care*, in many countries the home helps complain about the co-operation with hospitals and General Practitioners. The reason for the unwillingness of the GPs and the hospitals to co-operate is that home helps are viewed as professionals with a low status. Furthermore, the experts of nearly all countries reported problems in the co-operation between hospitals and home nursing. These problems concern the preparations for discharge, time-continuity between hospital care and home care and the lack of knowledge of hospitals about the possibilities of aftercare at home. In addition, in some countries (France, Germany, Greece and Spain) problems in the co-operation with General Practitioners were mentioned.

3.5 Conclusions

All member states of the European Union are confronted with an increase of the demand for home care. First because of socio-demographic pressures, like the ageing of the population, the fertility trend towards smaller family size and an increased female participation in the labour market. Secondly, because of the policy of substitution of home care for hospital care in order to control the health care expenditure.

However, there are large differences between the member states in the level of development of home care services. In countries like Denmark, the Netherlands, Belgium, Finland, Ireland, Sweden and the United Kingdom, home nursing and home help services are rather well developed, although in Ireland and the United Kingdom regional differences still exist in the supply of home care and in the level of co-payment for home help services by the clients. While in countries like Austria, Greece, Italy and Spain, home care is still in its infancy. In addition, there are large differences among the countries regarding the level of co-ordination of home nursing and home help services.

In general, there is a trend toward more co-operation between the two services, in a move towards efficient supply of home care, but much still has to be done in this area. A major problem in many countries is the separation between health and social services. Whereas home nursing is financed by general taxation or social insurance; home help services are usually administrated and financed by local government or sometimes by voluntary organizations. In general there are also large differences between the countries in the way home care is financed. In tables 12 and 13 (at the end of this chapter), the main features of organization and financing of home care in all countries are summarized. With regard to home nursing there seems to be a relation between the way of funding and the organizational structure. In member states where the organizations receive a fixed budget, based on the number of inhabitants or the demography of the catchment area, home nursing is mainly provided by one type of organization and is free accessible for the patients. In this situation there is little competition between the organizations, also because the catchment areas of the regional organizations do not overlap. On the other hand, in countries like Belgium, France and Germany, where organizations are reimbursed according to a fee-for-service principle and a referral of a doctor is required, home nursing is provided by different types of organizations and also by independent nurses. It seems that fee-for-service reimbursement stimulates competition between providers and a market oriented home care. In addition, a fee-for-service method of funding has also the consequence that mainly technical nursing procedures and some basic care like bathing the patient are reimbursed, which leaves little room for nurses to perform preventive and psychosocial activities and to provide more integrated care. In the Netherlands and the United Kingdom the financing of home nursing is in a transition period from budget funding to fee-for-service reimbursement. On the basis of the experiences in other countries one can expect that the nurses in the Netherlands and the United Kingdom will be confronted with changes in the content of their job: more time has to be devoted to (complicated) technical nursing procedures and less time will be available for preventive activities and psychosocial problems of the patients and their informal carers.

On the other hand, the countries resemble one another in the problems they face in home care. In many countries, there are waiting lists for home help services, mainly due to budget problems, low policy priorities or shortage of personnel. And also shortages of home nurses were reported.

In summary, it can be concluded that the unification of Europe with regard to the organization and financing of home care is still far away, but that the problems encountered in home care seem to ignore the borders of the member states. However, for social, economic and political reasons, home care is the best service to respond to the challenge of the ageing population. It is mostly not only more cost effective than intramural or residential care but it meets the aspirations of both politicians and older people to allow the latter to stay in their own homes for as long as possible.

Table 12
Overview of the organization and financing of home nursing in Europe

Country	Main providers	Medical referral required	Assessment of needs	Funding of organization	Co-payments by patients
Austria	Different organizations, varying between provinces. Mainly private non-profit organizations.	Yes, for technical home nursing care only.	By qualified nurse using a standardized form.	Fee-for-service: payment per nursing activity.	Yes, for general basic nursing care.
Belgium	One nationwide private non-profit organization (White/Yellow Cross), some smaller organizations and a large number of independent nurses.	Yes, for technical nursing care such as injections.	By home nurse using a national standardized form (Katz-scale).	Fee-for-service: per diem or per activity determined by level of dependency of patient.	Yes, mainly membership fee.
Denmark	Home care department of municipalities.	No	By social counsellor or nurse. No standardized assessment forms.	Fixed budget funded by national and local taxes.	No, except in some very specific cases.

32

Country	Organization		Assessment	Budget/Payment	Co-payment
Finland	Local health (and social) care centres (NHS).	Yes	By physician, health visitor or registered nurse. Standardized forms are used.	Budget determined by local authorities.	Yes, income- and household-related.
France	Mainly private non-profit organizations, some services by municipalities and a large number of independent nurses.	Yes	By nurse using standardized forms.	Fee-for-service (payment per activity) and budget for a fixed number of patients.	Yes, but mostly paid by additional insurance.
Germany	Mainly private non-profit organizations. In some regions, mainly for-profit organizations.	Yes	By physician in co-operation with head nurse, using standardized forms.	Fee-for-service.	No
Greece	NHS-organizations, private organizations (both for- and non-profit).	No	By physician, health visitor or visiting nurse. No standardized form.	NHS and Red Cross organizations: fixed budget; others: fee-for-service.	Yes, for all services.
Ireland	One type organization: Health Boards.	No	By public health nurse. No national standardized forms.	Fixed budget.	No

Country	Main providers	Medical referral required	Assessment of needs	Funding of organization	Co-payments by patients
Italy	Different organizations: NHS, social services of municipalities, private organizations (for- and non-profit).	No	Nurse, physician or special team. No national standardized forms.	Public organiza- tions: budgets. Private organiza- tions: fee-for- service.	Yes, in social services and private organizations. Not in NHS.
Luxem- bourg	Two large private non-profit organizations and four smaller ones (two non-profit).	Yes, for technical nursing activities only.	Physicians or specialized nurse. A special form can be used.	Mainly Fee-for- service; the four smaller ones also receive an additional state budget.	Yes, for general basic nursing care.
Nether- lands	The National Association of Home Care which consists of Regional Cross Associations or Home Care Organizations (all are private non-profit).	No	Home care nurse (in Regional Cross Associations); nurse, home help manager or special team (in Home Care Organiza- tions). No national standardized forms.	Fixed budget based on the number of personnel.	Yes, membership fee.

Country					
Portugal	Mainly NHS-health care centres and some private non-profit organizations.	No	Nurse or physician. No standardized forms.	Fixed budget based on historical costs with adjustments for inflation.	No
Spain	NHS-health care centres.	No	Nurse or physician using a standardized form.	Fixed budget.	No
Sweden	NHS-health care centres or social services of municipalities.	No, only in a few regions.	Registered nurse (in health care centres). Home help administrator (in social services). No standardized forms.	Fixed budget.	Yes
United Kingdom	Part of NHS: community unit of DHAs or independent Community Trusts (after reform of NHS).	No	By the team leader (a qualified nurse). No national standardized forms.	Old system: fixed budget based on number of inhabitants and demography of population. New system: fee-for-service.	No

Table 13

Overview of the organization and financing of home help services in Europe

Country	Main providers	Assessment of needs	Funding of organization	Co-payments by clients
Austria	Different organizations, varying between provinces. Mainly private non-profit organizations.	By a qualified nurse of a special governmental agency, with standardized forms.	Subsidized by province and municipalities and payment per hour.	Yes, depending on income.
Belgium	Social services of municipality and some private organizations.	By social worker or social nurse, using a national standardized form.	Subsidized by central government: based on number of personnel and clients.	Yes, depending on income and household composition.
Denmark	Home care department of municipalities.	By social counsellor or nurse. No standardized form.	Fixed budget, funded by national and local taxes.	No

36

	Provider	Assessment	Funding	Fees
Finland	Local health and social care centres, social welfare board of municipality and private non-profit organizations.	By leading home maker or social worker (social welfare) or health visitor or registered nurse (health and social centres). Standardized forms are used.	Budget determined by local authorities.	Yes, income and household-related.
France	Mixture of social services of municipalities and private organizations.	By social worker.	Funding by municipality (low-income group) or private insurance.	Not below a certain income. Otherwise dependent on old age insurance.
Germany	Mainly private non-profit organizations. Different organizations for services in addition to home nursing (*Sozial-stationen*) and for home help for elderly(MSDs).	Mostly by a nurse or social worker, using standardized forms.	Fee-for-service (by patient or insurance). For MSDs a global budget from municipalities is added, based on number of personnel and output.	Yes, except for home help in addition to home nursing.
Greece	Private organizations (both for- and non-profit).	By visiting nurse or social worker. No standardized form.	Fee-for-service. No funding by authorities or insurances.	Yes, in private for-profit organizations only.

Country	Main providers	Assessment of needs	Funding of organization	Co-payments by clients
Ireland	Mainly one public organization: Health Boards and some voluntary organizations.	By public health nurse or home help organizer. No national standardized forms.	Fixed budget.	Yes, but different regulations in health Boards.
Italy	Social services of municipalities and private organizations (for- and non-profit).	Large differences between organizations. No national standardized forms.	Social services: budgets. Private organizations: fee-for-service.	Yes, but large differences between organizations.
Luxembourg	Mainly private non-profit organizations.	By head of regional service: social worker or specialized nurse.	Mainly budgets financed by Ministry of Health and municipalities.	Yes, income-related.
Netherlands	The National Association of Home Care which consists of Home Help Organizations or Home Care Organizations (private non-profit).	Home help manager (Home Help); nurse, home help manager or special team (Home Care. No national standardized forms.	Fixed budget from central government based on number of inhabitants and age distribution in catchment area.	Yes, dependent on income and household composition.

Portugal	Social services of municipalities and some private non-profit social solidarity organizations.	Social worker. No standardized forms.	Fixed budget from central government, based on number of clients and types of services.	Yes, income-related.
Spain	Social services of municipalities.	Social worker. In some parts of the country a standardized form are used.	Fixed budget based on number of hours of care.	Yes, income-related.
Sweden	Social services of municipalities.	Home help administrator. No standardized forms.	Fixed budget from municipalities and central government.	Yes, dependent on income and number of hours of care.
United Kingdom	Social Services of municipalities and private organizations: both for- and non-profit.	Care manager (social worker). No national standardized forms.	Social services: budgets. Private organizations: fee-for-service.	Yes, different regulations exist.

References

1 STATISTISK SENTRALBYRÅ. Statistical Yearbook of Norway. Oslo-Kongsvingen: Statistisk Sentralbyrå, 1990.
2 OECD. Ageing populations: the social policy implications. Paris: OECD, 1990.
3 WALKER, A. Home care in Europe: current trends and future prospects. Brussels: European Association of Organizations for Home Care and Help at Home, 1991.
4 NIJKAMP, P., J. PACOLET, H. SPINNEWYN, A. VOLLERING, C. WILDEROM, S. WINTERS. Services for the elderly in Europe. A cross-national comparative study. Leuven/Amsterdam: HIV/VU, 1991.
5 VERHEIJ, R.A., A. KERKSTRA. International comparative study of community nursing. Aldershot: Avebury, 1992.
6 JAMIESON, A. (eds.). Home care for older people in Europe. Oxford/New York/Tokyo: Oxford University Press, 1991.
7 WITTE DE, L., KNOPS, H., PYFERS, L., et al. European services delivery systems in rehabilitation technology. Heartline C. Hoensbroek: IRV, 1994.
8 RAFFY-PIHAN, N. L'hospitalisation à domicile: Un tour d'horizon en europe, aux Etats-Unis et au Canada. Paris: Credes, 1994.

1 Home care in Austria

Cordula Wagner

1   The setting of home care

1.1   The country

In 1989, Austria applied for EU membership. It became a member in January 1995. The Austrian federal republic consists of nine fairly independent federal provinces, the so called *Bundesländer*. These provinces are divided into administrative districts (15 *Stadt-* and 84 *Land-politische Bezirke*). The formal head of state is the federal president who is directly elected for a period of six years. There are two chambers in the Federal Assembly: the National Council (*Nationalrat*) elected for four years by a form of proportional representation and the Federal Council (*Bundesrat*) elected by the nine federal provinces.

The population is unequally distributed over the country; e.g. 20% of the population live in Vienna.

After the Second World War, the economy of the country was successfully rebuilt.

Cordula Wagner

Population key figures (1990) [1,2]

Population in mln	7.8
Inhabitants per sq. km.	92
% Living in urban areas	58
% over 65 years	15.2
% over 75 years	7.1
Births per 1000	12.0
Deaths per 1000	10.6
Life expectancy (men)	72.6
Life expectancy (women)	79.2

1.2 The organization of health care

Health care in Austria is mainly the responsibility of the nine provinces and local authorities. The federal government (in particular the Ministry of Health, Sports, and Consumer Affairs) is only involved in the development of general health care policy and legislation, and technical supervision of health services and training [3]. The health care system is organized in a hierarchic way. The provincial government, assisted by a Health Advisory Council, appoints a supervising health officer (*Landessanitätsdirektor*) responsible for the whole province. Within the provinces, there are administrative districts with two main tasks in health care provision: supervising the local health authorities and the management of public health services such as centres for mother and child care, school health, and general health examinations.

Primary health care is provided by general practitioners (*Praktische Ärzte*) and specialists (*Fachärtze*) contracted by Health Insurance funds [3,4]. More than 90% of the GPs work in single-handed practice [1]. There is no personal list system. When needed, patients are referred by GPs or specialists to outpatient clinics of hospitals (*Ambulanzen*) or independent out-patient centres operated by social insurance agencies and providing medical specialist care (*Selbständige Ambulatorien*). These centres have short-term beds for diagnosis and treatment. A licence from the provincial authorities is required to run these facilities. In case of emergency, the clinics or centres are directly accessible to the citizens.

Until recently, the Austrian health care system was highly hospital-based [4]. Three types of hospital are situated in each of the nine provinces of Austria: general hospitals, specialist hospitals, and central hospitals. There are both public and privately owned hospitals. Public hospitals are run by federal, provincial or local authorities, and authorized independent bodies often related to the Health Insurance funds [5].

Health care figures (1990) [2]

Expenditure
Total expenditure on health
    Absolute per head in ppp$ 1383
    Percentage of GDP   8.3
Public expenditure on health
    Absolute per head in ppp$ 928
    Percentage of GDP   5.6

Manpower
Physicians per 1000 pop.   2.1
GPs per 1000 pop.   n.a
Qualified nurses per 1000 pop.   6.8

Hospital care
In-patient care
    Beds per 1000 pop.   10.2
    Admissions per 100 pop.   25.2
    Mean length of stay   11.9
Acute hospitals
    Beds per 1000 pop.   6.0
    Admissions per 100 pop.   20.5
    Mean length of stay   10.5
Nursing homes
    Beds per 1000 pop.   n.a

1.3   Health financing and insurance

More than half of the total health expenditure (55.6%) is financed by a social insurance scheme [6]. There are five schemes for different social groups [5]:
- ASVG (*Allgemeines Sozialversicherungsgesetz*) for employees or the unemployed and their relatives;
- GSVG (*Gewerbliches Sozialversicherungsgesetz*) for the self-employed;
- BSVG (*Bauern-Sozialversicherungsgesetz*) for self-employed in agriculture and forestry;
- B-KUVG (*Beamten-, Kranken- und Unfallversicherungsgesetz*) for civil servants;
- FSVG (*Freiberufliches Sozialversicherungsgesetz*) for the professions.

In addition to health care, the whole social insurance scheme also covers work accident- and pension insurance [3,4,5]. Social security premiums, which are income-related, are paid by the employers and employees (both 50%) or by the self-employed themselves. The level of the premiums is determined by the Ministry of Social Affairs. Although the schemes are only compulsory for all non-self employed, more than 99% of the population are enrolled in the social insurance system.

The actual administration is carried out by 24 autonomous Health Insurance funds [1,3]. They are organized at provincial level and responsible for collecting patient contributions and contracting care-providers. Although they work independently, they are supervised by the Ministry of Social Affairs [4,5].

Governments and local authorities (federal, provinces, communes) also contribute to health care expenditure via subsidies funded by general taxation. This counts for 25.2% of the total costs [6].

About 38% of the Austrian population have a private health insurance for additional health expenditure (largely special arrangements in hospitals) [5]. This private scheme only covers 6% of the total health care costs [6]. Finally, the remaining part of the health care expenditures (15.2%) consists of co-payments by patients: mainly for some dental care, drugs, and specific aids [6]. Nursing in special hospital wards also requires co-payments but they are often reimbursed by the private insurances [3].

Health services are provided in kind: bills are paid directly by the Health Insurance funds. Physicians need a contract with the Health Insurance funds to be reimbursed. The payment system (fee-for-service or capitation) differs among the provinces, although there are no large differences [1]. The financing systems of hospitals is very complicated because funds are obtained form different resources [4]. Accordingly, new policy measures have been discussed to simplify this system: one of the options is the introduction of the so called DRG (Diagnoses related groups) - payment.

1.4   Care for the elderly

As in all other West-European countries, the absolute and relative number of the elderly in the Austrian population is increasing significantly and continuously: especially the number of people over 75 [7]. About two thirds of this group are women: which is more than in most of the other countries.

Until the end of the 1980s, care for the elderly was mainly the responsibility of the informal care-givers mostly family members [8]. Until recently, there was hardly any national policy: no formal statement of the right of the elderly, nor a central office for old-age policies [9]. Furthermore, the amount of public services available in the welfare system was rather limited, especially in the field of community services. One of the major problems was the legal distinction between 'treatment' (cure) and 'need for care' [7]. Medical treatment was covered by the public health insurance without time limits. But, these insurances took no financial responsibility for care to people without medical treatment. So, until 1992, all expenditure on care was paid by the people themselves and the welfare system.

The increasing number of the elderly and the decreasing role of the family in the care for the elderly required new policies and adaptations in the organization and financing of formal care: both community and residential services.

There are large regional differences in the supply of care facilities: both in amount and in terms of organizational structure [8]. This is the result of the fact that the nine provinces are responsible for the welfare of the elderly and not the federal government. Furthermore, local authorities (the communes) quite often provide services themselves; often in local small- scale experiments [7,8].

The public sector often co-operates with private non-profit organizations. Especially in the field of community services, the role of this kind of organizations have been increasing in recent years. However, the impact of a few for-profit organizations is rather small because they provide relatively expensive services which can only be paid for by a small group of wealthy elderly patients.

In general the welfare system for the elderly (mainly non-medical care) is almost entirely financed by general taxation [9]. Since the beginning of the 1990s, some major reforms were introduced in the financing system. In 1992, the compulsory health insurance (see section 1.3) started to cover the expenses of technical home nursing services [8]. A year later, the federal government implemented the care allowance (*Pflegegeld*) paid directly to the older person by the pension insurance. The amount of payment depends on medical criteria and ADL-measurements. The patients' need for help is divided into seven levels. The basic idea of this policy is that each individual in need of care can buy it him/herself [9].

Community services As mentioned before, special community services for the elderly have only recently been developed in Austria. The concept is still in a developmental stage. A large variation exists between the provinces. In general, this field is dominated by private organizations which provide almost 80% of the services (74.4% by non-profit and 5% by for-profit organizations) [7]. Public organizations from provincial and, principally, local authorities provide fewer community services themselves. This might be related to the fact that the authorities have no legal obligation, such as for residential services, to guarantee this kind of service. Only in larger municipalities like Vienna and Innsbruck, is community care partly provided by the authorities themselves. The services are generally contracted out to private non-profit providers. The main non-profit organizations are traditional voluntary social welfare organizations (*Wohlfahrtsverbände*) such as the Red Cross, *Caritasverband* or local associations (*Vereine*) [7].

The services mostly consist of home nursing and home help (which will be discussed later), recreation and social schemes, and specific facilities such as meals-on-wheels.

One of the main policy goals is the integration of health and social services at the local level. In some parts of the country, local co-ordinating centres (*Sozial- und Gesundheitssprengel*) have already been established. Besides formal health and social care, they also co-ordinate many voluntary activities.

Residential services Care for the elderly in Austria is dominated by residential care. However, compared with other countries, a relatively low percentage of the elderly live in institutions: about 20% of the people over 80 [9]. This is mainly a result of the limited number of places available in nursing homes or old people's homes. To judge by the large waiting lists (e.g. in 1989 the waiting lists contained about 60,000 elderly throughout Austria), there is a considerable shortage of places [8]. Care activities in old people's homes are limited. Residents are expected to be relatively independent: they are responsible for their personal hygiene. Otherwise, they would be referred to a nursing home where total care is provided. In 1991, about 22,000 people were living in nursing homes: largely single women.

Contrary to the community services, residential services are mainly organized within the public sector (76.5% of the places compared with 21% private non-profit sector, and 2.5% for-profit sector) [7]. The institutions are reimbursed by the provinces for client-day charges. Old people's and nursing homes in the public sector are mostly larger, cheaper, and contain fewer single rooms than in the private sector [7]. Consequently, the resident populations differ: welfare recipients and members of lower social classes are more often living in public homes.

Capacity of residential services for the elderly in Austria (1989)*

	Number of places/beds per 1000 people over 65 years
Old people's homes	27.3
Nursing homes	18.7

*   Figures are estimates based on information from Badelt and Pazourek [7] and the OECD health date base [2].

2   The organization of home nursing

2.1   Organizations for home nursing

The development and the organization of home nursing differs considerably from one province to another. The federal government and the different provinces are responsible for regulating home nursing. Hitherto, every province has implemented its own system.

Nowadays professional home nursing exists nearly everywhere in Austria. In most parts of Austria four or more types of organization provide home nursing. Some of them provide home help services as well. Home nursing care is mainly provided by independent charity associations, but also by organizations which are set up by political parties and by self-organized groups in private business. In Vorarlberg, Tirol, Oberösterreich and Steiermark organizations are divided in regions. While in Niederösterreich, Burgenland and Salzburg, the organizations work throughout the whole province and compete with one another. In Vienna, one public (*Hauskranken-pflegefachdienst der Stadt Wien*) and eight private organizations provide home nursing.

The following associations provide home nursing:

- the *Österreichisches Rotes Kreuz*
- the *Österreichische Volkshilfe*

- the *Caritas der (Erz-)Diözesen*
- the *Niederösterreichische Hilfswerk*
- community based organizations
- local associations (*Vereine*)
- others like hospitals and church-based organizations [10].

In this section some examples of the differences between the provinces will be considered.

In Burgenland, there is a service called 'institutionalized neighbourhood help'. The volunteer neighbour takes responsibility for the care of an elderly person in the neighbourhood. He or she is supervised by a social worker and receives a nominal payment from the provincial government. Since 1984, the *Caritas der Diözese* has been developing home nursing care with qualified home nurses. Thus far, not every community has had professional home nursing care [10]. In Vorarlberg, another unique form of care is found: local associations (*Vereine*) provide home care for the sick and the elderly on a purely private basis. The whole population of the province can be reached by professional home nurses in co-ordination with informal family care using this decentralized system [10]. In Tirol, there are 50 non-profit local associations called *Sozial- und Gesundheitssprengel*, which provide home nursing and home help services and other social services for an area with between 3,000 and 28,000 inhabitants. 170 *Sozialstationen* in Niederösterreich organized by the *Caritas der Diözese* and local associations provide home nursing, home help services, meals-on-wheels, paramedical services and other welfare services. In Vienna, the public home nursing organization is divided into ten co-ordination centres (*Stützpunkte*) which are spread throughout the city. Every home nurse works at one or two co-ordination centres.

Though the market for home nursing is dominated by non-profit organizations, in recent years a growing number of nurses have decided to work freelance or have developed for-profit nursing organizations. For-profit organizations have developed mainly in urban areas. Most of the for-profit organizations did not, however, survive in Vienna. Despite of the attendance allowance (*Pflegegeld*), only a small group of patients can afford a private nurse.

2.2   Manpower in home nursing

Different types of nurses work in the community:

- Qualified nurses (*Diplomkrankenschwester/Krankenpfleger*): a generalist nurse with two years of hospital training. Some of them have specialized as home nurses in three to eight months of additional study or have followed management training.
- Geriatric aids (*Altenhelfer/in*), with two years of training. The division of labour between geriatric help and home nursing on one side, and home help and geriatric help on the other is not clear.
- Nursing assistants (*Pflegehelfer/in*), with one year of training, provide basic care.

In Vienna, there are 165 qualified nurses (some of them work part-time). To achieve a 1:5,000 nurse-to-population ratio, about 350 nurses (FTEs) would be needed. The ratio is now 1:9,300. In addition to the home nurses working for the public home nursing organization, in Vienna there are 263 (61,5%) home nurses working independently. There are only two *Altenhelfer/in* and six *Pflegehelfer/in* working in Vienna. In Vorarlberg, on the other hand, the nurse-to-population ratio is 1:4,590 [11]. In Tirol, a *Sprengel* with 8,000 inhabitants has one qualified nurse, one geriatric help, one family help and a group of 20 voluntary helps [12]. In Niederösterreich, 172 full-time qualified nurses are working in *Sozialstationen*. If every *Sozialstation* had two or three qualified nurses for circa 8,000 inhabitants, 184 qualified nurses would be needed [13].

2.3   Client population

In Vienna, 0.5% of the population have received some kind of home nursing care during 1993. According to estimates, about 88% of the patients were over 60, 73% were over 70 and 43% were over 80. In 1993, in Tirol 92% of the patients visited by a qualified nurse were over 60 years: 70% were female and 30% were male [14]. In Niederösterreich the mean age of patients is 80, two thirds are female [15].

An earlier study had shown that in 1985 more than half of the patients (52%) suffered from cerebrovascular problems, 57% from a skeleto-muscular system illness. Another large category (35%) had complaints of the central nervous system [10]. According to a recent study [15], about 41% of the patients had a hospital- or nursing home indication. Most of the patients suffered from several diseases which indicated that a large number of severe diseases were cared for at home.

2.4 Provision of services

In the provision of services, an important legal distinction is made between *Grundpflege* (helping the patient with basic needs including ADL-activities) and *medizinische Hauskrankenpflege* (technical nursing procedures as injections, stoma care, bladder washouts). The latter type of care is generally carried out by qualified nurses. The basic care like washing and dressing is carried out by *Pflegehelfer* and *Altenhilfen*. Because of the different organization and financial structure in home nursing in the different provinces, the provision of services also differs. In Niederösterreich the *Sozialstationen* and in Tirol the *Sprengel* provide integrated services for home nursing and home help. Potential patients do not have free choice in approaching a home nursing organization. The patient's Health Insurance fund has a contract with a particular home nursing organization or the care provider, who refers the patient to a home nursing organization, e.g. the general practitioner, is affiliated to a specific organization.

Generally, in Austria, a referral from a physician is needed for the reimbursement of technical home nursing care by the Health Insurance fund. Only patients who are able to pay a private nurse are free to choose any home nursing organization. Basic home nursing care is not covered by the Health Insurance funds.

First contacts between patients and home nurses are often initiated by general practitioners or by hospitals. In Vienna, 87% of first contacts are initiated by the general practitioner and 13% by the patient him/herself or his/her family. In Oberösterreich, patients contact a central co-ordination centre which assigns the patient to one of the four organizations.

After the patient has contacted the organization, a qualified nurse assesses the patient's needs and decides what type of care the patient is going to receive and during what period of time. When necessary, the home nurse is also allowed to determine the patients need for home help care. The standardized forms are used for the assessment which includes questions about the diagnosis, the therapy and therapists, activities of daily living, mental problems and social circumstances.

Home nurses operate from their own homes, the home nursing premises and nursing homes for the elderly. In Vienna, most of them work in a team with other care-providers as physical therapist, occupational therapist, social workers and home helps.

The Red Cross distinguishes three kinds of care depending on the time needed to help the patient. First, intensive care which means four to seven home visits a week and 24-hour access to the home nurse organization. 13% of the patients fall into this category. Second, normal care which means two to three home visits a week. This counts for 28% of the patients. Most of the patients (59%) belong to category three; they get one home visit a week [10].

In 1993 in Niederösterreich 45% of the patients needed care for periods of several weeks up to one year, 18% for two years, 12% for three years and 25% for more than three years. Nearly half of the patients (46%) receives between 10 and 20 hours help a month, 24% of the patients between 20 and 30 hours and 23% between 30 and 60 hours [13].

2.5 Problems and recent developments

In Vienna, there are no waiting lists for home nursing care because home help services take it over when necessary. If home help services did not take over, there would be a shortage of staff. The problem is that the home help services staff are not qualified to provide home nursing care. The public home nursing organizations in Vienna provides only technical home nursing care and the co-ordination centres of the social welfare services refer a lot of patients who actually need qualified home nursing care to home help organizations.

Another problem is the lack of knowledge in hospitals about the extramural health care options.

Finally, there are communication problems and conflicts about the division of labour between home nursing and home help organizations.

In some parts of Austria, a further growth of home nursing facilities is expected and the co-ordination between the different types of service will receive more attention. The main purpose is the establishment of an integrated care system. Home nurses will have a central position in this system. They are the intermediary between intramural and extramural health care institutions.

3   The organization of home help services

3.1   *Organizations for home help services*

Home help services are provided by different organizations in provinces. Officially the province is responsible for a network of social services pursuant to the legal guidelines (*Sozialhilfegesetz*). This responsibility is mostly delegated to organizations belonging to the *Freie Wohlfahrtspflege*. In Vienna, organizations at three different levels are concerned with home help services. At the first level, a governmental organization is responsible for the administration and finance of hospitals, nursing homes and home care services. Second, the *Magistratsabteilung 47 (MA 47)*, a governmental division, offers and co-ordinates home help services, and finances organizations in the field. At the third level, formal non-profit organizations deliver home help services, these organizations are called *Soziale Dienste*. In Niederösterreich the *Sozialstationen* and in Tirol the *Sprengel* are, as local associations (*Vereine*), engaged in providing home help services and home nursing. In the other parts of Austria nearly the same organizations mentioned in section 2.1 are providing home help.

Home help organizations cover all domestic health services, assistance in running the household, services for improving social contacts and meals-on-wheels. In Vienna, there also is a cleaning, washing, reparation and visiting service. This even includes looking after sick children.

3.2   *Manpower in home help services*

In Austria different types of home helps work for home help organizations. In Kärnten, these people work on voluntary basis only. In other provinces, the organization employs a small group of home helps, family helps and geriatric helps but depend for providing services on a much greater group of voluntary helps.

The following types of home help work for home help organizations:
- the family help (*Familienhilfe*), who has two years training, supports families where the mother is temporarily ill.
- the home help (*Heimhilfe*), who has a short training period of ten weeks or 400 hours, does housework, basic personal care and general support.
- the neighbourhood help (*Nachbarschaftshilfe*), who has no specific training or education at all, and works as a volunteer.

- in Vienna, the home helps who provide the visiting service have a about 20-hour training. Cleaning, washing and repair service staff has no specific training.

A lot of those working as home helps were formerly unemployed and have had periods of short training. Information on manpower is available for Vienna only. A total number of 3,520 home helps (*Heimhilfen*) work in Vienna (2,194 FTEs). The home-help-to-population ratio is 1:749.

3.3 Client population

In Austria 2.1% of the population aged 65 and older receive these services [9]. In Vienna 74% of the clients of home help organizations are 75 years or older, 16% are between 65 and 74 years old and a small group (10%) are below 65. Most of the clients (84%) are female and living alone (85%). Of the other clients, 14% live with a spouse only and 1% live with spouse and others [16]. According to a study in Tirol in 1993 [14], 92% of the clients, who received neighbourhood-help, were over 60 years of age. One third of the family help is given to clients up to 19 years of age and one third to older clients (> 60). In Niederösterreich 75% of the clients are women, 50% live on their own and the average age is 80. As mentioned in 2.3 about 41% of the clients have a hospital or nursing home indication [15].

3.4 Provision of services

The home help organizations provide temporary care for families or individuals at home. This care includes basic nursing care, home-making activities, pedagogical and psychological care, and *Betreuungsdienste* (keeping the elderly company, help with correspondence, taking clients to the doctor etc.).

Clients do not have free access to home help organizations, they always need a referral by the 'MA 47' (see for a description section 3.1). The 'MA 47' acts as an intermediary between the clients and to one of the home help organizations. There are no explicit criteria for this. Most of the clients are unaware that different organizations exist.

In 1993, the first contact between the home help organization and a client was initiated by the client him/herself or his/her family in 55% of the cases. In 22% of the cases a hospital or old peoples home initiated the first contact; in

9% this was done by a home nursing organization; in 3% by a general practitioner and in 2% by other professional care-providers.

After a client has sought contact, a qualified home nurse of the 'MA 47' visits the client at home and assesses the needs. At the same time the home nurse decides upon the type of help the client is going to receive and during what period of time. Ultimately the amount of help the client receives depends on the indicated level of dependency for the attendance allowance (*Pflegestufe*). During the assessment of the home nurse, it is possible that he/she determines that the client needs home nursing care. Standardized assessment forms are used to assess the need for home help services.

The home helps who actually provide the home help services work alone and operate from their own homes or a home help services building.

In Niederösterreich, the majority of clients (55%) receive help from the *Sozialstation* for more than one year. The number of hours, that the client receives varies from 10 to 190 hours a month [13].

3.5 Problems and recent developments

In Austria, none of the organizations which provide home help services have waiting lists. At this moment there is no shortage of home helps, but in the near future it is possible that, as a consequence of the increase in numbers of working women, the number of voluntary helps will decrease slowly. Up to now the system has depended on voluntary helps.

In Vienna there are some problems in co-operation between home help organizations and general practitioners, home nursing organizations and hospitals. The first problem is the lack of co-ordination between intramural and extramural care-providers, and between home helps and home nurses. Secondly, many general practitioners are unaware of the home help, home nursing and the visiting service options. Thirdly, the organizations have not defined or described their services. This makes is difficult to protect the field, and the result is that different types of organization provide the same services.

Recently the amount of services for a client has been related to the level indicated for the attendance allowance. Older people sometimes have difficulty in admitting their dependency. As a result they are assigned to a lower level on the attendance-allowance-scale, get less money and can ultimately not afford the help they really need. Secondly, home help services are becoming more client-oriented. In the past, most of the home helps were formerly unemployed. An important purpose of the organization was creating jobs. Another point is the payment system of the attendance allowance. Now, the client gets cash and it is quite easy to take advantage of it, so policy-makers are looking for an alternative method of paying the client. Finally, clients make higher demands upon the quality and the kind of service they receive. Many home help organizations are not prepared for this demands.

Empirical research among the urban elderly shows a clear preference for the further expansion of social services and not for payments for private, informal care [9].

4 Relations between home nursing and home help services

In all parts of Austria, except in Vorarlberg, home nursing and home help services were more institutionalized within the new *Sozialhilfegesetze* in the 1980s. Nowadays most of the organizations of the *Freie Wohlfahrtspflege* provide both services. In *Sozialstationen* and *Sprengel* several ambulatory care services, including home nursing and home help, were combined.

In those parts of Austria where one of the two services has been in existence much longer than the other, there are problems with the division of labour. If there are not enough qualified home nurses, geriatric or home helps provide basic care as well as some technical home care. In Vorarlberg the situation is different because of the long history of home nursing. There are more qualified home nurses than in other parts of Austria, so home nurses provide technical home nursing care as well as basic care and preventive care.

The co-operation between the two services depends on the initiative of the home nurses and home helps. For the future, organizations are striving for a clearer division of labour between home nurses and home helps.

5 The financing of home nursing

5.1 Payment and patients' insurance

There is one public insurance scheme for all; only one per cent of the population is insured privately.

In general, both for home nursing as well as for home help services, the Austrian system is based on the principle of subsidiarity: if there is informal service provision, no formal services are offered; if formal services are needed, the patient has to pay for them (except for technical home nursing activities which are reimbursed by the Health Insurance funds). The price for one hour home nursing services is ATS 450-480. In Vienna, if the service is provided by the public home nursing organization and Kärnten patients do not have to pay for the basic services of home nurses. In Vorarlberg every member of the *Verein* pays a membership-fee of ATS 300 but they do not have to pay for home nursing services separately. In general the proportion of out-of-pocket payments for the individual patient depends on his/her income. In 1993 in Niederösterreich most of the patients paid between ATS 80 and 90 an hour independently of the kind of services they received [13].

Until 1977 only patients with a hospital indication could get help from a qualified home nurse. But the Health Insurance fund was not obliged to bear the costs. Since 1977 the *Allgemeine Sozialversicherungsgesetz* is changed (*32. ASVG-Novelle*) and it is no longer necessary to have a hospital indication. Payment is still unresolved. Since 1992, professional qualified home nursing is covered by the health insurance system in order to release hospitals and nursing homes. It is important for reimbursement to have a referral from a practitioner. Basic nursing and home help are not covered by the public health insurance system. For patients who need basic care of other kinds of social services the *Sozialhilfegesetz* is appropriate. This means that home nursing will be provided in accordance with the *Soziale Diensten*.

So, two types of benefit are distinguished in the general social insurance law (*Allgemeine Sozialversicherungsgesetz* §151):
- specialized nursing (*medizinische Hauskrankenpflege*), technical nursing procedures as a support for medical treatment
- basic nursing (*Grundpflege*), personal care such as bathing, health monitoring, and so on.

According to the *Allgemeine Sozialversicherungsgesetz* §151 part 5 technical home nursing is an obligation (*Plichtleistung*) without time limits, a right, whereas basic nursing is a volunteer service by the Health Insurance fund. In practice home nursing care is limited to four to eight weeks.

5.2   Funding of the organizations

Beside the payment of the Health Insurance funds for technical home nursing activities the funding of the organizations differs slightly from province to province. This depends on the legal form of the organization. In Burgenland the institutionalized neighbourhood help is paid by the province. In Kärnten basic home nursing is paid by the province as part of the welfare services.

The sources of income of the organizations in the other provinces can be divided into:
-   subventions by the province and municipalities on the basis of the *Sozialhilfegesetz*;
-   out-of-pocket payment;
-   gifts;
-   the organization's own funds.

In Vienna, 46.5% of the income for home nursing organizations come from taxes, 42.5% from Health Insurance funds and 10% from patient's out-of-pocket payment.

The reimbursement of the home nursing organizations is based on a fixed budget (*Pauschale*). Health Insurance funds stated criteria that have to be met by the home nursing organization. Private organizations are reimbursed for the different home nurses activities by the patient. In Vienna 6% of the home nursing organizations operate on a for-profit basis.

5.3   Payment of the nurses

Nurses working independently are paid directly by the patient or have a contract with a specific home nursing organization which pays them on a fee-for-service basis.

All nurses employed by the home nursing organizations are paid a monthly salary. In 1993, the following wages were paid:
-   Qualified home nurse: between ATS 14,000 and 23,000.
-   Geriatric help: between ATS 12,000 and 15,000.
-   Nurse assistant: between ATS 12,000 and 15,000.

All wages are per month and based on full-time employment.

5.4 Problems and recent developments

A problem is the reimbursement of basic home nursing care. Since 1992 technical home nursing care has been insured by the Health Insurance funds, all the other forms of home nursing are still uninsured i.e. Health Insurance funds are free whether or not they reimburse the costs. In Vienna, the public home nursing organization has a monopoly because they can offer free home nursing within limitations of their staff. It is much more difficult to get a reimbursement for private home nursing organizations in Vienna.

Another problem is the home nurses' low salary. The wages of qualified nurses working in hospitals are higher than the wages paid by home nursing organizations.

A general problem is the decrease in state subsidies. This decrease is in part caused by the lack of financial and professional documentation by the home nursing organizations. Without the documentation they are not able to justify the financial support received.

6 The financing of home help services

6.1 Payment and clients insurance

In Austria there is one public insurance scheme for all. No private insurance schemes exist. Payment for home help services, as for home nursing, are based on the principle of subsidiarity. Clients have to pay for home help services themselves.

There are two main financial systems for strengthening informal care: first, direct payment for care from family members and neighbours (*Aufwandsentschädigung*) and second, indirect payment through attendance allowances (*Pflegegeld*) for dependent persons to be used for remunerating formal and informal help and care [9]. Since 1993 everybody, living in Austria, above the age of three and in need of continuous care for more than six months can ask for an attendance allowance from the pensions insurance [17]. The allowance is paid directly to the indigent person, independent of the reason for the handicap and the means of the person. Depending on the degree of need, an insurance physician determines the level of dependency (*Pflegestufe*) of the patient. The degree of need is determined by medical criteria and by the extent to which a person's capacity to live independently is reduced. The minimum payment is about ATS 2,500 per month; the maximum payment is ATS 20,000 for severely handicapped persons [9].

In 1993, two thirds of the care a patient in Vienna received could be paid from the attendance allowance and the patient had to pay one third from his/her own funds. The amount of the out-of-pocket payment depends on the income. Only clients with a monthly income below ATS 6,700 were not required to pay for the services. The price for one hour of home help service is ATS 300-350. In Vorarlberg patients pay a membership-fee. The average patient in Niederösterreich pays ATS 80-90 an hour [15].

For all clients there is a ceiling on the amount of care he/she is entitled to receive, but no official regulation determines the maximum. Clients do not need a referral by a doctor in order to be reimbursed for home help services, but in order to get the attendance allowance, a doctor from the pension insurance assesses the need for help and indicates the level of dependency.

6.2 The funding of the organizations

The funding of *Sozialstationen*, *Sprengel* and the *Vereine* in Vorarlberg has already been described in section 5.2. The *Soziale Dienste* in Vienna have the following sources of income: 75% from taxes, 12% from Health Insurance funds and 13% from clients out-of-pocket payment. The reimbursement of the organization is based on the number of hours care is delivered. Home help organizations do not have to meet any criteria in order to be financed.

6.3 Payment of the home helps

Home helps employed by home help organizations are paid a monthly salary or a fee for every hour. In 1993, the following wages were paid:
- Home help: between ATS 12,000 and 14,000.
- Personnel of the visiting service and for delivering meals: ATS 6,000 and 7,000.
- Personnel of the cleaning service: ATS 8,000 and 9,000.
- Personnel of the reparation services: ATS 10,000 and 11,000.

The wages for home helps are per month and based on full-time employment. The other personnel were paid a fee for every hour. Their wages are an average per month based on less than 40 hours a week.

6.4 Problems and recent developments

There are problems with the method of reimbursement of the home help organizations and the home helps. As in section 3.1 is mentioned the 'MA 47' finances the home help organizations. One of the problems is that the reimbursement for one hour of care does not always cover the real costs of the organizations. The second problem is the home helps' low salary. The salary for working in the evening and working on Sundays is the same as during the week. The trade union is trying to reduce these problems by negotiating with the home help organizations.

Acknowledgement
Information for this chapter was provided by:
Mrs. Regina Ertl
Mr. Mag. Peter Jakadofsky
Dachverband Wiener Pflege- und Sozialdienste
Wien

References

1 BOERMA W.G.W., F.A.J.M. DE JONG, P.H. MULDER. Health care and general practice across Europe. Utrecht: NIVEL, 1993.
2 OECD HEALTH DATA. Version # 1.5. Paris: OECD, 1993.
3 GROENEWEGEN, P.P., J. VAN DER ZEE, R. VAN HAAFTEN. Remunerating general practitioners in Western Europe. Aldershot: Avebury, 1991.
4 VREUGDENHIL, J.C., M. DE BRUINE. Gezondheidszorg in Europa: structuur en financiering van de gezondheidszorg in enkele Europeses landen. Rotterdam: BMG, 1992.
5 KEMENADE, Y.W. VAN. Health care in Europe. The finance and reimbursement systems of 18 European countries. Zoetermeer: Nationale Raad voor de Volksgezondheid, 1993.
6 SCHNEIDER, M., P. BIENE-DIETRICH, M. GABANYI, M. HUBER, A. KÖSE, L. SCHOLTES, J.H. SOMMER. Gesundheitssysteme im internationalen Vergleich: Laufende Berichterstattung zu ausländischen Gesundheitssystemen: Ausgabe 1992. Ausburg: BASYS, 1993.

7 BADELT C., J. PAZOUREK. Care for the elderly in Austria. In: Evers, A., I. Svetlik (eds.). New welfare mixes for the elderly, vol.2. Vienna: European Centre for Social Welfare policy and Research, 1991.

8 BADELT C., A. HOLZMANN. Care for the elderly in Austria: innovative projects on the local level. In: Evers, A., Svetlik I. (eds.). Balancing Pluralism: New welfare mixes in Care for the elderly. Aldershot: Avebury, 1993.

9 HÖRL, J. Eldercare Policy between the state and family: Austria. In: Bass, S.A., R. Morris (eds.). International perspectives on state and family support for the elderly. New York/London/Norwood: The Haworth Press, 1993.

10 FÜLÖP, G., E. SCHÄFER, R. FRISCH. Hauskrankenpflege in Öster- reich. Österreichisches Bundesinstitut für Gesundheitswesen: Wien, 1988.

11 BARBISCH, J., T. KREMMEL. Hauskrankenpflege in Vorarlberg. Amt der Vorarlberger Landesregierung: Bregenz, 1992.

12 AMT DER TIROLER LANDESREGIERUNG. Sollkonzept Sozial- und Gesundheitssprengel in Tirol. Amt der Tiroler Landesregierung: Innsbruck, 1991.

13 WIEGELE, B. Aufgaben und Wandel in der Ambulanten Altenhilfe. In Altwerden in Niederösterreich II "Altersalmanach 1994" edited by Amann, A., M. Kneusel, G. Nemeth, E. Urbas, B. Wiegele. Zentrum für Alterns- wissenschaften: Krems, 1994.

14 TRAWEGER, Ch. Jahresbericht der Sozial- und Gesundheitssprengel Tirol 1993. Universität Innsbruck: Innsbruck, 1994.

15 WIEGELE, B. Leistungsstrukturen der Ambulanten Dienste in Nieder- österreich - eine Bestandsanalyse. In Anspruchs- und Effizienzanalyse der Hauskrankenpflege in Niederösterreich edited by Amann, A., M. Kneusel, B. Wiegele. Zentrum für Alternswissenschaften: Krems, 1994.

16 Statistische Aufzeichnung Stadt Wien und Privater Anbieter in Wien: Wien, 1994.

17 Betreuung zu Hause, Soziale Dienste 1994;6:8.

2 Home care in Belgium

Jack B.F. Hutten

1   The setting of home care

1.1   The country

Belgium is one of the six initial member states of the European Community, the economic precursor of the European Union. It has been a hereditary constitutional monarchy since 1830. The king has only minor political power. The 212 member Chamber of Representatives is elected by proportional representation. The country consists of ten provinces and almost 600 municipalities. Probably more significant is the heterogeneity of its population, culturally as well as geographically. Roughly speaking, Belgium is divided between Flemings, the Dutch speaking population in the northern half, and Walloons who live in the southern part and speak French. Brussels is a third separate community, bilingual, with its own regional government. In the eastern part of the country there is a German speaking minority (1% of the population), yet with its own consultative parliament [1].

Over the past 20-30 years, Belgium has been developing into a federal state. An increasing number of tasks and responsibilities are delegated by the national government to the governments of the three communities: the Flemish, Walloon and Brussels communities. As regards health care, they are responsible for setting the minimum standards for health care provision,

62

management of social services, care for the elderly, health education, and home care. The central government is still involved in health insurance, planning of hospital care, professional education, and quality of care in general [2,3].

Population key figures (1990) [1,4]

Population in mln.	10.0
Inhabitants per sq. km.	327
% Living in urban areas	97
% over 65 years	14.9
% over 75 years	6.6
Births per 1000	12.6
Deaths per 1000	10.4
Life expectancy (men)	72.4
Life expectancy (women)	79.1

1.2 The organization of health care

Belgium has a highly privatized system of health care supply, which is very complex and relies for a great deal on private initiative [1,5,6]. With a large number of non-governmental organizations, struggling for independence and maintenance of their position, the organization is competitive in nature. Direct government involvement is limited to regulation and partial funding. Most health services are organized at the regional level.

The tasks of primary and secondary care are not well defined, which results in overlapping activities and competition among physicians [1]. Primary care is provided by numerous general practitioners (GPs) and by many specialists, in their private practice or in hospital out-patient departments. Patients are free to choose any doctor they like; no referral is required for a visit to a medical specialist. People can also apply for hospital admission, the need for which will be judged by a hospital doctor.

The physician density and the number of hospitals and hospital beds are quite high [1]. Most hospital beds are in private or semi private facilities: all function on a non-profit basis. Doctors are paid on a fee-for-service basis.

Health care figures (1990) [4]

Expenditure

Total expenditure on health		
Absolute per head in ppp$	1242	
Percentage of GDP	7.6	
Public expenditure on health		
Absolute per head in ppp$	1104	
Percentage of GDP	6.8	

Manpower

Physicians per 1000 pop.	3.4	
GPs per 1000 pop.	1.5	
Qualified nurses per 1000 pop.	6.5	('88)

Hospital care

In-patient care	
Beds per 1000 pop.	9.8
Admissions per 100 pop.	18.0
Mean length of stay	14.4
Acute hospitals	
Beds per 1000 pop.	5.6
Admissions per 100 pop.	17.0
Mean length of stay	10.0
Nursing homes	
Beds per 1000 pop.	2.3

1.3   Health financing and insurance

52% of Belgian health care are financed from social insurance premiums, 27% from taxes, 21% from direct payments and only 2% from additional private insurance [1,5].

There are two social health insurance schemes: one general scheme compulsory for all employees and their dependents and covering a broad range of risks and another scheme, also compulsory, covering only 'great risks' (mostly hospital care) for the self-employed. Nevertheless, about 70% of the self-employed take out a voluntary complementary health insurance covering ambulatory medical care, drugs, and protheses [6].

A key position in the insurance scheme is taken by the six Health Insurance Associations (mutualities) supervised by the National Sickness and Disability Fund (RIZIV). These mutualities are umbrella associations with different religious and political backgrounds: the Christian and Socialist organizations are the largest with 4.5 and 2.6 million insured respectively [5]. Mutualities are more than just the accounts department of health care, they are also entitled to take the initiative in the provision of care.

Despite the decentralized character, funds are centrally collected by the National Office of Social Security (ONSS/RSZ) and consist of premiums from employers, employees and self-employed as well as governmental subsidies for the benefit of the unemployed, the aged and the poor. Insurance premiums are income-related and set by negotiations between the medical profession and national social affairs authorities. The ONSS/RSZ is responsible for the distribution of these funds via the National Sickness Insurance Institution (INAMI/RIZIV) to the six Health Insurance Associations.

The remuneration system is based on the principle of reimbursement. Patients pay the bills directly and get (a part of) their money back from the local Health Insurance office. Hospital bills are mostly directly paid by the office.

A substantial part of health care costs is directly paid by the patients (co-payments: the so-called *ticket modérateur* or *remgeld*). The governments of the communities determine the amount of co-payment. For hospital admissions, patients have to pay a fee for the first day. Generally, patients have to pay 20-25% of the costs for primary care themselves. Widows, elderly people, handicapped and orphans have lower levels of co-payments. There is no maximum limit to the amount of co-payment for an individual patient.

1.4   Care for the elderly

Generally, services for the elderly are relatively well developed in Belgium [7,8]. The Flemish and Walloon communities have issued a decree, concerning the recognition and subsidy of services for the elderly, in 1985 and 1984 respectively [3]. Like in most of the European countries, the government stresses the importance of a higher degree of independence for the elderly allowing them to live in their own social environment as long as possible. This requires a more qualified care provided in the community [9]. Although professional home care has a high priority, the policy not only emphasizes professional care but also encourages informal care provided by family members, neighbours or friends [8]. However, for demographic reasons, the growth of the informal network is stagnating [3] and although there is a formal obligation for children to support their parents if indigent, a decreasing number of the elderly choose to live with their families [9]. The encouragement of home care implies cutting down the costs of hospital care by bed reduction and reconversion of acute hospital beds to beds in rest and nursing homes [3].

Community services. In addition to home nursing and home help services, which will be discussed later, other forms of community facilities are available for the benefit of elderly people. About 30% make use of 'meals-on-wheels' services [7]. Furthermore, one of every three municipalities has a 'service centre' (*dienstencentrum*). These centres provide hot meals, have bathing facilities and are very important meeting places for recreational activities. They are mainly subsidized by the government [3].

Residential services. In 1991, about 5.4% of the Belgian population over 65 lived in residential homes (old people's homes). More than 60% of the old people's homes are private organizations and about 25% work on a for-profit basis. It is estimated that about 70% of the total costs of old people's homes are paid by the elderly themselves, 16% are contributed by the public centres for social welfare (PCSW) and 14% by the social health insurance [7]. About 30% of the residents receive a contribution from the PCSW. There are main problems regarding living facilities (individual toilets, safety regulations) and the shortage of qualified personnel.

In Flanders especially, there is a tendency to increase the number of semi-residential services such as service flats, collective housing with services, day centres, and centres for night time relief. This policy is reflected in the planning standards for residential care. The former national planning standards of seven beds in old people's homes for 1,000 inhabitants are still used in the Walloon and Brussels communities, while the government of Flanders has replaced these standards by new ones: four beds in old people's homes per 100 elderly over 60 and three places in sheltered housing per 100 elderly over 60. A problem, however, with these living facilities is that they are more expensive and are therefore mostly occupied by richer elderly people.

In 1987, about one third of all hospital admissions involved people over 65. Hospitals also have special wards for elderly patients. Geriatric wards are meant especially for acute problems and specialized care. Special psycho-geriatric wards are available in general and psychiatric hospitals for the demented elderly. There is, however, an increasing shortage of beds in these kinds of wards. The shortage of services for the demented elderly or those with psychiatric problems is a major problem in Belgium [7].

Finally, there are long-stay wards in the hospitals: originally intended for continuous care and rehabilitation of the elderly with non-acute problems. However, these beds are more frequently used for the relief of the severely disabled elderly which increases the average length of stay and obstructs the circulation of patients. Consequently, the government intends to reduce these long-stay wards and encourages the replacement of the permanent care of the severely disabled elderly to rest and nursing homes associated with general hospitals or old people's homes.

Capacity of residential services for the elderly in Belgium (1990) [7]

	Number of places/beds per 1000 people over 65 years
Old people's homes	65.7
Service flats[1]	2.5
Rest and nursing homes	10.8
Geriatric wards	3.8
Long-stay wards	3.1
Psycho-geriatric wards	1.2

[1] Flanders only

2 The organization of home nursing

2.1 Organizations for home nursing

In Belgium, home nursing services are mainly provided by private organizations which work on a non-profit basis and an increasing number of independent nurses working in private practices. It is estimated that about 40% of the market are covered by independent nurses.

The largest organization is the White/Yellow Cross which covers the whole country and performs about 50% of all home nursing activities. The White/Yellow Cross is divided into three main organizational levels. The actual provision of care is organized at the local level. There are 180 local departments consisting of 20 to 40 nurses and lead by a head nurse. These departments are controlled and supported by the nine Provincial Cross

Associations which determine the number of nurses per region and contract the home nurses. The National Federation of White-Yellow Cross Associations is an umbrella organization which supports the provincial cross associations, develops policy in co-operation with the provincial cross associations and represents these in contacts with ministries, social associations and professional organizations.

Furthermore, there are a number of smaller organizations like Solidarity for the Family. This organization provides both home nursing and home help services, mainly in Eastern Flanders. Its catchment area is divided into nursing regions which are further divided into sectors in which about 20 nurses and one social nurse are employed [2]. The total nursing staff consists of about 120 employees. In the Walloon community, an equivalent organization exists namely the C.S.D.(*Centre des Soins à Domicile*).

Because other home care organizations are relatively small and more locally orientated organizations, our description of home nursing in Belgium will focus mainly on the White/Yellow Cross.

2.2 Manpower in home nursing services

In 1991, about 15,000 nurses were working in the Belgian home care: about 8,000 (53%) of them were working independently. A large number of nurses have part-time jobs. The White/Yellow Cross e.g. has contracted 4,800 nurses who represents 3,620 FTEs [10]. A comparative study in the Euroregion (the area around Maastricht, where the borders of the Netherlands, Belgium and Germany meet) shows that most Belgian home nurses work between 20 and 28 hours a week [11].

Three levels of nursing expertise can be distinguished in Belgium. *Graduate nurses* (*gegradueerd verpleegkundigen*) have had two years of basic training followed by one year's specialization in hospital nursing, psychiatric nursing, paediatric nursing or two years in social nursing. *Brevetted nurses* (*gebrevetteerd verpleegkundingen*) are trained for three years with a higher emphasis on the practical part of the job. The admission requirements for this training are less strict. Graduate and brevetted nurses are authorized to perform the same kind of tasks. The third, marginal group in home nursing care are the *brevetted hospital assistants* (*gebrevetteerd ziekenhuisassistentes*) with two year's training in the hospital. In practice, they can do the same tasks as other nurses, but must always be supervised by a graduate or brevetted nurse.

Most of the nurses employed by The White/Yellow Cross are brevetted (49%) or graduate (45%); only 6% are hospital assistants [10].

2.3   Client population

Vandenbroele et al. estimated that about 29.9 per 1000 inhabitants received home nursing care from The White/Yellow Cross [12]. Two out of three patients are women and the percentage of patients over 80 of age is increasing fast: to almost 36% in 1993. About one fifth of the patients are below 60 [10].

2.4   Provision of services

When a person is in need of home nursing care, he/she can contact a home nursing organization or an independent nurse directly. Theoretically, patients have free choice as to which home nursing organization they approach, but this choice is often restricted by the limited availability of different organizations in the region. However, recently the opportunity to choose between home care delivered by formal organizations and home care by private nurses has increased enormously.

About 80% of the first contacts with the White/Yellow Cross departments are initiated by the patient him/herself or his/her family, in 15% of the cases the hospital contacts the nursing organization and the general practitioner in the remaining 5% [2]. This does not mean that GPs only play a minor role. Most patients have a prescription from their physician because a formal authorization is required for all technical nursing activities such as injections, otherwise the health insurance associations do not reimburse these costs [2,11]. Only general nursing activities, such as ADL-support, are freely accessible for heavily dependent patients.

After the first contact, a nurse from the home nursing organization will visit the patient to assess the patient's level of care dependency. A standardized screeningform (*De aangepaste KATZ-schaal*) is used which includes six questions about activities of daily living and five additional items about mental problems and social circumstances [12]. The ADL-items are derived from the original Katz-scale [13] and include the degree of impairment with regard to bathing, dressing, moving, continence, going to the toilet, and nutrition. Orientation in time and place, restlessness, the living situation, availability of informal care, and living conditions (bathroom, hot water supply) are the other five aspects which are taken into account. The score of an individual patient determines the remuneration of the nursing services (see below) and the amount, type and duration of the home nursing activities needed.

There are no special professionals for the assessment procedure: all nurses who provide home care are also able to fill out the screeningforms. Accordingly, the assessment of needs, the actual provision of care and the evaluation of the care provided are mostly the responsibility of the same person.

The actual nursing care provided includes hygiene and other personal care, routine technical nursing procedures (injections, stoma care, bladder washouts), more complicated nursing activities (epidural anaesthesia, handling respirator, catherization), patient education, and the encouragement of informal care. ADL-assistance, injections and wound dressing are the activities most frequently performed by the Belgian home nurses during home visits [11,14].

Home nurses from the White/Yellow Cross work in teams co-ordinated by the local departments. In daily practice, most of them operate from their own homes because each nurse takes care of her own specific area.

2.5   Problems and recent developments

There are no waiting lists for home nursing in Belgium. Patients can immediately be helped because of the availability of a large supply of independent working nurses and an adequate planned nursing staff for home nursing organizations.

A few years ago, a shortage of nurses in home care organizations was reported [2]. However, since 1993 the situation has changed: there is even expected to be a surplus of nurses in the near future.

No problems in the co-operation between home nurses and other health care-providers such as general practitioners and hospitals are mentioned. Although the tasks of home nurses and home helps are strictly divided, there is some confusion about who is responsible for the hygiene care. The possible integration of home helps in formal established home care teams might also lead to more problems. However, the political debate about the integration of both home care disciplines is still going on.

3 The organization of home help services

3.1 Organizations for home help services

In general, the organization of home help services, mainly help with housework, is strictly separated from home nursing activities. Some exceptions are already mentioned, that is Solidarity for the Family in Eastern Flanders and the *Centre des Soins à Domicile* in the Walloon region which provide both home nursing and home help services.

Belgium has a number of formal home help organizations with their own catchment areas. Together they cover the whole country and have the same organizational structure in the Flemish, Walloon and Brussels communities. An important distinction must be made between public and private organizations. Although 76% of the home help services organizations are part of the public and 24% to the private sector [9,15], the latter accounts for almost 80% of the hours worked [16].

The Ministry of Social Welfare and the Family is responsible for the public home help services. The actual organization and responsibility of the provision of home help services is, however, at the local level. Each municipality should have its own PCSW which is in charge of social services in general and services for home help in the family and for the elderly in particular. The municipalities have the authority to control the budget of the centres. There are 589 PCSWs in Belgium. These centres own hospitals, old people's homes, and alternative housing units. They organize home help services, cleaning services, job services, service centres and meal distribution. The social function is mainly to grant the elderly with an insufficient income a benefit equal to the subsistence level and, if necessary, to contribute to the accommodation expenses in the institutions [3].

The principal professional home help organizations started about 40 years ago, having been based on charity and voluntary work [8]. Private home help organizations are still associated or linked with broader social organizations (e.g. the Christian Workers movement, Socialist movement) and organizations for more specific groups such as the Catholic Pensioners Union, other religious groups, and Health Insurance funds (mutualities). They are also organized at a local level and their catchment area is restricted. Examples of these kinds of organizations are Family Help (*Familiehulp*), Family Care (*Familiezorg*), and Solidarity for the Family (*Solidariteit voor het gezin*).

71

3.2   Manpower in home help services

Home helps are mainly involved in housework [8]. There are no gradations in the qualifications of the home helps. However, since the end of 1970 long-term unemployed people (unemployed for least two years) were able to be employed in community jobs, e.g. in the so called cleaning services (*poetsdiensten*). The cleaners are attached to the home help organizations and can be considered as a separate type of home help which requires no specific qualifications.

Recognized home helps, the family and elderly helps, are supposed to have an adequate level of educational. Vocational training at upper secondary level is required, for instance training as a family social-worker, family and health worker, children's nurse or a training in an acknowledged training centre for home-help workers. The training must include moral, psychological, hygienic, social and domestic knowledge and include 500 hours of theoretical training and 150 hours of practical training in various health and social institutes. In addition to this, home helps must also participate in some in-service training every two years [17].

Statistical figures about the volume of workers in home help services are only available for the Flemish community. In 1992, 9,944 professional family and elderly helps and 6,949 cleaners were registered. About 80% of the cleaners worked part-time (total FTEs: 4,801) and 53% of the helps (total FTEs: 8,023).

3.3   Client population

In 1992, 46,649 clients received home help services in the Flemish community: 70% were over 65. This accounts for 0.8% of the total population or 3.8% of elderly people. Only figures of 1989 are available for the Walloon community: 1.2% of the total population or 4.4% of the elderly received home help services from professional organizations.

According to the Yearly Report of Family Help, the largest organization in the Flemish community, about 75% of their clients are female, most of them live alone (46%), and a majority (58%) are over 75 [18].

The client population of home help services is characterized as the most vulnerable category of elderly people, that is the oldest among the elderly living alone, without children, financially weak and with a multi-pathological state of health [9].

3.4   Provision of services

Theoretically all clients are free to choose the organization for home help themselves. However, in some regions there are only one or two professional organizations able to provide home help services. No formal referral is needed. So potential clients can contact the home help organizations themselves. In 54% of the cases the client him/herself or his/her family firstly applies for home help. Hospitals and social workers of Health Insurance funds and PCSWs are also important initiators (respectively in 13 and 15% of the cases). It is important to notice that only 4% of the clients are recruited by home nurses or GPs [18].

The needs of the potential client are assessed through a so called social investigation performed by a social worker (or social nurse) who is responsible for the first contact with the client, the work schedule of the home helps and the follow-up. Since 1994, the so called BEL-profile scale (*Basis Eerste Lijn*) is applied by all subsidized services. This scale consists of the same items as the Katz-scale, discussed before for the home nursing activities, completed by some specific items concerning household activities. The income of the client is also part of the social investigation not to determine the needs of care but because it is used to calculate the level of co-payment by the client. The decision about the type of home help care to be provided and the period of care is made by the service managers or special committees of the organizations.

The next step is the actual provision of home help services by home helps employed by the organizations. All home helps and cleaners operate from their own homes; not from central working units like health centres, hospitals or old people's homes. About 80% of the Flemish home helps work alone, 20% are part of community teams [16]. The work of cleaners is limited to the cleaning of the house. Home helps provide a larger range of care, i.e. housework (preparing meals, washing dishes, washing and ironing, and cleaning), hygienic and other personal care (bathing, ADL-help), moral support (counselling and advice), general and family support (shopping, going for a walk, administrative support), and occasionally encouraging help from family members, neighbours or friends. In practice, the same organizations will provide cleaning as well as home help to the same client.

Home helps provide an average of 11 hours help per week per family, generally the help is spread over two days [12]. The cleaning services deliver help an average of four hours a week per family. The majority of patients receive help one day a week, but there is also a considerable group who only receive cleaning help once in 14 days [12]. This is probably due to the fact that travel costs are not subsidized and therefore need to be kept to a minimum [8].

3.5 Problems and recent developments

Some of the new clients of home help services have to wait before they actually receive home help. About 10% of the potential clients are placed on a waiting list and the waiting time varies between one and six months. Shortage of personnel and the increasing number of applicants for home help services are the most important causes. One of the main policy measures to reduce the size of the waiting lists was the introduction of cleaning services by long-term unemployed people. This policy increased the hours available by almost 40%. A growth of the number of subsidized hours by home helps was also achieved in the period between 1989 and 1993; a growth of 6.7% was established and in 1994 a growth of 3.0% is expected. Thirdly, a choice was made to reduce the frequency of help for individual clients from 296 hours a client per year in 1986 to 236 hours in 1991 [18].

Problems were also reported regarding the co-operation with all other professional care-providers. Home help is still considered as a low status job which mainly involves of cleaning services.

There is too an overlap with the tasks of home nurses who also provide a lot of ADL-supportive activities. This can lead to conflicts at the homes of their clients.

4 Relations between home nursing and home help services

Generally, home nursing and home help services are separately organized. Only a few organizations provide both kinds of home care. However, in the actual provision of care co-operation between home nurses and home helps is increasing. Home helps sometimes assist home nurses in the daily care of the patient (especially with hygienic tasks) and occasionally signal problems which they discuss together. A survey in a specific region of Flanders shows that 2.8% of the home nursing clients also received home help services and 18.3% of the home help clients also received home nursing care [12].

Most professional and even informal home care-providers are now urged to participate in 'team meetings' on shared clients in the context of the 'co-operation initiatives' (*samenwerkingsinitiatieven*) which are co-operative structures for several home care organizations and GPs, organized both locally and regionally [2,3]. These co-ordinating structures are partly subsidized by the Flemish government. They started since 1987 and now about 60 of them are functioning in Flanders. In the Walloon community there is a parallel development.

5   The financing of home nursing services

5.1   Payment and patients' insurance

As mentioned above, there are two public health insurance schemes. One general scheme compulsory for all employees, covering a broad range of risks. Secondly, there is a scheme compulsory for the self-employed only covering 'great risks'. With regard to home nursing there is no out-of-pocket payment. However, patients have to pay a membership fee to the White/Yellow Cross, which varies between BEF 500 and 1,000 per family per year. The actual costs of home nursing activities are paid directly by the Health Insurance funds to the home nursing organizations or the independent nurses. The self-employed patients have to pay full costs including the membership fee. In Belgium, there are no national or other regulations stating the maximum amount of care a patient is entitled to receive.

5.2   Funding of the organizations

The White/Yellow Cross organization works on a non-profit basis. The government provide subsidies for the personnel, co-ordination and management. Governmental subsidies are only paid if the personnel accounts for at least five full-time equivalents. Co-operation initiatives are subsidized on the condition that GPs take a part in them, in addition to teams of nurses, home help services, social services and three representatives of other disciplines. Furthermore, the initiative has to cover a population of at least 25,000 people. However, these subsidies are only a minimal part of the total income of the home nursing organizations. Most of the funding (about 94%) is provided by the Health Insurance funds [2]. The patient's membership fees only account for 3.5% of the income of the White/Yellow Cross.

By law only well-defined nursing tasks can be reimbursed by the health insurance funds, no other activities carried out by home nurses are paid for. Reimbursement requires a formal prescription from a doctor, except for ADL help.

The remuneration is fee-for-service based. Technical nursing care, such as injections, are paid per item of service (nomenclature). Other activities are paid per diem depending on the level of care dependency of the patient. The fact that the dependency level is assessed by the nurses using a standardized form including items regarding physical, mental and social functioning (*de aangepaste Katz' schaal*) has been discussed. Three patient categories are distinguished and the payment system differs for each group:

1. *Less dependent patients*: fee-for-service reimbursement according to a list, which contains technical nursing procedures only. Prevention, caring activities and psychosocial guiding are therefore not reimbursed for these patients.
2. *Moderately dependent patients*: low reimbursement per day of care, about BEF 500 a day.
3. *Highly dependent patients*: high reimbursement per day of care, about BEF 950 a day.

The reimbursements per day are all in. So, the technical nursing procedures are not reimbursed separately.

The home nursing organizations do not have direct influence on the tariffs and budgets which are determined by the RIZIV and the professional nursing organization.

5.3   Payment of the nurses

Nurses working independently are paid directly by the Health Insurance funds or they have a contract with a specific home nursing organization which pays them on a fee-for-service basis. All nurses employed by the home nursing organizations are paid a monthly salary. In 1993, the following wages were paid:

-   Graduate nurses: between BEF 60,000 and 100,000.
-   Brevetted nurses: between BEF 55,000 and 86,000.
-   Brevetted hospital assistants: between BEF 51,500 and 80,000.

All wages are per month and based on full-time employment.

5.4   Problems and recent developments

Between 1991 and 1993 (social agreement regarding the revaluation of nurses' salaries) the salaries of nurses were increasing by 15.57%, the tariffs only increased by 10%. This leaves the home nursing organizations with a budgetary deficit of more than 5.5%. Consequently, the National Federation of the White/Yellow Cross Associations has recently started negotiations with the Social Insurance funds to increase the tariffs by 3% and also discuss a structural reduction in the wages with the nursing trade unions.

6   The financing of home help services

6.1   Payment and clients' insurance

The largest part of the cost of home help services in Belgium is financed by general taxation: 75% by the community governments and 5% by local or provincial authorities. However, all clients have to pay co-payments which account for about 20% of the costs [19].

The level of the client's contribution depends on the net family income and the composition of household (e.g. number of household members). Exceptions are possible for low income groups such as widows, orphans, invalids and pensioners, but they generally also have to pay the lowest level of contribution BEF 19 per hour. In 1991, the average contribution by the clients in the private non-profit sector was BEF 82.3 per hour and in the public sector BEF 75.6 per hour. A part of the client's contribution (30%) is reimbursed to the client through the 'complementary insurance schemes' of the Health Insurance funds.

In the Decree of the Flemish Executive Committee of 1988, specific regulations on the allocation of home help services were established. There are no limitations to the amount of help that *can* be provided for the first 13 weeks. From the 14th week home help is limited to 32 hours a week for each person. Occasionally, the organizations can decide to deviate from this regulation. However, this policy is going to change in the near future. The minister of Social Welfare and the Family wants to cancel the limitations and let the organizations decide how they are going to spend their subsidized hours. In practice, however, the services themselves already make their own agreements about the minimum and maximum amount of home help which can lead to a large variation in services between the organizations [8].

6.2   Funding of organizations

Home help organizations need to be authorized by the Ministry of Social Welfare and the Family to receive governmental funding. The subsidies consist of two parts. Firstly, organizations receive a fixed budget toward overhead costs such as administration, co-ordination costs, and wages of the social workers and managers. The level of the budget is based on the number of clients, home helps and cleaners. The second part is an allowance toward wages and operating costs of the actual work in the families at a certain rate per hour.

To receive an allowance by the government, the organizations have to meet the following criteria:
- total working hours must not exceed the quota that can be subsidized;
- a social inquiry must be carried out to estimate the needs of the applicant before the help is actually granted;
- home help must be provided in the residence of the applicant.

An officially recognized organization employs at least three full-time home helps and can be subsidized for the following staff members:
- one full-time social nurse for every 150 families who receive help;
- one extra half-time social nurse for every additional 75 families;
- one manager for every 150 home helps.

Since 1980, the number of hours that can be reimbursed has been fixed by the government. Each organization has a certain quota of subsidized hours which is stated at the level of provision for 1979. In addition to budgetary considerations, this regulation was intended to force the organizations to be more selective with the provision of help.

An extension of these hours is possible in the context of the IBF (Interdepartmental Budget Fund) and the operation which intended to support employment of long-term unemployed (see section 3.2).

6.3   Payment of the home helps

The wages and social insurance contributions of the cleaners are paid by the state through the Ministry of Employment. Home helps are directly

78

contracted by the authorized home help organizations. On the average, cleaners are paid BEF 43,270 and home helps earn BEF 53,545 a month (both salaries are gross income, 5 years of seniority based on full-time work).

6.4 Problems and recent developments

Because the reimbursement by the Ministry of Social Welfare and the Family is not based on the actual costs, home help organizations have to rely on other sources of income which are uncertain and unpredictable (incidental subsidies from municipalities or provinces) and tend to take clients with a higher personal contribution (those with a higher income) first. Due to the higher level of clients' dependency, there should be a greater role for management which should be paid for. In a recent policy paper by the minister a higher contribution to training and management expenses was promised [20].

There is also a debate about the level of the co-payments by the clients. In general, they are considered too low. However, the contribution of two income families is considered too high.

There are also problems reported regarding the salaries of the home help workers. In particular, mention is made of the difference between salaries in the private and public sector: home helps working for the public organizations earn about 15% more, due to extra salary components. The last upgrading of the salaries of workers in the private sector was in 1988. The wage scales were harmonized, but extra payments such as extra supplement (Christmas bonus) at the end of the year were not taken into account.

A recently published policy paper on the care for the elderly, by the Flemish minister of Social Welfare and the Family, notes future developments and proposed policy [20]. Most of the proposals are related to the cost and payment system. First, the government wants a more simple and transparent system of subsidies, with fewer subsidizing agencies, and a new client contribution system. As the old system only takes incomes into account, some groups with low income but a relatively large amount of property (pensioners) are ahead. Harmonization of the client contributions in home care and those in residential care has also been proposed. Although the government gives priority to the financial support for home care organizations, hospital care remains the main item in the total expenditure on health. Elderly patients stay in acute hospitals longer than necessary because

Jack B.F. Hutten

there are not enough alternatives in the community and secondly, because hospital treatment is free, unlike home help services.

Other important policy objects are a controlled growth of provision, the integration of special employment schemes (IBF) in the financing system and better co-ordination between home help, cleaning, and home nursing services.

Acknowledgement
The questionnaire about home nursing in Belgium was drawn up by Mr. L. Geys (Head Nursing Department, National Federation of the White-Yellow Cross organizations, Brussels). Mr. G. Hedebouw (Project leader Home Care and Care for the Elderly, HIVA, The Catholic University of Leuven, Leuven) provided information about the home help services.

References

1 BOERMA, W.G.W., F.A.J.M. DE JONG, P.H. MULDER. Health care and general practice across Europe. Utrecht: NIVEL, 1993.
2 VERHEIJ, R.A., A. KERKSTRA. International comparative study of community nursing. Aldershot: Avebury, 1992.
3 PACOLET, J., C. WILDEROM (eds.). The economics of care of the elderly. Aldershot: Avebury, 1991.
4 OECD HEALTH DATA. Version # 1.5. Paris: OECD, 1993.
5 SCHNEIDER, M., R.K.H. DENNERLEIN, A. KÖSE, L. SCHOLTES. Health care in the EC member states. Health Policy Special Issue. Health Policy; 1992, 1+2, 113-123.
6 KEMENADE, Y.W. VAN. Health care in Europe. The finance and reimbursement systems of 18 European countries. Zoetermeer: Nationale Raad voor de Volksgezondheid, 1993.
7 NIJKAMP, P., J. PACOLET, H. SPINNEWYN, A. VOLLERING, C. WILDEROM, S. WINTERS. Services for the elderly in Europe. A cross-national comparative study. Leuven/Amsterdam: HIV/VU, 1991.
8 BARO, F., L. MOORTHAMER, G. DE BRUYNE, H. VAN DEN BERGH, K. MAGITS. Home-care services in the Flanders, Belgium. In: Jamieson, A. (eds.). Home care for older people in Europe. Oxford/New York/Tokyo: Oxford University Press, 1991.

9 DOOGHE, G., L. VAN DEN BOER, L. VAN DER LEYDEN. De leefsituatie van de bejaarden, CBGS-mongrafie 1988/1. Brussel: Ministerie van de Vlaamse Gemeenschap, 1988.

10 YEARLY REPORT NATIONAL WHITE-YELLOW CROSS FEDERATION. Brussel: 1993.

11 ZEE, J. VAN DER, K. KRAMER, A. DERKSEN, A. KERKSTRA, F.C.J. STEVENS. Community nursing in Belgium, Germany and the Netherlands. Journal of Advanced Nursing; 1994, 20, 791-801.

12 VANDENBROELE, H., A. BODE, A. LEUS, H. VAN LOON. Het screenen van kliënten in de thuiszorg. Brussel: Nationale federatie van de Wit-Gele-Kruisverenigingen, 1993.

13 KATZ, S., A.B. FORD, R.W. MOSKOWITZ, B.A. JACKSON, M.W. JAFFE. Studies of illness in the aged: the index of ADL: a standardized measure of biological and psychosocial function. Journal of the American Medical Association; 1963, 914-919.

14 GEYS, L., H. VAN LOON. Wat voeren verpleegkundigen uit in de thuis-verpleging? Frequentie van verpleegkundige handelingen in het Wit-Gele Kruis; koncepten en cijfers ter financiering van de thuisverpleging. Brussel: Nationale Federatie Wit-Gele Kruis, 1989.

15 PROVINCIALE WELZIJNSCOMMISSIE ANTWERPEN. Naar een geintegreerd beleid voor thuisverblijvende bejaarden. Antwerpen: 1986.

16 LANNOYE, H. ET AL. Het personeel in de bejaardensector in Vlaan-deren. Leuven/ Antwerpen: HIVA/RUCA, in press.

17 FLEMISH COMMUNITY. Het besluit van 22 juni 1988 van de Vlaamse Executieve tot regeling van de erkenning en subsidiering van de diensten voor gezins- en bejaardenhulp en van de opleidingscentra voor gezins- en bejaardenhulp. Antwerpen: 1988.

18 YEARLY REPORT FAMILY HELP. Brussel: Familiehulp, 1991.

19 MINISTRY OF FINANCE AND BUDGET. Begroting gezondheids-instellingen, welzijn en gezin (unpublished document). Brussels: 1994

20 MINISTRY OF SOCIAL WELFARE AND THE FAMILY. Policy paper on elderly care. Brussels: May, 1994.

3 Home care in Denmark

Jouke van der Zee

1 The setting of home care

1.1 The country

Denmark was the first Scandinavian member state of the European Union; it entered the Union in 1973 together with the United Kingdom and Ireland.

In this constitutional monarchy, a king or queen is the ceremonial head of state. The one-chamber parliament, the *Folketing*, is elected for a period of four years and delegates much of its authority to local government; the 16 counties and the 275 communities that have decision authority on resource allocation to social services, health care, infrastructure and education.

The standard of living in Denmark is among the highest in Europe, as are the tax rates, necessary to pay for the welfare system [1].

Population key figures (1990) [1,2]

Population in mln.	5.14
Inhabitants per sq. km.	119
% Living in urban areas	87
% over 65 years	15.1
% over 75 years	7.0
Births per 1000	12.6
Deaths per 1000	11.6
Life expectancy (men)	72.0
Life expectancy (women)	77.7

1.2 The organization of health care

Overall responsibility for health care lies with the Ministry of Health. The National Board of Health has an important role in the co-ordination of the system and advises the minister [1]. Social services (of which home help forms a part) belong to the domain of the Ministry of Social Affairs. The planning and management of health care facilities and staff are largely decentralized to the counties (*Amt*) and municipalities (*Kommune*), which regularly develop plans for health policy and development of health care services in their own territories. Planning and provision of social services have also been decentralised to the community level. The central government may issue guidelines as to the content of regional plans. The hospitals and a great deal of the out-patient care sector, including general practice, are within the competence of sixteen regions (the city of Copenhagen is one of them) each with 250,000 to 550,000 inhabitants. The remaining primary care facilities, like most of the preventive care, all sorts of adapted and sheltered housing facilities, nursing homes, community nursing and home help services, belong to the domain of the municipalities.

General Practitioners have a central role in the Danish health care system [1]. Most of the population (about 95%) are listed with a particular general practice. Access to specialist or hospital care is only possible, except in cases of emergency, after a formal referral of a GP. In 1993, there was one GP per 1600 inhabitants [1]. GPs are independent practitioners who have contracts with the counties. They are paid via a mixed remuneration system, a capitation and 'fee-for-service' part for each patient, which is aimed at keeping patients in primary care as long as possible [1,3].

Secondary care is mostly provided by hospital-based salaried medical specialists. A limited number, mainly ophthalmologists and E.N.T. specialists, work as independent private practitioners. GPs refer patients to the admission department of a hospital that will allocate the patient to a specific physician.

In 1990, there were 106 general, specialized and categorial hospitals. Most of them were public organizations; a few are in the hands of patient unions and only two were privately owned [1].

Health care figures (1990) [2]

Expenditure

Total expenditure on health		
Absolute per head in ppp$	1051	
Percentage of GDP	6.3	
Public expenditure on health		
Absolute per head in ppp$	870	
Percentage of GDP	5.2	

Manpower

Physicians per 1000 pop.	2.8	
GPs per 1000 pop.	0.7	
Qualified nurses per 1000 pop.	6.4	('89)

Hospital care

In-patient care		
Beds per 1000 pop.	5.7	
Admissions per 100 pop.	21.2	
Mean length of stay	8.0	
Acute hospitals		
Beds per 1000 pop.	4.7	('89)
Admissions per 100 pop.	20.5	
Mean length of stay	6.6	
Nursing homes		
Beds per 1000 pop.	n.a.	

1.3 Health financing and insurance

About 85% of the system are financed by taxation (mainly local and regional taxes); the remaining 15% are paid by the patients themselves [1,4]. The counties can levy a proportional income tax, and they are free to determine the rate. Communities also raise funds by taxing incomes, property and industrial estates. Health expenditure is a major part of the regional budgets; about two thirds of its total are spent on it. The central authorities apply a system of grants to equalize and supplement local resources. Regions with a lot of elderly persons, bad housing and other factors associated with increased health needs receive extra money from the state.

The health insurance system covers the whole population [5]. There are two different schemes which people can choose freely. Group one insured people, 95% of the population, have access, almost free of cost, to comprehensive health care including free medical care from the GP and free specialist care after referral. People in the other scheme, group two insured, have the freedom to consult GPs or specialists of their choice without limitations but they are charged for 50% of the costs of out-patient care.

1.4   Care for the elderly

With the exception of acute hospital care, psychiatric institutions and general medical care (GPs), which are the county's responsibility, all remaining care for the elderly is organized by the municipality (*Kommune*). This implies that a broad range of facilities can be offered, while, according to priorities determined at community level, the emphasis can be on residential services, home care or other facilities. However, in general, absolute priority has been given to home care and sheltered housing. The Social Security Act of 1973 stresses the explicit obligation of the communities to organize home help services for the elderly and restricted the further development of all types of institutional care for the elderly [6,7].

Community services. Besides home nursing and home help services which will be discussed later, there are all sorts of additional community services for the elderly, such as meals-on-wheels, alarm systems, transport services, assistance with shopping, gardening and snow clearance. The elderly pay only a limited or symbolic contribution for these kinds of services. Furthermore there are day centres (*Dagcentre og daghjem*) which provide day care. This can be in the form of a short stay in a nursing home (respite care) or day care with the night spent at home.

Residential services. In 1988, 6.9% of the population over 65 years lived permanently in special housing facilities for the elderly [6]. This percentage is expected to drop quickly because the public housing policy for the elderly is de-emphasizing the traditional types of residential and semi-residential care facilities to provide appropriate care through better housing conditions. Since 1988, there has been a building stop for traditional institutions for the elderly and handicapped [8]. The underlying principal is a clear distinction between housing facilities on the one hand and the service and care functions on the other hand. This will prevent the elderly having to move when their needs for care change.

There are still a number of traditional residential services such as nursing homes (*Plejehjeme*) for the elderly impaired in need of extensive nursing care and personal and practical assistance, sheltered housing facilities (*Beskyttede boliger*) for the elderly needing less care, and collective service flats (*Lette kollektivboliger*) or pensioners flats (*Kommunale pensionistboliger*) reserved for the elderly and handicapped. Furthermore, adapted flats for the disabled and elderly in non-profit housing (*Aeldreegnede boliger i almenyttigt byggeri*) are still constructed and many of the old nursing homes have been or are going to be modernized and changed into these kind of flats.

The new housing facilities are owned by municipalities and non-profit housing associations. However, in both cases, the allocation decision is the responsibility of the municipalities.

The elderly used to pay for nursing homes with their (state-)pensions in exchange for pocket money. Since 1989 it is possible to separate the housing and service function. This means that the elderly in traditional residential homes can choose whether they wish to make use of a particular kind of service. For housing the maximum contribution is 15% of income; in such cases, services are purchased according to need. The maximum contribution is 15% of income for service-flats and sheltered housing.

Capacity of residential services for the elderly in Denmark (1988) [6]

	Number of places /beds per 1000 people over 65 years
Service flats	4.8
Pensioners flats	38.0
Flats for disabled	25.0
Sheltered housing	8.5
Nursing homes	61.0
Geriatric wards	1.3

2 The organization of home nursing

2.1 Home nursing organization

In Denmark home nursing (*Hjemmesygepleje*) is provided by the community in the same department as home help services.

At national level the association of communities (*KL, Kommunerne Landsforening*) negotiates with the nurses' association about general guidelines for the relationship between the number of head nurses, nurses and assistant nurses at community level. Communities are, however, not obliged to adopt these guidelines literally.

2.2 Manpower in home nursing services

Home nursing services are provided by home nurses and assistant nurses. There are no specific nursing gradations or levels of expertise distinguished. The protected title 'nurse' is received after four years of post-high school education. Community nursing organizations provide extra schooling for these nurses, provided they have at least two years of practical experience in institutional nursing. Since 1991 there is a combined education programme for assistant nurses. There is one year common both to future home helps and assistant nurses; after that year a further 1.5 year qualifies for assistant nurse.

In 1992, 8,914 nurses and assistant nurses were working in home care in Denmark. More than the half of them (55%) had part-time jobs. In total, there were 7,065 FTEs available in home nursing services [9].

There is a trend towards a strong increase of nurses working in Danish home care: from one nurse per 345 elderly people in 1977 to one nurse per 114 of the elderly in 1992 [9,10]. The policy to stop building nursing home beds and increase home nursing is clearly visible in these figures.

2.3 Client population

In 1989 there were 222,231 patients receiving home nursing care [11]. More than 70% of them were over 67 years of age. In 1991, 7.3% of the population over 65 were patients of the home nursing scheme [12]. There was, however, a considerable turnover of patients. For each 1,000 of people over 66 there were 257 home care episodes.

The official statistics do not contain much information on client characteristics. More can be derived from the ACRE-survey conducted in 1986 [13]. Twelve percent of the total population over 70 used home nursing services in 1986 (9% of the males; 13% of the females); this number increased from 7% (70-74) to 11% (75-79) and 23% (80-95).

2.4 Provision of services

The demand for home nursing care is generally initiated by health professionals. Approximately one quarter of the new patients (23%) are referred by the General Practitioner; while almost 40% stem from the hospital; the latter figure varies from 34% in West- and North Jutland to 58% in Frederiksberg [11]. An official authorization by a physician (GP or hospital doctor) is required in case of a medical treatment such as injections or medication. No such medical authorization is needed for social, caring and preventive activities [14].

The assessment procedures of home nursing needs can differ between the communities. Hospitals often use the services of a social counsellor (*Socialraadgiver*) for the estimation of the home care required and the contacts with the home care-providers. In other cases (Copenhagen e.g.) there are fixed agreements such as after discharge there will be a nurse assessing home care needs on the same day or the day after. In general, there is no formalized assessment: nurses assess the need for care and provide it themselves or have it provided by assistant nurses and/or home helps.

No detailed information about the type of service provided is available (surveys will be carried out in december 1994). The official statistics give numbers of visits only and not the actual activities. The number of visits in 1989 was 10,124,004; an average of 45.6 per patient (almost one visit per week), this number varying from 40.6 visits in North Jutland to 56.2 visits in the Copenhagen suburbs (Frederiksberg) [11]. Home nursing services were mostly provided during daytime (74% in 1989); 18% in the evening and 8% during the night.

There is no official list with activities linked to the professions of nurse and assistant nurse. In general the typical functions of home nurses include the usual activities like giving drugs and injections, wound care and giving health advice [7].

Patients discharged from hospitals, where the length of stay per admission decreases continuously, will, usually be cared for and treated by nurses.

However, assistant nurses perform a full range of nursing and home help activities (if that is more convenient and reduces the number of persons the patient has to deal with) for the chronically ill.

2.5   Problems and recent developments

The Social Law states that each community shall have adequate facilities for care for the elderly, such as nursing homes, sheltered housing, home nursing and home help. The Law does not state how many facilities of each kind should be provided. This is up to the communities themselves. As there also is no formal and detailed division of labour between the home care professions, this might lead to a preference for the lowest paid home helps and so threaten the quality of home care. However, this is not the case, according to our sources. First, there is a shortage of fully qualified nurses, which encourages an efficient deployment of personnel. Secondly, each community is obliged to publish figures on supply and utilization of all sorts of facilities for the elderly. Citizens can compare the services provided with the amount of taxation and, if not satisfied, try to get support for change.

Although supply of home nursing was almost doubled since 1988, the year Denmark stopped building nursing homes, obligations have increased too. Twenty-four-hour service is an possible option now in most communities, although no extra budget is available for that service; extension of it will be at the expense of regular services.

The decreasing length of stay in hospitals and the tendency to discharge patients before the weekend also increases workload of the home nurses; in some cases and some places this could cause friction. Hospitals prefer to discharge patients before the weekend and both the community nursing services and the home help services also prefer service delivery during the week.

3   The organization of home help services

3.1   Organizations for home help services

As already mentioned, home help and home nursing are organized within the community. Essential for the organization of health care and social security in Denmark is the supply of a comprehensive and integrated set of services ranging from institutional care (nursing homes) to home help and from specially adapted housing facilities to concrete adaptations in existing dwellings. Since the building-stop for nursing homes in 1988, there is an increased emphasis on home care facilities like home nursing and home help.

Home help, in its turn, belongs to an even wider range of services: neighbourhood work (*Omsorgs-arbejde*) that includes services like gardening, snow clearance, meals-on-wheels and public transport for which modest co-payments (for meals-on-wheels the cost of ingredients only, not those of preparation) are charged.

3.2 Manpower in home help services

Traditionally home helps used to have little formal training (just basic education and some additional courses). Since 1992, however, a new educational programme has started, combined with the training for assistant nurses. One year's training is sufficient to become home help.

In 1992, there were 32,078 FTEs home helps available in Denmark [9]. Most of the home helps (62%) had a part-time job. There has clearly been a considerable increase of the number of home helps in the last 20 years. In 1972, there were 13,800 home helps available for 600,000 persons over 65 (one home help per 43 elderly persons); in 1984, the number increased to 25,500 over 749,000 (one home help per 29 elderly persons); in 1992 there were 37,932 home helps for 803,973 persons over 65 (one home help per 21 elderly persons) [7,9,11,12].

3.3 Client population

In 1992, 145,100 people over 67 years of age (20.5%) received home help services in Denmark [12]. The next table shows that utilization of home help services increases considerably with age.

Table 1
Households in age categories receiving home help services

Age	Percentage of households receiving home help services	
	1984[7]	1987[6]
67-69	6	-
70-74	11	15
75-79	22	28
80-84	34	44
> 85	38	61

Background information about the clients of home help services can be derived from the already mentioned ACRE-study of 1986 [7,13]. In this study some determinants of home help utilization appeared more important than others: geographical area did not make any difference, whereas social class, social network contacts (unexpectedly!) and help from spouse did. Single persons received more professional help, as did persons with low household income and the more help received from the social network, the more home help became available. Finally person with worse health and lower functional ability received more professional home help. When the Social Security Act was drafted, it was decided that a person's economic position should not have an influence on receipt of home help. Nevertheless low income households receive more professional help.

The following combination of factors shows interesting results (combination of age, sex and living alone or with others).

Jouke van der Zee

Table 2
Percentage of the elderly receiving home help by demographic characteristics in combination, 1984 [7,13]

Characteristic		Percentage receiving home help	
Living alone	Men, 70-79 yrs	35	41
	Men, 80-95 yrs	54	
	Women, 70-79 yrs	26	35
	Women, 80-95 yrs	48	
Living with others	Men, 70-79 yrs	9	12
	Men, 80-95 yrs	26	
	Women, 70-79 yrs	15	22
	Women, 80-95 yrs	58	

Men living alone received more often professional home help than females in these circumstances. With regard to the people living with others (mostly spouses) the opposite difference was shown. These results reflect the fact that women perform more tasks in the household, whether they have a spouse or their age.

3.4 Provision of services

The provision of home help usually is decided by taking into account the need for home nursing as well; the co-ordinating home nurse (visiting nurse) evaluating the combined needs.

In the Social Security Act of 1972 the following home help activities have been described [7]:
- housework such as cleaning, cooking, bed making, washing and ironing;
- assisting with -going to the toilet, -dressing, -washing, -bathing, -hair combing and other aspects of personal hygiene;
- shopping and -outdoor walks.

It is clear that home help in Denmark involves substantially more than just cleaning the house. Personal care such as dressing, washing, bathing are activities assigned to assistant nurses in most countries; while accompanying a disabled or frail elderly person on outdoor walks and taking care of shopping is usually not included in home help activities in other countries that are more strictly limited to cleaning activities. The ACRE-study described practical work of Danish home helps in more detail. It showed that cleaning takes most of the time, followed by conversation, shopping, cooking, and washing (see table 3).

Table 3
Home help's reported use of time during one week [7]

	Percentage of working time
Cleaning	37.2
Conversation	13.1
Shopping	12.0
Cooking	10.1
Washing	8.2
Outdoor walks	3.7
Personal hygiene	3.5
Dress and undress	2.4
Other	9.8

Most families received less than six hours of care per week, but the amount of help increased with age [7].

According to our sources, cleaning is a hot issue in home help provision. Cleaning windows for instance is not considered as a home help task and certainly if a healthy near-family member like a spouse is present cleaning is supposed to be the client's responsibility.

3.5   Problems and recent developments

The low level home help training was regarded as a problem in Denmark, which is understandable considering the extensive range of tasks performed by Danish home helps. The new and combined education programme for assistant nurses and home helps is targeting this problem.

Although there are no waiting lists (according to law the community is obliged to provide home help services), studies like the ACRE-survey reveal that there certainly are unmet needs. The determinants of these unmet needs are not very different from the determinants of fulfilled needs, which implies some restraint or shortage in the provision of home help services [7].

The shortage of nurses in Denmark and the decreasing length of stay in hospitals, which requires the first attention of the nurses to be directed to discharged hospital patients influence home help services indirectly. The home helps take care of a great deal of chronically ill patients and provide services that in other countries are definitely outside the home help domain.

4 Relations between home nursing and home help services

Unlike most other countries home help and home nursing are two of a kind; they are part of the same organization and their activities are employed complementarily.

As the elderly and chronically ill have a high preference for one single help, home helps provide quite a range of services to this group.

Nurses usually are in charge of need-assessment and allocation of a broad range of services.

In the new education programme a common ground for both home helps and assistant nurses is provided.

5 The financing of home nursing and home help services

Where in most other member states of the European Union two separate sections are needed; in Denmark, the financing of both services is similar.

5.1 Payment and client's insurance

Until mid-1989, home help was free for low-income pensioners with co-payment for the higher incomes (where home help was less than six hours a week, if more it was free anyway). Since that date it became a service free of charge for those needing it chronically with the option of charging those receiving care for a short period only.

Their is some varying co-payment for acute home help of non-permanent character (usually for younger persons after accidents or illnesses) and for additional services like gardening.

5.2 Funding of the organizations

Local and national taxation form the funding sources; communities are obliged to provide home nursing and home help, but, the amount of services is not determined centrally but left to the communities (as is the taxation level).

The costs of home nursing and home help were in 1993 DEK 1,142 million and DEK 4,197 million [9].

Communities have some freedom to allocate budgets; so there are differences both in supply and utilization of home help and home nursing services. Annual publication of these data, however, forms a stimulus to active citizens to compare their community with its neighbours.

5.3 Payment of home nurses and home helps

All community nurses and home helps are employed by the local communities. In 1994, the gross salaries of home nurses was DEK 234,373. The home helps earned DEK 191,315 a year.

Acknowledgement
Mr Peter Sanderhof of the Ministry of Social Affairs and Mrs Lene Holländer of the Copenhagen Community were our major sources. As is clear from this text, we used previous comparative and descriptive studies with gratitude.

References

1 BOERMA, W.G.W., F.A.J.M. DE JONG, P.H. MULDER. Health care and general practice across Europe. Utrecht: NIVEL, 1993.

2 OECD HEALTH DATA. Version # 1.5. Paris: OECD, 1993.

3 DELNOY, D.M.J. Physician payment system and cost control. Utrecht: NIVEL, 1994.

4 KEMENADE, Y.W. VAN. Health care in Europe. The finance and reimbursement systems of 18 European countries. Zoetermeer: Nationale Raad voor de Volksgezondheid, 1993.

5 SCHNEIDER, M., RK-H. DENNERLEIN, A. KÖSE, L. SCHOLTES. Health care in the EC member states. Health Policy Special Issue. Health Policy; 1992, 1+2, 113-123.

6 NIJKAMP, P., J. PACOLET, H. SPINNEWYN, A. VOLLERING, C. WILDEROM, S. WINTERS. Services for the elderly in Europe. A cross-national comparative study. Leuven/Amsterdam: HIV/VU, 1991.

7 HOLSTEIN, B.E., P. DUE, G. ALMIND, E. HOLST. The home help service in Denmark. In: Jamieson, A. (eds.). Home care for older people in Europe. Oxford/New York/Tokyo: Oxford University Press, 1991.

8 BOLL HANSEN, E., J. JORDAL-JØRGERSEN, A. KOCH. Fra pleje-hjem till hjemmepleje, AKF, Amtener og kommunerses Forskningsinstitut, AKF Forlaget, 1991.

9 DANMARKS STATISTIK. Social sikring og retsvaesen. Kopenhagen: Danmarks Statistik, September 1993.

10 ABRAHAMSON, P. Welfare for the elderly in Denmark: from institutionalization to self-reliance. In: Evers, A., I. Svetlik (eds.). New welfare mixes for the elderly, vol. 2. Vienna: European Centre for Social Welfare Policy and Research, 1991.

11 Statistik om virksomheden i hjemmesygeplejen 1989, Primær sundhedstjenestatistik III:13:1990. Sundhedsstyrelsen, Copenhagen: 1990.

12 MINISTRY OF SOCIAL AFFAIRS. Pensioner in Denmark: main features of Danish old age policy and care for the old. Kopenhagen: Ministry of Social Affairs, 1992.

13 HOLSTEIN, B.E., G. ALMIND, P. DUE, E. HOLST. The elderly in Denmark. Health and social situation. Institute of Social medicine. University of Copenhagen, 1988.

14 ROSSUM, H.J.L. VAN. Effects of Preventive home visits to the elderly. dissertation, Maastricht, University of Limburg, 1993.

4 Home care in Finland

Jack B.F. Hutten

1 The setting of home care

1.1 The country

Finland is a fairly young state. After centuries of foreign control, the country became an independent republic in 1917 and the constitution was adopted two years later. The president is elected for a period of six years. The one chamber parliament consists of 200 members who are chosen for a four year period.

Finland has a low population density and most of the people live in the south and west: the north is very sparsely inhabited.

Forestry has traditionally been the major economic activity. Nowadays the share of metal industry and engineering in the economy is almost equal to that of the forestry. The recent membership of the European Union is expected to bring new economic impulses, especially to compensate the lost of the intensive trade with the former Soviet Union.

Jack B.F. Hutten

Population key figures (1990) [1,2]

Population in mln.	5.0
Inhabitants per sq. km.	15
% Living in urban areas	60
% over 65 years	13.2
% over 75 years	5.7
Births per 1000	13.1
Deaths per 1000	9.8
Life expectancy (men)	71.4
Life expectancy (women)	79.3

1.2 The organization of health care

Health care in Finland is mainly a part of the public services. Only in the field of out-patient care is an additional private sector active [1]. At national level the Ministry of Social Affairs and Health decides about general priorities and approves a national four year plan for public health care and social services [3]. There are twelve provincial departments of Social Affairs and Health, but the local authorities (in particular the Health Boards of the communes) are responsible for the actual provision of the health care services. Big municipalities have there own health care organizations, while smaller municipalities have joint organizations supplying health services in several communes (municipal federations). Local authorities make their own plans for periods of four years. Since 1992, the influence of the central government on the local plans has decreased: the central direction of municipal policies by the state has reduced considerably. Municipalities can provide services not included in the national plan, of course without a state subsidy [3]. Furthermore, state subsidies are not longer earmarked which gives the municipalities more autonomy in the allocation of this money between different policy areas. The provision of health care is organized within hospitals and primary health care centres which are controlled by a board of publicly elected municipal politicians [5].

Since 1972, primary health care has been a major priority in Finnish health policy. Primary care is provided by the 223 health care centres [1,4]. Every municipality has a health centre, either of its own or shared with neighbouring municipalities. The term health centre is not related to one specific building, but refers to an independent organization supplying health care. These centres provide a full range of primary care services including dental care, physiotherapy, laboratory and X-ray facilities, an emergency unit, a maternity and child health unit, and even a local hospital for acute and chronic patients. The average number of beds in health centre hospitals is 100 [6]. Most centres employ at least four general practitioners and several primary care nurses. The centres account for almost three-quarter of the patient contacts in primary care. The remaining patients are seen in private practice or by a hospital out-patient department in acute cases. The GP only makes home visits to those of the elderly or chronically ill who are entitled to 'home care'. All other home visits are made by community nurses. Until recently, there was no personal doctor system: all GPs in a centre had a collective responsibility for the patients. However, nowadays, the centres have been reorganized so that each doctor has his/her own personal list of patients and is personally responsible for his/her patients [1]. In 1993, about 36% of the Finnish population were involved in this new system [5].

Historically, hospital bed supply is fairly high in Finland. However, recently, the number of beds (especially in psychiatric wards) has been diminished [1]. For in-patient medical treatment the country has been divided into 21 'hospital regions'. Each region has a central hospital where the most common specialities are available. Highly specialized medicine is practised in the five University Hospitals. Furthermore, there are a large number of smaller district hospitals. Only a small minority of the hospitals are privately owned. No distinction is made between hospitals for acute patients and hospitals for chronic cases. Most chronic patients stay in health centre hospital, except for those who are in need of specialized medical care. Hospital out-patient departments are only accessible after patients have been referred by a health centre (except in case of emergency).

As mentioned before, the private sector mainly focuses on out-patient care. It covers about 20% of the total ambulatory services by physicians; in special areas such as obstetrics and psychiatry over 50% [3].

Jack B.F. Hutten

Health care figures (1990) [2]

Expenditure

Total expenditure on health	
Absolute per head in ppp$	1291
Percentage of GDP	7.8
Public expenditure on health	
Absolute per head in ppp$	1046
Percentage of GDP	6.3

Manpower

Physicians per 1000 pop.	2.4
GPs per 1000 pop.	1.1
Qualified nurses per 1000 pop.	10.2

Hospital care

In-patient care		
Beds per 1000 pop.	12.5	
Admissions per 100 pop.	23.3	('89)
Mean length of stay	18.2	
Acute hospitals		
Beds per 1000 pop.	4.3	
Admissions per 100 pop.	16.3	
Mean length of stay	7.0	
Long-term care		
Beds per 1000 pop.	9.7*	

*   4.7 in old people's homes and 5.0 in health centre hospitals [7,8]

1.3   Health financing and insurance

In the public sector, on the average, half of the cost of hospital care and the local health centres is financed through communal taxes and half by the central government. In wealthier municipalities, the percentage contributed by the central government is lower than in the poorer ones (varying from 29 to 66%) [3,4]. Furthermore, the entire Finnish population is covered by a public health insurance run by the National Social Insurance Institute (NSI). This compulsory scheme is funded by premiums paid by employers and employees on the one hand and subsidies from the state or local authorities on the other hand. This insurance scheme mainly covers drugs prescribed by a physician, examinations and treatment performed in the private sector, and dental care for young adults. Most of these services require some co-payment from the patients [1,4]. As regards medicines, percentages can vary between 50 and 100% reimbursement, depending on the related diagnosis. In 1991, co-payment contributed about 7% to the total health care expenditures [3].

Since the beginning of the 1990s important reforms have been introduced in the health care financing system [4,5,9,10]. In January 1993, the allocation of central grants to municipalities or municipal federations changed radically. Previously state subsidies were earmarked for specific purposes. The specific state subsidies for health care have been replaced by a block grant which covers education, welfare and health care expenditure. The level of the grant is calculated taking into account the number of inhabitants, age distribution, morbidity rates, population density, geographic area, and the economic situation of the municipality [5,9]. Block grants are paid to individual municipalities only and not to federations of municipalities as before [10].

In the old situation, hospitals received state budgets (covering 60% of their total expenditure) directly from the central government and the remaining amount from the local authorities [4]. Funding was based on the number of beds available, not on occupancy rates. Nowadays all financial resources are allocated through the municipalities which operate as purchasers of care for the entire population [5]. As a consequence, they can decide how to spend their money more autonomously.

Traditionally physicians, in hospitals as well as in primary care, work on a salary basis in the public system. They are, however, free to run a private practice in their spare time. In private practice, a fee-for-service system is used. For reasons of efficiency, a new remuneration system has been introduced recently. In primary care, an experimental contract has been developed dividing physician's remuneration into three components: basic salary (60%); a capitation fee for patients on the list with three or more visits in the previous year (20%) and fee-for-service payment for other patients (20%) [5]. This system is of course closely related to the development of the personal doctor system mentioned above.

1.4   Care for the elderly

Since 1950, the proportion of the elderly in the Finnish population has been increasing rapidly [11]. In 1993, 13.7% were over 65 [12]. This figure is expected to double in the first half of the next century [13].

101

Finland is considered as a social welfare state. During the past few decades, care for the elderly was mainly provided within the public system; the informal network (relatives and friends) played a less important role [11,14]. This is related to the fact that participation of Finnish women in *full-time* employment is the highest in the Western world. But, the situation is changing nowadays: relatives are becoming more involved in the care for the elderly. People who take care of elderly patients are eligible for a home care allowance; the actual amount of money varies from one local authority to another [14].

During the past 20 years, the care system for the elderly was strongly based on institutional services. For financial and social reasons (people prefer to stay in their own home as long as possible) more community oriented services have been developed recently. Nowadays old-age policy is focused on an increasing co-operation, integration and co-ordination of health care services on the one hand and social welfare services on the other hand.

Community services The national program, formulated in 1988, emphasises the need of short-term and part-time treatment. Opportunities for day care and treatment of a clients for a maximum period of three months in a old people's home had to be increased. In 1993, a sort of day care service was available in 40% of the municipalities [11]. Besides home nursing and home help services (which are discussed in the following sections), there are several supportive services developed for the elderly, such as meals-on-wheels, bathing services, and transport services.

Residential services Institutional care of the elderly is provided mainly in old people's homes as part of the social services and in health centre hospitals which are part of the primary health care services. The number of long-term patients (more than 90 days in hospital) in general hospitals is rather small; they are mainly involved in acute care.

In 1991, about 5.5% of the elderly over 64 years were in long-term institutional care: 3.4% in old people's homes and 2.1% in health centre hospitals [7,8,15]. Very old people in particular were in permanent care: 1.3% of the people between 65 and 74, 7.4% of the people between 75-85, and 27.7% of the people 80 years or older lived permanently in institutional services [7,8,15].

Since the 1970s, the number of places in old people's homes decreased considerable. In 1992, 26,715 places were available, compared to 31,000 in the late 1970s [11,15,16]. Taking into account the rapid growth of the elderly population, the proportional decrease is even larger.

The majority of the old people's homes are owned by municipalities; about 8.5% are run by private associations and nonprofit organizations [16]. These private homes are mostly occupied by those of the elderly in relatively good health. Emphasis is on residential services and less on medical treatment. Municipalities contribute to the operating costs of private homes according to the number of places. The residents themselves have to pay the monthly fees. Those of the elderly who cannot afford this can apply for housing allowances to the municipalities.

Old people's homes owned by the municipalities are mostly larger than the private services. They provide more medical services. The staff consists mainly of qualified nurses (75%) and auxiliaries who have completed a nine-month basic training course. The level of the fees for institutional care depends own personal income of the elderly.

Furthermore, new experiments with forms of sheltered housing for the elderly are reported.

Capacity of residential services for the elderly in Finland (1992) [16]

	Number of beds/places per 1000 people over 65 years*
Old people's homes	39

* Specific figures of other services are not available because they are part of the total health care supply which means that they can be used by all age groups. There were e.g. 4.7 beds per 1000 population in health centre hospitals which are mainly occupied by elderly people [15]. In 1991, 19.2 per 1000 people over 65 years were admitted in health centre hospitals [15].

2 The organization of home nursing

2.1 Organizations for home nursing

As described in the previous sections, health care is mainly the responsibility of the 460 Finnish municipalities. The actual care is often part of the activities of health centres, but some municipalities contract private organizations for specific tasks such as home nursing care.

At the moment, there are two different organizational structures in home nursing care. In 69% of the municipalities, health care (home nursing) and social services (home help) are strictly separated. The local authorities appoint a health board which puts a health manager in charge of the health centre. In the remaining 31% of the municipalities health care and social services are part of the same organization. This does not necessarily mean that the actual provision of the services is also integrated. The health board is replaced by a social welfare and health board, and the health and social care centres provide home nursing as well as home help services.

2.2 Manpower in home nursing services

At the end of 1992, a total of 7,377 nurses worked in Finnish home care [17]. There are three kinds of nurses. The majority (62%) are health visitors or public health nurses (*terveydenhoitajat*). The remaining part is almost equally divided among registered nurses (*sairaanhoitajat*) and practical nurses (*perushoitajat*). Most of the nurses (estimate: 96%) are full-time workers. They are employed by health centres or municipalities; none of the nurses work independently in home care.

Table 1
Figures about nurses (FTEs) working in home care in Finland,
end of 1992 [17]

	Total number	Number of inhabitants per nurse
Health visitor	4,604	1,103
Registered nurse	1,360	3,733
Practical nurse	1,413	3,593
Total	7,377	688

The duration of training depends on their previous education. Practical nurses receive a 1.5 years training (for matriculated students) or 2.5 years (for comprehensive school graduates). This is respectively 3.5 years and 4.5 years for the two other types of nurses.

There are also a small number of specialized nurses working in home care.

2.3   Client population

The official registration of services counted 71,384 patients in home nursing care, during 1993. That is 1.4% of the national population. In total, they received 2,087,952 visits by a nurse.

A survey among 11,257 patients in home nursing care, conducted in 1991, provides more background information [18]. Most of the patients were female (74.1%). Furthermore the data show that home nursing services are mainly used by the elderly. Only 11 percent were below 65. The very old, 80 years and older, were the largest group (46.4% of the total).

2.4   Provision of services

As in other countries operating a public health care system, patients do not have a choice of whom to approach for home nursing care. Finland has no internal health care market with different (private) providers. The municipalities decide which organizations (e.g. their own health (and social) care centres or private organizations) will provide the actual care. In addition, a formal referral by a physician is always required. In most of the cases, this will be the general practitioner who is attached to the health centres that also provides the home nursing care. The survey among home nursing patients shows that most patients (45%) were at home at the moment they were referred [18]. This means that generally the patients themselves or their family, and GPs were the main initiators for home nursing care. About 26% were admitted previously to a health centre hospital, and 25% came from a hospital. Acute illness was the main reason for the admission to home nursing care, but social reasons were also often mentioned (58% of all cases) [19].

As already mentioned, a referral by a physician is always required. He/she therefore can be involved in assessment of the patient's needs. However, this is mostly done by a nurse; health visitor or registered nurse. They can also determine the patient's needs for home help services. Standardized forms are used for the assessment and the development of an individual care and service plan. These forms contain personal characteristics (e.g. age, sex, education), information about living conditions and social circumstances, and scales of activities of the daily living. In the end, the total assessment procedure gives the care-providers a total picture of the patient's needs for home care; including both home nursing and home help services. The actual decision about the type and amount of care is made by the physician or the health visitor and not by the other types of nurses.

Home nurses operate from health (and social) care centres. They sometimes work alone, but often in teams of varying composition. On special occasions, e.g. difficult or special patients, a multi-professional team can be formed including physicians, nurses, home helps and social workers.

The general tasks of home nursing services are formally described in three point:

- to give medical and nursing care at the patient's own home;
- to assist with all activities of daily living;
- to plan and co-ordinate the care of the patient in co-operation with home help services to keep the patient living in his/her own home as long as possible.

With the exception of more complicated nursing care, the three types of nurses are qualified to perform the same kind of tasks. However, in the daily practice there is a clearer differentiation. All three types are involved in routine technical nursing procedures such as injections and dressings. One of the main activities in this respect is the provision of medicines. Hygienic and other personal care (bathing, dressing, etc.) are mainly done by practical or registered nurses. The activities of health visitors and registered nurses extend towards more complicated technical nursing procedures (handling respirator, catheterization), patient education, counselling (e.g. concerning psychological or social problems), and the evaluation of the care provided. However, it must be mentioned that complicated technical nursing procedures in home care are more restricted than in many other countries: e.g. epidural anaesthesia at home is not allowed. Sometimes, practical or registered nurses are involved in housework, but this is mainly done by home helps (see 3.4).

2.5 Problems and recent developments

No waiting lists for home nursing care are reported. According to the social and health managers of municipalities, the needs for home nursing care and number of personnel have stabilized recently [20]. There is only a small increase of the level of patient dependency. A few years ago, there was a lack of qualified personnel. But, nowadays, there is increasing unemployment in the nursing profession which leads to an abundance of professionals.

There are three important developments in Finland related to home nursing care.

First, the process of the substitution primary and home care for institutional care. There is a growing need for home care: professional as well as informal (by relatives, neighbours and friends). A large part of the personnel of institutions will therefore gradually be moved to primary or home care.

Secondly, there is the process towards integration of health and social services. The former sectoral service structure has been transformed into small-area-responsibility. The health care and social welfare boards of municipalities will be merged. An increasing number of municipalities will be operating health and social care centres. So, both kinds of services will be provided within the same organization. This, however, does not necessarily mean that social and health services are actually integrated. In 1994, this process had already been completed in 31% of the municipalities; in 30% specific plans were already developed [21]. In future, the centres will consist of a broad range of public activities such as home nursing and home help services, housing, and environmental aspects. This idea of regional responsibility will be implemented in every municipality before the end of 1996.

Finally, in the autumn of 1993 a new training was started in the field of home care: the basic qualification in social and health care. The training period is 2.5 years. The first students will graduate at the beginning of 1996 and will start to work in a new basic integrated profession in both social and health care.

3   The organization of home help services

3.1   Organizations for home help services

As mentioned in section 2.1, in 31% of the municipalities home help services are provided by health and social care centres. In the other municipalities, the social welfare board is responsible for these services. They appoint a social manager or social secretary who is in charge of the daily activities.

About 90% of the services are provided by municipal organizations; 10% by private organizations which are contracted by the municipalities, such as the Central Union for the Welfare of the Aged, the Finnish Red Cross, National Association of the Disabled, and the Association for Old Aged and Neighbours Service.

A leading home maker or home service advisor is generally in charge of the municipal home help service. These services are involved in three main tasks:
- domiciliary care (provided by home makers and home helps);
- supporting services such as meals-on-wheels, transport services;
- payment of home care allowances to individuals for care of the elderly or disabled.

This chapter focuses on the first task.

3.2 Manpower in home help services

In 1992, there were 792.5 permanent functions led by home makers. They are in charge of the whole service. The actual work within the homes is done by two types of personnel: home makers (*kodinhoitaja*) and home helps (kotiavustaja). Home helps have limited training consisting of some basic courses. Home makers receive a vocational training for a period of 2.5 years (comprehensive school graduates) and two years (for matriculated students).

In 1993, 4,467 home helps (3,424 FTEs) and 7,462 home makers (6,198 FTEs) were working in home care (these unpublished figures are based on the information in [12,15]. This means that there one home help per 1,483 inhabitants and one home maker per 819 inhabitants.

3.3 Client population

Based on the official KETI-figures, it is estimated that about 7% of the Finnish population had received official home help services in the year 1993: 6.8% provided by the municipal services and 0.2% by private organizations [22].

The age distribution of the clients shows a deviant picture compared to many other countries. 35.5% of the clients were under 65 years of age; 16.3% between 65 and 74, and 48.2% were 75 years or older. It is interesting to notice that home help services in Finland are not exclusively used by the elderly. Families with young children in particular often use these services: e.g. when parents are in need of care, but also when children are ill and parents have to go to work. Most of the applicants are female (65%) and more than half (52%) live alone [22].

3.4 Provision of services

Because home help services are part of the public social service, all inhabitants of a municipality can approach one formal organization for home help. This is mainly their own municipal service or, in some cases, a private organization under contract to the municipality. There is no competition in this field.

No figures are available about who initiates the first contact with the home help services. It can be done by the clients themselves or their families, and health care professionals (GPs, nurses and hospitals). No formal referral is required.

In big municipalities, the assessment of the client's needs is the responsibility of the leading home maker; in smaller municipalities this is part of the work of social workers. Furthermore, in health and social care centres, home nursing and home help needs are assessed in one procedure.

The same standardized assessment form as described in section 2.4 is used including e.g. personal characteristics, social background features, and activities of daily living. The form is also used to formulate a care and service plan, and to determine the client's fee.

In general, the professional who is involved in the assessment decides, together with the client, the number of hours and period of care.

In the daily practice, home makers and home helps operate from a home help service office or health and social care centres. They can work as soloists as well as in teams. Help is available for 24-hours, seven-days-a- week.

The tasks of home help and home makers do not differ largely. They are mainly involved in housework and assistance with personal hygiene. The first include e.g. cleaning, providing meals (including shopping), and care for clothes (washing, repairs, ironing). Assistance with all kinds of activities of daily living, bathing, dressing, help with the lavatory can be done by a home help or home maker, but also by someone with a nursing background (see 2.4). Moral support is also a part of the work of home helps and home makers. They are not allowed to do any simple technical nursing procedure like wound care or pressure sores and are not involved in the assessment and evaluation of the provided care.

3.5 Problems and recent developments

In section 2.5, three important developments regarding home care in Finland had already been described: substitution of home care for institutional care, the principle of small-area responsibility, and the introduction of a new occupation for home care (basic qualification in social and health care).

There are, however, also some specific problems in the field of home help services. It is not possible to provide home help immediately when the need occurs. On the average people have to wait for two days (maximum is eight days) [20]. There is, nowadays, no shortage of personnel any more. Although the majority of municipalities maintain the same number of home help personnel, about 25% have reduced the number recently. This leads to a higher workload, also strengthen by the fact that the level of dependency of the clients has increased rapidly over the years. Furthermore, the increasing demand for home help by the elderly leads to a decrease in child care and assistance to young families.

There are important problems regarding the co-operation and communication between home help personnel on the one hand and other care-providers on the other hand. There is hardly any exchange of information and little personal contact between the formal care-providers. In the field of care for the elderly, co-ordination and concrete arrangements between health and social services are still poorly developed. This has negative implications for the continuity of care [10].

4   Relations between home nursing and home help services

The amount of co-operation between home nurses and home help personnel differs greatly among municipalities. As mentioned before, in 31% of municipalities, home nursing and home help services are part of the same organizational structure. In this situation a joint social welfare and health board is responsible for both kinds of service, and the actual provision is done by health and social care centres. This is still mainly an organizational integration. It does not necessarily mean that more intense co-operation has also been established between health and social workers in the daily practice. However, it stated that a joint organization is an important condition for improving this co-operation.

Nowadays, nurses and home helps/makers sometimes work in teams or discuss shared patients occasionally. This is mainly by telephone, informal meetings at the client's house, or through a note (message) book. But, the extension of integration in health and social services and the improvement of communication and exchange of information are still important goals in home care. The introduction of a new integrated basic qualification in social and health care is an important step forward. As well as the fact that before the end of 1996 the principle of small-area responsibility will have been implemented in all municipalities. When the local authorities are responsible for the whole range of activities, this may facilitate stricter co-operation in the daily practice setting.

5 The financing of home nursing services

5.1 Payment and patients' insurance

Home nursing care is provided by the municipalities. All inhabitants have access to this services which are mainly funded by municipal taxes, state subsidies, and the health insurance scheme. There are no private insurance schemes for the costs of home nursing care.

The public system does not completely cover the costs for home nursing activities. All patients have to pay additional fees themselves. For occasional nursing care, a fee of FIM 30 per visit by a nurse is charged. When a longer episode of care is required, all patients have to pay a percentage of the costs. The level of co-payment depends on monthly income and the size of the family and varied, in 1994, from 11 to 35%. There is no legal maximum amount of care determined.

5.2 Funding of the organizations

As mentioned in section 1.3, municipalities receive a block grant from the central government. They are free to allocate this money among different areas of interest such as education, health, and social services.

5.3   Payment of the nurses

All nurses are employed by the centres and are paid a monthly salary. Their incomes are determined in official wage scales. Health visitors and other specialized nurses earn between FIM 7,529 (start) and 9,792 (end) a month. Registered nurses have a salary between FIM 6,729 and 8,752 a month. Practical nurses start with FIM 6,102 and end with 7,936 a month.

5.4   Problems and recent developments

Until the end of 1992, although provided locally, the social welfare and health services had been very highly controlled by the central government. From the beginning of 1993, the principle of earmarked state subsidies has changed into a block grant system. Each municipality receives a payment calculated by a formula taking into account population size, age distribution, morbidity rates, population density, land areas, and the financial capacity of the municipality. Education, several kinds of social services and health care need to be financed by this grant. Each municipality will therefore determine itself how the money is spent. There are, of course, different options like expansion of primary health centres or contracting out services to private care-providers (e.g. private hospitals). This will lead to a larger variation of social and health care services within the country. The state subsidy reform is a major shift of decision-making power from the Ministry of Social Affairs and Health to the municipalities, although the former still has strong control over capital investment. There are, however, concerns that some municipalities may not succeed in providing an adequate amount and mix of services because of economic restrictions due to the recession.

In general, the salaries of the nursing personnel have been considered as rather low compared with other occupations. The trade unions have started negotiations recently to increase the salaries. In February 1995, the first nation-wide strike of nurses took place, but because of the recession and the lack of financial resources it was difficult to reach an agreement.

6 The financing of home help services

6.1 Payment and clients' insurance

Home help services are part of the public social service system which is the responsibility of the municipalities. Everyone has a right to apply for these services when needed. There are no private insurance schemes which cover the costs of these services.

All clients have to pay a fee which is based on their income and the number of persons in the household; the fees vary between 11 and 35% of the total costs. The costs are based on the care and service plan.

6.2 Funding of organizations

The home help services are financed by state subsidies, local taxation, and client's fees. The grant from the central government is not earmarked any more and can be spend in different ways. It is therefore difficult to produce exact figures about the funding of home help services. In 1991 (this is before the important state subsidy reform), about FIM 1,843 million were spent on home help services for the elderly: 42% were paid by state subsidies, 46% by municipal taxes, and 12% by the users [12]. Home care for children and families cost FIM 372 million: 45% state subsidies, 48% municipal taxes, and 7% user's fees [12].

Some municipalities contract private organizations for home help services.

6.3 Payment of the home helps

There is an official salary system for home makers and home helps. Their monthly salaries depend on education, experience, and in which municipality they live. Home helps start with FIM 5,427 or 5,667 (in more expensive municipalities) a month, and end with FIM 7,058 or 7,370 a month. The wages of home makers vary between FIM 6,102 or 6,729 and 7,936 a month [12].

6.4 Problems and recent developments

The most important developments were already discussed in section 5.4. Home help and home maker are professions with low social status and low

113

wages. Trade unions are trying to increase the salaries but it seems difficult because of restricted financial resources due to the general recession in the country.

Acknowledgement
The information in this chapter is provided by Mrs. Anja Noro, MSc (health care), researcher at the National Research and Development Centre for Welfare and Health (STAKES), Helsinki.

References

1 BOERMA, W.G.W., F.A.J.M. DE JONG, P.H. MULDER. Health care and general practice across Europe. Utrecht: NIVEL, 1993.
2 OECD HEALTH DATA. Version # 1.5. Paris: OECD, 1993.
3 HÄKKINEN, U., K. LUOMA. Determinants of expenditure variation in health care and care of the elderly among Finnish municipalities. Themes from Finland. Helsinki: STAKES, 12/1994.
4 KEMENADE, Y.W. VAN. Health care in Europe. The finance and reimbursement systems of 18 European countries. Zoetermeer: Nationale Raad voor de Volksgezondheid, 1993.
5 HERMANSON, T., S. ARO, C.L. BENNET. A letter from Finland. Finland's health care system: universal access to health care in a capitalistic democracy. JAMA, 271, 1994, 24, 1957-1962.
6 VERHEIJ, R.A, A. KERKSTRA. International comparative study of community nursing. Aldershot: Avebury, 1992.
7 STAKES. Vanhainkotien asiakaslaskenta 2.12.1991. Tilastotiedore 1994:1.
8 STAKES. Potilaslaskenta terveyskeskuten vuodeosastoilla 2.12.1991. Tilastotiede 1994:2.
9 KOKKO, S. State subsidy reform in the Finnish social welfare and health services. Dialogue, 1993, 6-8.
10 MINISTRY OF SOCIAL AFFAIRS AND HEALTH. Health for all by the year 2000: revised strategy for co-operation. Helsinki: Ministry of Social Affairs and Health, Publication series 1993:9.
11 HEIKKINEN, R.L. New challenges for elder care in Finland. In: Olson, L.K. (eds.). The graying of the world: who will care for the frail elderly? New York/London/Norwood: The Haworth Press, 1994.
12 STATISTICS FINLAND. Statistical yearbook of Finland, 1993

13 VALKONEN, T., T. NIKANDER. Vanhojen ikäluokkien koon ja rakenteen muutokset. In: Jylhä, M., P. Pohjolainen. Vanheneminen ja elämänkulku: sosiaaligerontologian Perusteita. Mänttä: Weilin ja Göös, 1990.

14 SIPILÄ, J. Home care allowances for the frail elderly: a contradictory innovation. In: Evers, A., I. Svetlik (eds.). Balancing pluralism: new welfare mixes in care for the elderly. Aldershot/Vienna: Avebury/European Centre Vienna, 1993.

15 NAWH. Facts about Finnish social welfare and health care. Helsinki: NAWH, 1994.

16 SOSIAALI- JA TERVEYSMINISTERIÖ. Sosiaaliturva Suomessa 1992. Sosiaali- ja terveysministeriö, Sosiaaliturva 1994:2.

17 STAKES. Sosiaali- ja terveydenhuollon KETI-tietoja vuodelta 1992, 27.5.1994.

18 STAKES. Kotisairaanhoidon asiakkraat 2.2.1991 ja käynnit vuonna 1991. Tilastotiedote 1994:4.

19 LOUNAMAA, A., A. NORO. Yksin asuvat iäkkäät naiset valvotun kotisairaanhoidon suurin potilasryhmä. Dialogi, 1, 1994, 13-14.

20 MARJAMÄKI, P. Avopalvelujen toimivuus palvelurakennemuutoksen näkökulmasta. In: Laatupalveluihin kohtuukustannuksin. Palvelurakennehankkeen seurantaraportti II. Sosiaali- ja terveysministeriön Monisteita 1994:2.

21 SIHVO, T., M. LINDQVIST, Muutossuunnat kunnissa. Tietoja sosiaali- ja terveydenhuollon menoista, säästöistä, rationalisoinnista, priorisionnista ja karsinnasta lamavuosina 1992 ja 1993. Helsinki: STAKES, raportteja 135, 1994.

22 STAKES. Sosiaali- ja terveydenhuollon KETI-tietoja vuodelta 1993 (unpublished).

5 Home care in France

Robert A. Verheij

1 The setting of home care

1.1 The country

With a population of 56.4 million and an area of over 550,000 square kilometres, France is one of the largest countries of the European Union. Contrasts between urban and rural parts are sharp. On the one hand there are unpopulated areas and on the other hand there are highly urbanized areas like Paris and surroundings. The country is highly centralized; in many respects Paris is the nerve centre [1]. However, as we will see below, as regards the care for elderly people, the system suffers from a lack of cohesion and problems of co-ordination.

Population key figures (1990) [1,2]

Population in mln.	56.4
Inhabitants per sq. km.	102
% Living in urban areas	74
% over 65 years	13.8
% over 75 years	7.0
Births per 1000	13.1
Deaths per 1000	9.2
Life expectancy (men) ('89)	73.0
Life expectancy (women) ('89)	81.1

1.2   The organization of health care

The health care system in France has a rather fragmented structure. The main governmental body in French health care is the Ministry of Health and Social Affairs. Below the national level, there are 22 regions and 95 *départements* and numerous municipalities that are to a certain extent involved in the financing and organization of health and social services. Considerable decision-making power is delegated to the various Health Insurance funds that operate under the national public health insurance scheme (*Caisse Nationale Assurance Maladie*, CNAM) [1].

Home help services are part of the social services in France. With regard to social services, important roles are again played by the Ministry of Social Affairs at the national level, and again by the regions, the *départements*, and the municipalities. After 1984, with the introduction of decentralization, social services became the responsibility of the *départements*. In addition, old age insurance (*Caisse Nationale Assurance Vieillesse*, CNAV) plays an important role in the theatre of health and social care.

Secondary care is provided in public hospitals, for-profit private hospitals and non-profit private hospitals. Out-patient specialist care is provided in out-patient clinics, attached to hospitals. Hospitals and out-patient care are accessible without GP-referral.

Primary health care is provided by both general practitioners and independent specialists. Most GPs work alone in private practices. Community nursing care is provided by private (non-profit) organizations or by the local authorities but there are many independent nurses working on their own account.

Robert A. Verheij

Health care figures (1990) [2]

Expenditure

Total expenditure on health		
Absolute per head in ppp$	1528	
Percentage of GDP	8.8	
Public expenditure on health		
Absolute per head in ppp$	1137	
Percentage of GDP	6.6	

Manpower

Physicians per 1000 pop.	2.7	
GPs per 1000 pop.	1.0	
Qualified nurses per 1000 pop.	5.4	('89)

Hospital care

In-patient care	
Beds per 1000 pop.	9.7
Admissions per 100 pop.	23.3
Mean length of stay	12.3
Acute hospitals	
Beds per 1000 pop.	5.2
Admissions per 100 pop.	21.0
Mean length of stay	7.0
Nursing homes	
Beds per 1000 pop.	1.2

1.3   Health care financing and insurance

There are three main types of health insurance in France:
- Compulsory insurance (*Régime Générale* of the *Caisse Nationale Assurance Maladie* (CNAM) for all employees, pensioners and the unemployed. The *Régime Générale* is operated by many local and regional *Caisses Assurance Maladie* (CRAM). In 1982, 80% of the population were covered by this general scheme [1,3]. The insurance is based on the reimbursement principle: patient pays provider and claims a refund.
- Special schemes for agricultural workers, miners, seamen, civil servants and railway employees.
- Private supplementary insurance (*Mutualité*). This supplementary schemes covers 58% of the population and re-insure co-payments and cover risks that are not covered by the *Régime Générale*.

Coverage of health care costs under the *Régime Générale* varies according to the type of service from 65% for diagnostic tests to 100% for certain types of drugs. GP and dental services require 25% co-payment (*ticket moderateur*); paramedical services 25%; first thirty days of hospital stay 20%; and 60-30% for certain other types of drugs.

1.4 Care for the elderly

This study focuses on home help and home nursing services. However, these are not the only services especially directed towards elderly people, although they are the most important ambulatory services for the elderly [4].

As regards ambulatory services, home help and home nursing are complemented by whole array of other services. A telephone alarm system has been organized in several *départements*. Much technical medical help is given by medical auxiliaries working independently [5]. Respiratory care is an example of this [3]. Usually the patient has to finance this type of home care him/herself. Regarding social activities there are senior citizen's clubs and *foyer restaurants*. Meals-on-wheels, and home improvement services are available in some areas [4,5].

As far as residential services are concerned Spinnewyn distinguishes medical-social institutions and hospital services [4]. The medical-social sector includes private and public old people's homes (*maisons de retraite*) as well as *logements foyers*. The latter can be translated as sheltered housing, in which the elderly are offered optional facilities like a restaurant, laundry and home care. *Hospices publics* which can be circumscribed as old fashioned old people's home have largely disappeared [6] or transformed into *maisons de retraite*. Long-stay hospitals exist for the elderly who need long-term medical attention.

Recent developments in the care of the elderly comprise the CANTOUS, small residences for the demented elderly and MAPAD/MARPA, small-group housing programmes for those of the elderly who have lost their autonomy [4,6]. The creation of care-co-ordinators was mentioned by Spinnewyn [4] as a new development. However, Henrard [5] concludes that "their funding, initially subsidized by the state for a short period, was not taken over by local financing, so that most of the posts have been withdrawn" (p.114).

Finally, there are cash-payments to cover home help services when such services are insufficient in number (see also section 3.1) and there are tax deductions for those who care for and give housing to a person 75 years or older and have resources below a certain ceiling.

Capacity of residential services for the elderly in France (1986) [4]

	Number of places/beds per 1000 people over 65 years	
Sheltered housing	14.9	
Old people's homes and hospices	40.1	
Long-stay hospitals	7.3	
Medium-stay hospitals	5.3	('82)

2 The organization of home nursing

As regards home nursing in France, a distinction can be made between two types of care that are financed and administered separately. *Soins à Domicile pour Personnes Agées* (SAD) is the most important one. It is comparable to what is usually considered home nursing and it concentrates on elderly people. The other type is *Hospitalisation à Domicile* (HAD), which constitutes a much more specialized type of care, concentrating on patients who have been discharged from hospital. In many cases SAD and HAD are delivered by the same organization, by the same people, on a different funding base. Reimbursement for HAD is about three times that of SAD.

The number of places under HAD is relatively small, 3,972 in 1992 [7], versus 47,468 under SAD in 1992 [8]. Unless otherwise stated therefore, we mean SAD by the term home nursing.

2.1 Organizations for home nursing

There are two types of home nursing organization. One type (31%) is established and run by the municipality; in some cases through the local hospital. The other has come about through private initiative (69%). Usually the municipality has a large say in these private organizations. A total number of 1,199 organizations existed in 1990, having grown from 713 in 1985 [9].

In terms of services delivered, there is much variation, irrespective of the organizational structure of the organization. In some cases, a whole list of services, varying from meals-on-wheels to maternity care is delivered via home nursing. In other cases, only home nursing is provided. About 60% of all home nursing services provide an other service as well. The combination of home help, meals-on-wheels and tele-alarm is the most popular one [10]. The geographical scope of services also varies. There are services covering a whole *département*, but also those that cover only one municipality.

In addition to organizations for home nursing with salaried workers, there are a large number of independent nurses *(libérales)*. In many cases independent nurses are hired by home nursing organizations.

2.2 Manpower in home nursing

In France, nurses receive a three-year's in-service training. Although there are many options for specialization after graduation, community nursing is not one of them. To become a chief nurse *(infirmière coördinatrice)* in either hospital or home nursing, an eighteen month course is required. Second level nurses *(aides soignantes)* require a one year's training but in practice the sometimes have no such training.

In April 1991 there were 1,357 *infirmières coördinatrices* and 900 *infirmières salariées*. The number of active *infirmières libérales* in that period was estimated at 6,300 and the number of *aides soignantes* amounted to 7,900; the larger part of the latter work part-time. In 50% of all organizations, the *aides soignantes* worked less than 30 hours a week on average.

Table 1
Nursing and other personnel in home nursing agencies,
and independent nurses (April 1991) [10]

	number	average working week	no. of inhabitants per FTE nurse
inf. coördinatrice	1,357	32 h.	51,953
inf. salarié	900	27 h.	92,840
inf. libérale	6,300	n.a.	n.a.
aide soignante	7,900	28 h.	10,198
total	16,457	-	-

The home nursing organizations are paid according to the number of places for patients they are allowed to offer. The average number of places per 1,000 inhabitants > 75 is about 10. This figure has almost doubled since 1984.

121

Departmental differences are striking, however. About 20% of the departments have fewer than seven places per 1,000 inhabitants over 75, and 17% have more than 15 places.

2.3   Client population

Most home nursing clients are women and the elderly: 70% are female. The mean age is 82 years; 84% are over 75 and 47% are at least 85. During one week in April 1991, a total number of 17,178 persons were receiving home nursing care, 0.15% of the total population above 60 years of age [9]. Henrard estimates that only 10% of all 500,000 people who are dependent 'just for the activities of daily life' benefit from organized home nursing, which "necessarily implies that independent nurses, and especially the informal support of family and the neighbourhood, play a predominant role" [5].

For most of the clients home nursing is not the only care they receive. 46% of the clients receive home help services as well and 33% receive physiotherapy [9].

2.4   Provision of services

In theory each client has a free choice as to which home nursing organization or independent nurse to turn to. This choice is constrained, however, by the fact that supply is very low in some areas and there is not much to choose from and by people's insurance (public/private).

First contact with home nursing services is, in about 40% of the cases, established by the patient's family, 30% by a GP and 30% by hospital or nursing home (educated guesses). A referral by a GP or hospital physician is always required. Official assessment is carried out by one of the nurses. This assessment serves only an administrative purpose since the nurse has to stick to the content of the doctor's referral. It is sent to the Health Insurance company for authorization. Standardized assessment forms are used for this, on which the level of dependency of the client is indicated. In deciding upon the type of care that has to be given, the nurse cannot deviate from what the GP has stated in his/her referral.

The actual care is then usually provided by *aides soignantes*. This comes as no surprise, since the average number of salaried nurses per organization is less than one. Tasks of these *aides soignantes* include hygienic and other personal care, psychosocial activities and encouraging help from family members and other carers. Home help type of care like preparing food and drinks is not part of their work.

2.5   Problems and recent developments

Statistics on waiting lists are not kept. Some organizations are relatively flexible, because they provide such a variety of services that there will always be some way to help a specific client. In some regions - on the other hand - there may be no home nursing organization at all, let alone one to keep statistics on waiting lists. However, it is clear that there are large regional differences in the distribution of home nursing organizations and that must imply shortages. Good co-operation with independent nurses was suggested as a way to overcome possible waiting lists. If such co-operation exists, one can count on a larger, more flexible workforce.

Compared to other European countries, the home nursing workforce in France is rather small. Even in the unlikely event that independent nurses were all to work full-time (see also table 1), the number of inhabitants per nurse would be almost 7,000. It is hardly likely that this difference is entirely due to differentiation among nursing staff. The distribution of services is also unequal: two thirds of them are located in the greater Paris area [4].

Other problems are sometimes present in co-operation with general practitioners, in that they (GPs) do not always appreciate the importance of co-operation with home nursing organizations. The same applies to hospitals, although substitution is gaining momentum and some hospitals even provide home care on their own initiative. As regards home help services no problems were reported. Here, usually co-operation is very fruitful.

3   The organization of home help services

3.1   Organizations for home help services

Home help services are part of the social services in France. Henrard [5] distinguishes two sectors that are responsible for delivering home help services. The first is the public sector. It is financed by the *département* and provided by the municipalities. These services are part of the compulsory assistance for the poor [5,11]. About 30% of all hours of home help services are financed by the *département* [9]. If there is no home help service in a local community, or if this help is (temporarily) unavailable, the elderly person can get an allowance to buy this help (this allowance corresponds to a maximum of 60% of what it would actually cost). The other sector is the private sector. Provision is ensured by associations financed by old-age insurance and complementary pension schemes for those of their members who have a higher level of resources than the social assistance ceilings. Above a certain income level home help services are no longer financed by the *département* but have to be insured through old-age insurance funds like the *Caisse Nationale Assurance Vieillesse* for salaried workers and complimentary pension schemes. They provide about 45% of all home help hours [9].

According to the CNAV [12], there are about 725 *communes* not covered by a home help service. This may imply a shortage but it can also reflect the uneven distribution of people and especially the elderly over the communes. On average the number of unserviced communes has rapidly shrunk from 4,293 in 1983 and is stabilizing now. The remaining 725 communes constitute only 2% of the total number of communes in France and they are probably very sparsely populated.

3.3   Manpower in home help services

Most home helps are women between 45 and 60 years of age. A minority have had specific training and there are no statutory training requirements, though training is subsidized by the central government. In 1986, there were about 100,000 home helps, accounting for about 40,000 full-time equivalents [5]. This amounts to an average of 1,410 inhabitants per full-time home help.

3.3   Client population

In 1988 a total number of 490,000 people received home help service at some time that year, with some source of financing [9]. This is 3.5% of the population above 65 years of age.

In 1992 about 78% of the home help clients financed through CNAV were female. More than 70% were over 75. The number of people receiving home help services amounted to 4.26% of the total number of the people receiving a pension from CNAV [12].

3.4   Provision of services

As implied above, clients do not have a free choice as to what home help organization to turn to. Below a certain income-level, they have to turn to the municipality (financed by the *département*). Above that level help must be sought from the private sector. This does not always imply that you have to go to another organization, however. It may well be that there is one organization, that receives money from both the municipality/*département* and from old-age insurance companies.

In practice clients are often referred by social workers or general practitioners but this is not officially required. In 75% of the cases the reason is a health problem. Assessment is carried out by a social worker. He/she also determines the amount of care that will have to be given. Home helps usually work on their own, not in a team.

The work of home helps includes cleaning the home, laundering and ironing. In some instances hygiene care is also given, but this is not the rule. Though frequently performed, moral support, stimulating informal care and family support are not officially part of the home help's task.

3.5   Problems and recent developments

Official waiting lists are not kept. There are waiting lists for residential care, though, making it likely that home help services are also scarce and there may be a shortage of them.

As is the case with home nursing, general practitioners are reluctant to co-operate with home help services. The co-operation with home nursing is usually not a problem and, as regards hospitals, there are some cases of excellent co-operation.

A problem may be the uncontrolled increase of the third person allowance *(allocation compensatrice)* which is paid by the *département* but controlled by the state, causing co-ordination difficulties [6].

4   Relations between home nursing and home help services

It was mentioned above, that in many cases, home help services and home nursing are provided by the same organization. However, joint assessment of care is very rare. The same applies to home nurses and home helps taking part in the same team. It is more common to have regular meetings in which shared patients are discussed.

At the policy level, home help and home nursing suffer from problems of co-ordination because of different systems of financing.

5 The financing of home nursing

5.1 Payment and patients' insurance

The patient has to be over 60 or handicapped and has to be referred by a GP or hospital physician in order to receive home nursing. The *régime générale* reimburses 70% of the patient's cost for the nursing performed by independent nurses. The other 30% have to be paid by the patient himself (*ticket modérateur*), unless the patient has complementary insurance, which is often the case. There is no co-payment for patients under SAD. Patients are entitled to a maximum of four thirty-minute visits or two six-hour visits a day [13].

5.2 Funding of the organizations

Organizations have to apply individually to health insurance funds to get authorization to offer a specific number of 'places' for HAD or SAD patients. That number is fixed, although applying patients are not always turned down if this number is (temporarily) exceeded. The organization receives a lump sum according to the agreed number of places.

5.3 Payment of the nurses

Nurses employed by the home nursing organizations are paid a salary. Nurses earned a gross income of FRF 7,878 a month on a full-time basis and *aides soignantes* FRF 6,745 in one of the organizations that were taken into consideration by Verheij and Kerkstra [3]. According to Gabanyi et al. [14] the starting net salary of nurses was FRF 6,300 in 1991. Independent nurses (if not contracted by an organization) work on a fee-for-service basis. Services are then reimbursed according to the *nomenclature des actes professionels* in which each activity is assigned a price [3].

5.4   Problems and recent developments

In fact, there are no problems reported in the financing of home nursing as such. Although questions may arise as to the quantitative sufficiency, Henrard [5] concludes that "the beneficiaries appear to be well targeted" (p.110). The problems that do exist have to do with a lack of consistency in the financing of home care as a whole: home nursing and home help services. This subject will be discussed in section 6.4.

6   The financing of home help services

6.1   Payment and clients' insurance

Home help can either be obtained through social welfare or through private insurance. The difference is a particular income level. In order to be granted home help services in the public sector, patients should not earn more than about FRF 3,000 and total assets should not be more than FRF 250,000 [6]. Above this ceiling provisions are ensured by associations financed by old-age insurance (like CNAV) and complementary pension schemes. Also within the private sector, there is a ceiling to the amount of resources a possible patient is allowed to possess. Above that ceiling one has to pay for everything oneself. Ceilings may vary from one insurance scheme to another.

Within the private sector as well as the public sector, the maximum number of hours of home help a person is entitled to is 30 hours a month [5].

6.2   Funding of the organizations

As mentioned before, an organization can be largely financed by the *département* or by private insurance companies. The *département* is responsible for about 30% of all hours of home help that are provided, and private insurance companies take care of 45%. The rest can be attributed to various other sources [9]. Organization-specific figures are not available.

6.3   Payment of the home helps

Aides ménagères earn a net income of about FRF 5,000 on a full-time basis. *Aides ménagères* who have been trained for the job earn about FRF 2 more per hour than *aides ménagères* without such training.

6.4   Problems and recent developments

According to Henrard [5] the most important problem in home help services is targeting the available resources to the right people. From other research he concludes that "only 35 percent of those in need actually receive home help, and of those receiving home help only 60 percent need this service" (p.107). He raises questions about the distribution criteria that suffer from poor information, difficulties of access, quantitative insufficiency and poor use of existing services due to imprecise distribution criteria [5].

Furthermore, Henrard observes an increase of the number of beneficiaries, accompanied by a steady decrease in the number of hours per beneficiary. The increase in beneficiaries has taken place particularly among those who need relatively few hours of help (less than two hours) per week. This makes it even more unlikely that people with severe disabilities will benefit from home help services.

In June 1991 a report was published by the central government in which several measures were proposed to cope with the growing demand for home care (home nursing and home help) and the increasing problems of co-ordination within home care [3,15]. Measures included the financial and organizational integration of medical and social services; reimbursement dependent on the level of care dependency and measures to encourage informal care, together with an overall increase of the home care capacity. However, these revolutionary plans stranded in the first half of 1994 because of the protests from the elderly themselves who would have to finance it all.

Acknowledgements
The information presented in this chapter was provided by the following persons and institutions:
Mrs C. Niclausse, CASSPA, Soissons.
Professor J.C. Henrard, Université René Descartes, Laboratoire Santé et Veilleissement, Paris.
Caisse Nationale d'Assurance Vieillesse (CNAV), Paris.
Service des statistiques de études et des systèmes d'information (SESI), Paris
Centre de recherche d'étude et documentation en économie de la santé (CREDES), Paris.

References

1 BOERMA, W.G.W., F.A.J.M. DE JONG, P.H. MULDER. Health care and general practice across Europe, Utrecht: NIVEL, 1993.
2 OECD HEALTH DATA. Version # 1.5. Paris: OECD, 1993.
3 VERHEIJ, R.A., A. KERKSTRA. International comparative study of community nursing. Aldershot: Avebury, 1992.
4 SPINNEWYN, H. France. In: Nijkamp, P., J. Pacolet, H. Spinnewyn, A. Vollering, C. Wilderom, S. Winters, S. (eds.) Services for the elderly in Europe. A cross-national comparative study. Leuven: Commission of the European Communities, 1991.
5 HENRARD, J.C., J. ANKRI, M.C. ISNARD. Home care services in France. In: Jamieson, A. (eds.). Home care for older people in Europe. Oxford: Oxford University Press, 1991.
6 MINISTÈRE DES AFFAIRES SOCIALES ET DE L'INTÉGRATION. Vieillir en France. Paris: Ministère des affaires sociales et de l'intégration, Secretariat d'état à la famille, 1993.
7 COM-RUELLE, L., N. RAFFY. Les patients hospitalisés à domicile en 1992. Paris: CREDES, 1994.
8 SESI. Annuaire des statistiques et sociales. Edition 1993. Paris: Service des statistiques des études et de systèmes d'information (SESI), 1993.
9 SESI. Annuaire des statistiques sanitaires et sociales. Edition 1992, Paris: Service des statistiques des études et des systèmes d'information (SESI), 1992.
10 SESI. Les services de soins a domicile, enquête SSAD 1991. Documents statistiques no.168. Paris: Service des statistiques des études et des systèmes d'information (SESI), 1993.
11 SESI. Dépenses et bénéficiaires d'aide sociale. Resultats 1991, Paris: Service des statistiques des études et des systèmes d'information (SESI), 1994.
12 CNAV. L'action sociale pour les retraités aide ménagère à domicile. Statistiques 1992 (édition août 1993). Paris: CNAV, 1993.
13 France. Health Policy; 20, 1992, 148-160.
14 GABANYI, M., S. MAY, M. SCHNEIDER. Absicherung des Pflegerisikos am Beispiel ausgewählter europäischer Länder. Bonn: Bundesminister für Arbeit und Sozialordnung, 1992.
15 BOULARD, J.C. Rapport d'information no. 2135 sur les personnes âgées dépendantes 'Vivre Ensemble'. Paris: Assemblée Nationale, 1991.

6 Home care in Germany

Diana M.J. Delnoij

1 The setting of home care

1.1 The country

Germany is a federal state, consisting of sixteen *Länder*: eleven in the former Federal Republic of Germany (FRG) and five in the former German Democratic Republic (GDR). The sixteen *Länder* each have their own national legislation. The chancellor (the head of the federal government) is elected by parliament (the *Bundestag*) on the nomination of the federal president. On the 3rd of October 1990, the German Democratic Republic formally joint the Federal Republic of Germany. In the Bilateral Unity Treatment it was agreed that the social jurisdiction and the legislation of the old Federal Republic, as well as the respective institutional system, were to be assumed by the five new Federal States. This integration of a former communist state into West Germany's market system is a gigantic operation accompanied by great difficulties and huge costs (which were greatly underestimated before the start of the process). Although Germany is a dominant economic power in Europe, the unification continues to demand considerable financial efforts. Problems also arise from the significant cultural gap between the eastern and western *Länder* [1,2].

Population key figures (1990) [1,3]

Population in mln.	78.7	
Inhabitants per sq. km.	221	
% Living in urban areas	84	
% over 65 years	14.9	
% over 75 years	7.2	
Births per 1000	13.3	
Deaths per 1000	11.1	
Life expectancy (men)	72.6	('89)
Life expectancy (women)	79.0	('89)

1.2 The organization of health care

The German health care system is characterized by Kirkman-Liff [4] as "a decentralized system with private practice physicians (for ambulatory care) and independent, mostly non-profit hospitals". In Germany, a distinct division is made between institutional care (provided by salaried hospital doctors) and non-institutional, ambulatory care. Ambulatory care physicians cannot treat hospitalized patients, and hospital physicians cannot treat ambulatory patients. This also implies that hospitals do not have outpatient clinics for specialty ambulatory care.

Within ambulatory care, provided by so-called *niedergelassene Ärzte*, no further division is made between GPs and medical specialists. Patients are not obliged to be listed with a general practitioner. Health Insurance funds provide their members quarterly with a health insurance certificate, the so-called *Checkkarte* (the former *Krankenschein*), with which patients may consult any physician who has a contract with the Health Insurance fund. Handing in the certificate ties patients to one specific provider for the period in which the *Krankenschein* is valid (three months).

Health care figures (1990) [3]

Expenditure

Total expenditure on health		
Absolute per head in ppp$	1522	
Percentage of GDP	8.3	
Public expenditure on health		
Absolute per head in ppp$	1090	
Percentage of GDP	6.0	

Manpower

Physicians per 1000 pop.	3.1	
GPs per 1000 pop.	1.2	
Qualified nurses per 1000 pop.	5.2	('89)

Hospital care

In-patient care		
Beds per 1000 pop.	10.4	
Admissions per 100 pop.	20.9	
Mean length of stay	16.5	
Acute hospitals		
Beds per 1000 pop.	7.5	
Admissions per 100 pop.	18.5	
Mean length of stay	13.4	
Nursing homes		
Beds per 1000 pop.	9.6	('88)

1.3 Health financing and insurance

The institutional structure of the German health care system has two historical roots. At the end of the nineteenth century, social laws including health insurance were introduced for workers. The concept of Health Insurance funds originated in Germany when in 1881 a Social Insurance Act was passed by the Bismarck administration, introducing compulsory insurance for low-paid industrial workers. The social welfare for the non-working part of the population was dealt with on the local level by churches, communal bodies and private charity associations [2].

In 1993, most Germans obtained their health insurance through membership in one of 1,241 *gesetzliche Krankenkassen* (Statutory Health Insurance funds). Virtually all Germans with a salary or wage income below DEM 64,800 are obliged to join a *Krankenkasse*. Approximately 93% of the population are covered [5]. The remaining 7% are privately insured. Another 8% of the population have *supplementary* private insurance.

German law requires that Health Insurance funds provide a comprehensive benefits package, including ambulatory and hospital care; maternity, dental, and preventive care; physical therapy; drugs and family planning; rehabilitation; eyeglasses; medical appliances; home health care; fitness tests and work therapy (including spa visits). Apart from these service benefits, health insurance includes certain cash benefits for maternity leave, paid leave for care of a sick child, sick leave and burial allowances.

Above a certain income ceiling there are co-payments for the cost of drugs, inpatient hospital care and dental care.

Health insurance benefits do not include long-term nursing care. Long-term nursing care will be covered by the new *Pflegeversicherung* (nursing care insurance) which will be introduced in 1995 (see section 5.4).

1.4 Care for the elderly

The ageing of the population has taken place more rapidly in Germany than elsewhere in the European community. Social conditions for the elderly in the old Federal Republic have improved over the past decade, but, at the same time, they have become more differentiated. Income after retirement is made up (in various proportions) by rebates from the statutory Federal Pension Insurance Scheme for workers and employees; of state, industrial or professional pension schemes; of social security benefits; and of income from personal means. The existing old-age and social welfare schemes can lead to an insufficient level of income for those who have always earned low wages [2].

In the old Federal Republic about 1.2 million elderly are cared for at home by family members. Another 450,000 are in nursing homes (*Altenpflegeheime*), 70% of those depend on welfare [6]. About 4% of the elderly, not necessarily in need of care, live in homes for the elderly (*Altenheime*). Old people's homes do not have a very good reputation in Germany: they are generally seen as "terminal homes".

The German system of care and welfare in the eleven *Länder* of the old Federal Republic is characterized by an institutionalized form of co-operation between the public bodies engaged in the field of care and various welfare associations (private initiative). During the past twenty years, the so-called *Sozialstationen* (Social Stations), providing community nursing and often home help care as well, have become the most important community-based care-providing institutions [2,8]. The first *Sozialstationen* were established in 1970 in Rheinland-Pfalz. The state of Berlin was one of the last to start a programme of *Sozialstationen* in 1982, though in the state of Bremen, for example, *Sozialstationen* do not yet exist. The services that are provided elsewhere by *Sozialstationen* are in Bremen delivered by *Dienstleistungszentren* (service centres).

In the former GDR special problems arise in the care for the elderly. For one thing, there has been a considerable amount of migration of people of working age from the old GDR to the former FRG. The average age of those remaining has increased markedly as a result of that process. About 4.5 to 5% of the elderly in the former GDR live in old people's homes. The buildings in which these homes are located, are generally old (often pre-war) and as such, the constructions lack modern facilities and comfort, by Western standards along rate. Home nursing was provided by *Gemeindekranken-schwestern*. In addition to that, many companies would take care of their pensioners, e.g. by providing meals from the canteen. Since 1990, *Sozialstationen* have been introduced in the former GDR.

In Germany, several types of organization are involved in providing ambulatory care for the elderly. They are referred to in general as *Ambulante sozialpflegerische Dienste* (organizations for ambulatory social and nursing care). In 1993, there were 6,250 *Ambulante sozialpflegerische Dienste* that together employed 49,808 people. This total number of organizations can be divided into:
* *Gemeindekrankenpflegestationen*
* *Haus- und Familienpflegestationen*
* *Sozialstationen*
* *Mobilen Sozialen Hilfsdienste*
In 1993, in West-Germany there were 2,061 organizations for the separate provision of either home nursing (*Gemeindekrankenpflegestationen*) or of "traditional" home help services (*Haus- und Familienpflegestationen*, providing home help mainly in families with children under twelve, where the mother is hospitalized, has recently been discharged from hospital or is temporarily incapable of attending to the home and the family for other reasons). The number of these separate organizations had decreased with about 30% (there used to be 2,919 in 1990). At the same time, the number of integrated

organizations for home nursing and home help (*Sozialstationen*) and of *Mobilen sozialen Hilfsdienste* (providing help at home mainly for elderly, in contrast to the "traditional" home help services) had grown, from 2,869 in 1990 to 3,295 in 1993. In the former GDR, the total number of 894 organizations for home help and nursing care consisted predominantly of *Sozialstationen*, of which in 1993 there were 666 [11].

Capacity of residential services for the elderly in West Germany (1986) [8]

	Number of places/beds per 1000 people over 65 years
Old people's homes	13.6
Service flats	7.3
Nursing homes	4.1
Multilevel homes	21.5

2 The organization of home nursing

2.1 Organizations for home nursing

Though it is possible to give a general outline of home nursing and home help services in Germany, it should be noted that the details of the organization of home care vary greatly throughout the country. The regulations determined in federal law are, of course, the same throughout the republic, but since the implementation of legal guidelines is left to private initiative, the actual care provision differs from state to state.

Social care and welfare services are provided mainly by independent charity associations, but also by self-organized groups and by private business. Home nursing is provided by so-called *Gemeindekrankenpflegestationen* (organizations for home nursing only) and increasingly by the *Sozialstationen* (providing a broad range of ambulatory services, including home nursing and home help services). In 1993, there were 1,072 *Gemeindekrankenpflege-stationen* and 3,069 *Sozialstationen* in Germany as a whole.

The size of the population that is served by a *Sozialstation* varies between 12,000 and 50,000 depending on the size of the *Sozialstation* and the degree of urbanization. Usually, *Sozialstationen* in urban areas serve a larger number of inhabitants [7].

In the state of Berlin, the number of staff employed by *Sozialstationen* varies from 12 to over 100, though exact figures are difficult to obtain because of the wide range of employment arrangements involved [9].

The totality of all forms of social support on a non-statutory, non-profit making basis in Germany is called the *Freie Wohlfahrtspflege*. Within the *Freie Wohlfahrtspflege*, the welfare associations have combined to form six national umbrella organizations:
- the *Diakonisches Werk* (of Protestant denomination)
- the *Caritas* (of Catholic denomination)
- the *Arbeiterwohlfahrt*
- the *Zentralwohlfahrtsstelle der Juden in Deutschland* (of Jewish denomination)
- the *Deutsches Rotes Kreuz*
- the *Deutscher Paritätischer Wohlfahrtsverband*

Though the market for home nursing is dominated by non-profit organizations, in recent years a growing number of nurses have decided to work freelance or have developed for-profit nursing organizations [9]. For-profit organizations have developed mainly in urban areas. E.g. in Hamburg, 60% of home nursing are delivered by for-profit providers.

2.2 Manpower in home nursing

Four types of qualified nurses work in the community:
- *Krankenschwester* (male: *Krankenpfleger*), a nurse generalist with three years of education. Many of them have specialized as a community nurse (*Gemeindeschwester*) in one additional year of study (which can be entered after having worked in their profession for at least two years [7]).
- *Kinderkrankenschwester*, specialized in care for children, three years of education
- *Altenpfleger(in)*, specialized in care for the elderly, two to three years of education
- *Krankenpflegehelfer(in)*, auxiliary nurse, one year of education

There seems to be quite a lot of variation in nurse-to-population ratios throughout the country. Except for Berlin, there is a shortage of (qualified) community nurses. In 1990, there were some 10,000 community nurses [7].

A typical Social Station employs eight to ten nurses, either generalists or nurses specialized in care for the elderly. This staff is assisted by volunteers and nursing aides, who perform basic nursing procedures and home help services [12]. In 1993, all the *Sozialstationen* in Germany employed 20,599 full-time and 15,644 part-time employees. *Gemeindekrankpflegestationen* employed 1,887 full-time and 1,182 part-time employees.

2.3 Client population

According to a study published in 1990 [10], about 50% of the *Schwerpflege-bedürftige*, patients with a need for intensive nursing care (see also section 5.1), were over 80 years old and 85% were over 65. About half of them suffered from illnesses of the central nervous system, 43% from cerebrovascular illnesses. Approximately 40% had both. Another large category (26% of the patients) had an illness of the skeleto-muscular system. About 75% of the *Schwerpflegebedürftige* were visited daily, about 20% weekly. Of patients that were visited daily, 25% received more than one visit per day [10].

An earlier study had shown, that in 1986 there were 56 *Sozialstationen* in Berlin, that had 6,054 patients to whom they paid 40,036 visits totalling 36,453 hours of care during one week in October [7]. A later case-study [9] indicated that by 1990, there were 70 *Sozialstationen* in Berlin that provided home care for about 10% of the total population over 70 years of age. The case-study also showed that 57% of people with a high level of need did not receive any home-care services during the year studied [9].

The same case-study indicates that there seems to have taken place a shift in the focus of activities of *Sozialstationen*. At the outset they were intended to be institutions for short-term intervention and acute nursing care. Today they have in fact become long-term care facilities. Another study [7] points in the same direction: about 90% of the patients cared for by *Sozialstationen* are chronically ill.

2.4 Provision of services

In the provision of services, a quite important legal distinction is made between *Grundpflege* (helping the patient with basic needs including ADL-activities) and *Behandlungspflege* (specialized, technical nursing procedures) (see also section 5.1). The two types of care are generally carried out by *Krankenschwestern*, and with the exception of technical nursing by

Krankenschwesterhelferinnen and *Altenpflegerinnen*. Home visits take about 80 to 90% of the total working time of these nurses. Apart from that, they spent about 5% of their time on consultation hours and 5-10% on administrative activities (qualified nurses more than auxiliaries) [7].

80% of the patients cared for by *Sozialstationen* are visited once a day from Monday through Friday, 15% twice a day, and another 5% are visited three times a day. An average house-call takes about 20 minutes, leaving very little time for talking or rehabilitative procedures [12].

First contacts between patient and home nurse are often initiated by the family or neighbours, but also by general practitioners or by hospitals, which contact the *Sozialstation* a few days before discharging a patient. Officially, the assessment is done by either a physician, whose orders are needed for reimbursement of home nursing by the Health Insurance funds. Physicians however, closely co-operate with head nurses of Social Stations in assessing patients. Usually, the head nurse of the *Sozialstation* also decides which level of expertise is needed and who is going to deliver the care. Normally, care is given by the nurse serving the specific area in which the patient lives. Since doctor's orders are needed for reimbursement, assessment forms (which are used in all *Sozialstationen*) are adapted to this. A case study from Berlin [9] shows that *Sozialstationen* differ in the procedures by which patients are assigned to nurses. Some centres try to ensure continuity of care (a patient always has the same nurse), others prefer staff rotation or group care-giving [9].

2.5   Problems and recent developments

General problems that the federal Ministry for Labour and Social Affairs (*Bundesministerium für Arbeit und Sozialordnung*) recognizes are [12]:
- *Sozialstationen* predominantly care for patients with a high need for nursing care. This implies that they take over from informal care-givers at a very late point, so that often patients are admitted to a nursing home in a stage in which they could have stayed at home, provided that the necessary ambulatory care provisions had been available.
- During the night and in weekends, care is provided by *Sozialstationen* to a very limited degree only. At the same time, in many towns competitive behaviour prevents the establishments of agreements between ambulatory care-providers on availability around the clock.

A case-study in Berlin [9] indicates that other health and social institutions are still not very much aware of the range of services that *Sozialstationen* have to offer. It should be noted, however, that the state of Berlin was the last to introduce *Sozialstationen* (in 1982). Other problems that were mentioned [9], are:

- poor service co-ordination (the actual condition of a patient often remains unknown until the first job has been done)
- poor timing (hospital tend to discharge patients at midday on Fridays)
- restricting job definition (a number of tasks that are grossly underrated in tariff lists, has to be carried out before the actual nursing can commence)
- general practitioners' unwillingness to co-operate
- arbitrary and increasingly bureaucratic care allocation
- low training standards, specifically among home-care assistants.

These problems occur in the highly populated area of Berlin. It is not clear, of course, to what extent they are also found in the rest of Germany.

3 The organization of home help services

3.1 Organizations for home help services

Home help services are provided by three types of organizations. "Traditional" home help services are provided by *Haus- und Familiepflege-stationen* (of which there were 623 in 1993) and by *Sozialstationen*. In the former GDR, domestic services, hot meals, and cultural activities used to be provided by a semi-governmental organization called *Volkssolidarität* (People's Solidarity). Now, the five *Wohlfahrtsverbände* are engaged in providing home help services through their *Sozialstationen*.

Additional home help services mainly for elderly people are provided also by *Mobilen sozialen Hilfsdienste*. In 1993, there were 1,050 *Mobilen sozialen Hilfsdienste* in all of Germany. These are organizations that also belong to the *freie Wohlfahrtspflege*, represented on the federal level by the six umbrella organizations mentioned in section 2.1. Although *Mobilen sozialen Hilfsdiensten* do not provide traditional home help services, they are of vital importance in German home care: they provide services such as 'meals-on-wheels' and cleaning services, which enable the elderly (and chronically ill) to stay in their own homes, instead of being admitted to nursing homes or old people's homes. For that reason, *Mobilen sozialen Hilfsdienste* are also described in this chapter, although the range of services they offer is different from what is usually defined as 'home help services'.

3.2 Manpower in home help services

"Traditional" home help services
Two types of personnel work in "traditional" home help, which is provided by *Haus- und Familienpflegestationen* and by *Sozialstationen*:

- the *Haus- und Familienpflegerin* (home and family help), who has two year's training (one year in school, one year of practice) and provides care mainly in 'problem' families.
- the *Haus- und Familienpflegehelferin* (home and family help aide), who has usually attended a variety of short training courses and provides care in families without further social problems.

In 1993, *Haus- und Familienpflegestationen* employed 2,308 full-time and 4,116 part-time workers.

'Mobilen sozialen Hilfsdienste'
For the *Mobilen sozialen Hilfsdienste* in all of Germany, a total number of 1,339 full-time and 1,753 part-time salaried employees is reported for 1993. However, these do not include the large number of volunteers and *Zivildienstleistenden* (conscientious objectors to military service) that work in this particular area of ambulatory care. In all of Germany, in 1994 there are 103,041 *Zivildienstleistenden*, about 60% of whom are employed in home care (12,1% in *Mobilen sozialen Hilfsdienste*).

Information on manpower in *Mobilen sozialen Hilfsdienste* (MSDs) is available in more detail for 34 MSDs belonging to the *Arbeiterwohlfahrt* in the state of North Rhine Westphalia [13]. A survey shows that on August 1, 1993, 1,004 people (924 FTEs) were working in these 34 MSDs, among which 496 *Zivildienstleistenden*. Apart from *Zivildienstleistenden* about one third of people working for MSDs in North Rhine Westphalia consist of participants in special programmes for the unemployed, such as *Arbeitsbeschaffungs-maßnamen* (ABM) or *Arbeit statt Sozialhilfe* (ASS). Of all the employees, 45% were specifically educated to work in ambulatory social or nursing care, 40% had no professional training, and another 10% had a training for other than social or nursing professions.

3.3 Client population

"Traditional" home help services
Clients of traditional home help services, families with children as well as elderly people.
'Mobilen sozialen Hilfsdienste'
The client population of the 34 MSDs in the survey mentioned earlier [13], consists for 82% of people over 65 years of age. 72% of the clients are women, more than half of the clients are widow(ers) and live on their own. About 40% of the clients have a *Schwerbehindertenausweis*, a document indicating disability.

3.4 Provision of services

Traditional home help services
The traditional *Haus- und Familienpflege* provides temporary care for families or individuals at home. This care includes basic nursing care, pedagogical and psychological care, and homemaking services. Typical of traditional home help services is its diversity as far as the provision of services is concerned.

'Mobilen sozialen Hilfsdienste'
All of the 34 MSDs included in the survey in North Rhine Westphalia [13], provided:
- information and advice on social and other ambulatory services
- homemaking services (help with cooking meals, doing the dishes, tidy up and so on)
- so-called *Betreuungsdienste* (keep elderly company, help with correspondence, accompany clients to their doctor and so on).

About 70% of the MSDs also provided some basic nursing care, such as help clients getting dressed. Only 38% of the MSDs provided shopping and cleaning services.

The majority of clients received help from a MSD for more than six months, 60% of the clients were visited five times a week or daily. Another 20% were visited three to four times a week.

Diana M.J. Delnoij

3.5 Problems and recent developments

'Mobilen sozialen Hilfsdienste'
The main problems of MSDs are financial ones, which shall be described in section 6.4. According the *Arbeiterwohlfahrt Bezirk Westliches Westfalen e.V.*, however, there is also a need for more qualified personnel in MSDs.

4 Relations between home nursing and home help services

Before 1970, there used to be separate organizations for home nursing and home help services. Home nursing was provided mainly by nuns or by Protestant Diakonessen. By the end of the 1960s, due to a process of ongoing secularization, a shortage of qualified nurses had developed. In order to be able to employ nurses and create better working conditions, the concept of *Sozialstationen* was introduced in 1970 in Rheinland-Pfalz. From there, *Sozialstationen* have spread over the rest of the country. In *Sozialstationen* several ambulatory care provisions, among which home nursing and home help, were combined. The general impression exists, that this has put a greater emphasis on home nursing care, whereas the traditional home and family help has become somewhat less important.

5 The financing of home nursing

5.1 Payment and patients' insurance

In general, both for home nursing as well as for home help services, the German system is based on the principle of subsidiarity: if there is informal service provision, no formal services are offered; if formal services are needed, the family has to pay for them (except for services that fall under health insurance); only if the family cannot pay, formal providers (social welfare) take over the costs [9].

Before 1989, nursing services in Germany were provided under health insurance only as a complete substitute for hospital care or if it enabled an early discharge. Two types of benefits are distinguished in §37 of the federal nursing law (*Sozialgesetzbuch V*):

- specialized nursing (*Behandlungspflege*), technical nursing procedures as a support for medical treatment,
- basic nursing (*Grundpflege*), basis personal care such as bathing, health monitoring, making of bed and so on.

Specialized nursing is a so-called *Ist-Leistung* (a necessary service), whereas basic nursing is optional, a so-called *Kann-Leistung*. This means that, as far as health insurance is concerned, only the need for specialized nursing allows for the provision of basic nursing. Specialized nursing itself is seen as an adjunct to medical treatment [9].

A third type of benefit is under certain conditions reimbursed by health insurance: according to §38 of the above mentioned law, home help (*Haushaltshilfe*) is provided (only) in addition to specialized nursing in families with a child under twelve years of age (see section 6.1).

In addition to that system, since January 1, 1989 patients with a need for intensive (nursing) care who live at home (the so-called *Schwerpflege-bedürftige*) are entitled to 25 home visit (of maximally one hour each) from a professional nurse per month, not exceeding the value of DEM 750 per month per case (§53 and §55 of the *Sozialgesetzbuch V*). It is possible to be visited more than once a day. During the home visit, the services delivered can include both basic care (e.g. washing the patient), as well as homemaking services (e.g. cooking and cleaning).

It is also possible to apply for cash benefits (instead of service benefits in the form of a home nurse). The maximum amount of cash benefits a patient can receive per month for care usually provided by relatives, is DEM 400. §56 Of the above mentioned law has created the option for informal care-givers to apply for a substitute in the form of a professional nurse during their vacation. The substitute is reimbursed for a period of maximally four weeks up to a value of DEM 1,800. The costs are refunded on the condition that the informal care-giver has provided care over a period of twelve months [2].

Nursing care under the health insurance system is generally offered for a period of four weeks. It is provided as a statutory service instead of hospital treatment and/or as a discretionary service to ensure the effects of medical treatment. It is provided in case in household member can deliver the service [9].

5.2 Funding of the organizations

One of the reasons explaining the success that *Sozialstationen* have had since 1970, is the financial promotion of these organizations by different states and health insurance programs. Dieck and Garms-Homolová [9] describe the situation as follows: "The network of finance running to different organizations is rather intricate. It is not that organizations other than social stations are excluded from it, but it is safe to say that the social stations are well in the middle of this web" [p. 128].

For 1993 the sources of income of *Sozialstationen* are roughly estimated as follows:

state taxes	10-20%
private insurance companies	< 5%
Health Insurance funds	65%
out-of-pocket payment	10%
umbrella organizations	< 10%

Out-of-pocket payment and payment from insurance companies or Health Insurance funds to *Sozialstationen* is made on a fee-for-service basis.

5.3 Payment of the nurses

Nurses receive a salary, the level of which is determined in negotiations between their employers and the *Gewerkschaft Öffentliche Dienste, Transport und Verkehr*, Germany's second largest trade union. In 1994, a 22-year old *Krankenschwester* who has just finished school and starts to work in home nursing receives a gross salary (i.e. before taxes) of DEM 3,154 per four weeks plus a bonus for working nights, sundays and holidays. After two years on the job her salary would be increased to DEM 3,402 plus bonuses (before taxes).

5.4 Problems and recent developments

An important development is the introduction of the *Pflegeversicherung* (nursing care insurance) starting in 1995. Starting January 1, 1995, premiums will have to be paid for the new insurance. From April 1, 1995, onwards home nursing will reimbursed and from July 1, 1996, onwards the benefits package will also include long-term nursing care in homes. Carriers of the new *Pflegeversicherung* are the Health Insurance funds. Publicly insured will enter insurance with their *gesetzliche Krankenkassen* (Statutory Health Insurance funds), privately insured will be obliged to take out a *pflegeversicherung* with their insurance company.

Those eligible are people who, due to physical or mental illness, are (partly) unable to attend to activities of daily living for at least (unexpected) six months. Three categories of need are distinguished:

- category I: *erheblich Pflegebedürftige*, people who need help with at least two activities of daily living once a day and who need home help services several times a week. For this category, as far as ambulatory care is concerned, benefits consist of service benefits (professional home care delivered in kind) up to a maximum of DEM 750 a month, or cash benefits, with which a patient can buy is own home care, up to a maximum of DEM 400 a month.

- category II: *Schwerpflegebedürftige*, people who need help with activities of daily living at least three times a day and who need home help services several times a week. For this category, service benefits may not exceed DEM 1,800 a month; cash benefits may not exceed DEM 800 a month.

- category III: *Schwerstpflegebedürftige*, people who need help with activities of daily living 24 hours a day and who need home help services several times a week. For this category, service benefits may not exceed DEM 2,800 a month; cash benefits may not exceed DEM 1,300 a month. For long-term care in nursing homes, service benefits may not exceed DEM 2,800 a month as well.

The assessment of patients in order to determine to which category they belong, will be the responsibility of the medical advisors of the Health Insurance funds (carriers of the new insurance). The new insurance is financed out of premiums that, in principle, are paid for 50% by employees and for 50% by employers. However, in order to "buy" employers' consent to the introduction of the insurance, one national holiday will be cancelled in 1995. The possibility is left open to abolish a second national holiday later on, when necessary due to the inclusion of long-term nursing care in homes (scheduled for July 1, 1996).

Since the new insurance is not yet functioning, it is difficult to predict its effects. The *Arbeiterwohlfahrt* however, foresees some problems with the new *Pflegeversicherung* [14]. Firstly, the maximum amounts set by government are too low compared to the average real costs of nursing care, especially as far as care provided in nursing homes is concerned. Further, the *Arbeiter-wohlfahrt* has serious doubts on the ability of medical advisors (experts on "cure", rather than on "care") to assess a patient's needs for nursing care. The fact that an overall expenditure cap is imposed on the new care insurance, finally, could have a negative effect on the quality of care, according to the *Arbeiterwohlfahrt* [14].

6 The financing of home help services

6.1 Payment and clients insurance

Payment for home help services, as for home nursing, are based on the principle of subsidiarity (see section 5.1). Clients have to pay for home help services themselves, and only if they or their children cannot afford this, social welfare will take over the costs.

"Traditional" home help services
Under certain conditions, home help is provided under the health insurance system in addition to ambulatory nursing care. It is delivered to households with a child under the age of twelve (or a handicapped child), where the mother is hospitalized, or has recently been discharged from hospital, and where no other family member can take over (compare section 5.1). This quite narrow regulation prevented the reception of home help by the elderly, until a new law in 1982 opened up for home help as a discretionary service proved for the elderly and funded by health insurance. Though even today, elderly people are not the target group of this type of home help service, because home help for the elderly is mainly provided by *Mobilen sozialen Hilfsdienste*.

Yet, the elderly are no longer excluded from home help services under health insurance [9]. Apart from that, the 1991 arrangement with regard to *Schwerpflegebedürftige* (described in section 5.1) can be taken as a sort of revival of traditional community care, in which basic nursing and home help are combined for patients who do not clearly fit into the system directed towards the acutely ill [9].

'Mobilen sozialen Hilfsdienste'
The price of home help services provided by *Mobilen sozialen Hilfsdienste*

(MSD) varies greatly. Information is available for 34 MSDs belonging to the *Arbeiterwohlfahrt* in the state of North Rhine Westphalia [13]. In 1993, home help services provided by a professional home help aide cost between DEM 24.50 and 41.70 per hour (average DEM 31.00); provided by *Zivildienstleistenden* it was cheaper, on average DEM 10.50 per hour. Housekeeping services (e.g. cleaning) provided by MSDs were somewhat cheaper, on average DEM 18.00 per hour for *Zivildienstleistenden* and DEM 9.15 for participants in programmes for the unemployed (ABM/ASS).

6.2 Funding of the organizations

Home help services under health insurance are generally provided by *Sozialstationen*. For funding of *Sozialstationen* see section 5.2.

'Mobilen sozialen Hilfsdienste'

Mobilen sozialen Hilfsdienste (MSD) are funded by a variety of sources. Information is, again, available for the 34 MSDs of the *Arbeiterwohlfahrt* in North Rhine Westphalia [13]. The staff of MSDs is in some cases financed out of a state budget; sometimes municipal funds are added to it. Further municipal funding is made available for running the MSD. This funding takes the form of a global budget in the majority of cases, but can also be based on the number of employees of a MSD, the output of an MSD (hours of service provision), or a percentage of the total costs of running the MSD.

Apart from that, MSDs charge fees per hour for services provided. These fees are either paid the clients themselves, or by social welfare or health insurance (under the conditions described earlier). On average, MSDs in North Rhine Westphalia are funded by these fees (the so-called *Leistungsentgelten*) for 20.5% of their total costs. Around this average, however, quite a lot of variation exists: the costs of one MSD are covered for over 60% by fees for service, the costs of another for less than 10%. 17 of the 34 MSDs are funded between for 10 and 30% by fees for services.

6.3 Payment of the home helps

Home helps are paid by means of a salary, which is lower than that of community nurses (exact data not available). Of course, *Zivildienstleistenden* and participants in unemployment programmes earn even less.

147

6.4 Problems and recent developments

The main problem with home help services lies in their funding. MSDs do not have a solid financial base, but instead, depend heavily on volunteers, participants in unemployment programmes and conscientious objectors to military service. Federal cuts in the funding of e.g. *Zivildienstleistenden* or the unemployment programmes can therefore endanger the provision of services by MSDs [13].

Acknowledgement

Information for this chapter was provided by:
Mrs. Doris Wagner
Arbeiterwohlfahrt Bundesverband
Bonn

References

1 BOERMA, W.G.W., F.A.J.M. DE JONG, P.H. MULDER. Health care and general practice across europe. Utrecht: NIVEL, 1993.

2 EVERS, A., I. SVETLIK. New welfare mixes in care for the elderly, Volume 3: Canada, France, Germany, Italy, United Kingdom. Vienna: European Centre for Social Welfare Policy and Research, 1991.

3 OECD HEALTH DATA. Version # 1.5. Paris: OECD, 1993.

4 KIRKMAN-LIFF, B.L. Physician payment and cost-containment strategies in West Germany: Suggestions for medicare reform. Journal of Health Politics, Policy and Law; 15, 1990, 1, 69-99.

5 GROENEWEGEN, P.P., J. VAN DER ZEE, R. VAN HAAFTEN. Remuneration of general practitioners in Western Europe. Aldershot-Brookfield: Avebury, 1991.

6 UNITED STATES GENERAL ACCOUNTING OFFICE (GAO). 1993 German health reforms, new cost control initiatives, report to the Chairman, Committee on Governmental Affairs, U.S. Senate, GAO: Washington, July 1993.

7 VERHEIJ, R.A., A. KERKSTRA. International comparative study of community nursing. Avebury: Aldershot-Brookfield, 1992.

8 NIJKAMP, P., J. PACOLET, H. SPINNEWYN, A. VOLLERING, C. WILDEROM, S. WINTERS. Services for the elderly in Europe: A cross-national comparative study. Leuven: VU Amsterdam / KU Leuven, 1991.

9 DIECK, M., V. GARMS-HOMOLOVÁ. Home-care services in the Federal Republic of Germany. In: Jamieson, A. (ed). Home care for older people in Europe, a comparison of policies and practices. Oxford/New York/Toronto: Oxford University Press, 1991.

10 BRANDT, F., R. SCHWEIKART. Häusliche Pflegehilfen für Schwerpflegebedürftige; Zwischenbericht zum Modellversuchs de Bundesministers für Arbeit und Sozialordnung. Saarbrucken: Institut für Sozialforschung und Sozialwirtschaft e.V., 1990.

11 BAGFW. Gesamtstatistik, stand 1.1.1993.

12 BUNDESMINISTERIUM FÜR ARBEIT UND SOZIALORDNUNG. Pflegeversicherung kommt (Informationsschrift), Bonn.

13 Arbeiterwohlfahrt Bezirk Westliches Westfalen e.V.. Situation Mobiler Sozialer Dienste bei der Arbeiterwohlfahrt Bezirk Westliches Westfalen e.V., Ein Positionspapier, Stand: 08/1993.

14 Arbeiterwohlfahrt Pflegeversicherung - Ein neues Zeitalter?, Sonderdruck aus: Theorie und Praxis der sozialen Arbeit, nr. 6, Juni 1994.

7 Home care in Greece

Wienke G.W. Boerma

1 The setting of home care

1.1 The country

Greece is situated in the extreme south-east of Europe. The country's location is somewhat isolated from the remaining countries of the European Union to which it was belonged since 1981. This geographical isolation has been enhanced since 1992 by the war in former Yugoslavia. Recent history since the 1930s has been turbulent, full warfare and brutal administrations. Since the monarchy was abolished in 1974, the country has been a republic. Greece is relatively scarcely populated; almost one third of the Greek populations live in the Athens conurbation. The archipelago of many small islands are an obstacle to communications between different parts of the country.

In the past, many Greeks emigrated to Western Europe for economic reasons. Many treasures from ancient times and the attractive islands in the Aegean Sea, combined with the favourable climate, make Greece quite popular for holidays. The tourist industry is an important economic factor.

Population key figures (1990) [1,2]

Population in mln.	10.2
Inhabitants per sq. km.	78
% Living in urban areas	63
% over 65 years	13.9
% over 75 years	6.3
Births per 1000	9.8
Deaths per 1000	9.1
Life expectancy (men)	75
Life expectancy (women)	79

1.2   The organization of health care

The health care system in Greece can probably best be typified as an incomplete National Health System. This system was introduced in 1983 as an intended remedy against the many shortcomings of the health services. In those days there were considerable inequalities in the access to and quality of care; uneven distribution of health resources, oversupply of doctors, a severe shortage of nurses and almost total absence of primary medical care. As a result of the inadequacy of the public system, a high proportion of health consumption was in the private sector [1,3,4,5].

The highest responsibility for health care is with the Ministry of Health, Welfare and Social Insurance. Central and regional authorities are advised by the Central Health Council. This council identifies priorities and develops policy strategies. Members of the council are representatives of the health professions, trades unions and laymen appointed by the authorities. One of the aims of the National Health System was to reduce the involvement of doctors in both public and private practice and to improve primary care by the development of health centres. The many categorial Health Insurance funds, which vary considerably in size and wealth, remained in existence. The largest fund, called IKA, has its own health centres and medical posts, mainly in the cities. The other funds provide care from public hospitals and by contracting private practitioners. With respect to health services, rural areas are underserved, among other reasons because only part of the intended number of health centres has been completed. Health Insurance funds still have the opportunity to contract-out services to the private sector. That is why the provision of health care is characterized by a mix of public and private supply, which is unusual (to this extent, at least) in most National

Health Systems [6]. The public (state) supply is free and provided mainly by hospitals and health centres. The Health Insurance funds are also suppliers, sometimes with facilities of their own but mostly by means of contracted private supply [1]. The Greek National Health System has been called a 'labyrinth of institutional structures, multiple standards and sectional interests that owes its formation more to chance than intention' [7]. It seems to be difficult to change the well-known shortcomings of the system. Most important are: unequal access to services of members of different Health Insurance funds, underdevelopment of services in rural areas, too much hospital orientation and underdevelopment of primary care, inadequate services by IKA polyclinics in the cities (too crowded), inefficiency and fragmentation due to absence of planning, almost complete absence of prevention and health promotion, growth of the - uncontrollable - private sector despite restrictive policy intentions, too many doctors and lack of nurses. Doctors, as well as facilities, are quite unevenly distributed. Athens, with 31% of the population, has 56% of the physicians and 48% of the hospital beds [1,7,8].

Health care figures (1990) [2]

Expenditure

Total expenditure on health		
Absolute per head in ppp$	400	
Percentage of GDP	5.4	
Public expenditure on health		
Absolute per head in ppp$	308	
Percentage of GDP	4.1	

Manpower

Physicians per 1000 pop.	3.4	
GPs per 1000 pop.	n.a	
Qualified nurses per 1000 pop.	3.4	

Hospital care

In-patient care		
Beds per 1000 pop.	5.1	
Admissions per 100 pop.	12.6	('89)
Mean length of stay	9.8	('89)
Acute hospitals		
Beds per 1000 pop.	n.a	
Admissions per 100 pop.	n.a	
Mean length of stay	n.a	
Nursing homes		
Beds per 1000 pop.	0.3	('89)

1.3   Health financing and insurance

In the financing of health care a range of (compulsory) Health Insurance funds have an important role. The oldest and largest, called IKA and covering urban employees, was created in 1937. Other funds date from the 1960s. Despite strong formal state control, the funds differ widely in the packages they provide, the standards of care, rules for eligibility and levels of contribution. With one exception, the funds are financed by contributions from their members: employees pay one third of the premium and the employer two thirds. But avoidance of contribution seems to be common place. The state is an indirect financier, not only by subsidizing the public hospitals and health centres but also by subsidizing deficits resulting from too low price setting by the ministry. Insured patients are basically entitled to use hospital out-patient and in-patient care and care provided in health centres free of charge. In many other cases there are co-payments (e.g. for drugs).

Many people use private services for which considerable direct payments are made [1,4,7]. It can be concluded that, at present, the health financing system does not have a sufficient level of distributional justice and that (...) "public spending on health has distributive implications that, quite separately from the effects of service use, directly oppose the stated aims of public policy" [7].

1.4 Care for the elderly

For several reasons the elderly population has received more and more attention from policy-makers. As in other countries, their proportion has grown and will continue to grow during the next decade. But, in addition, social and economic changes in the Greek society justify this attention. As a result of increased mobility and a higher degree of participation of women in the labour force, opportunities for the care of the elderly in families have been diminished. Government policy has a number of focal issues. Since services should be adapted to local needs the organization must be at decentralized level. Secondly, the elderly should retain an active role in society as far as possible. This implies that they remain independent in their own environment as long as possible. There should be a shift from permanent residential protection towards more open protection [9,10].

In Greece, there is no comprehensive system of services for the elderly. For temporary medical services the regular supply of hospitals, specialists and

GPs can be used. For longer term care, there are a limited number of public and private old people's homes; however these are not accessible to frail elderly people. Institutes for chronic disease provide another opportunity for longer term care; however, these are for all age groups. As a result of the changed government policy, all over the country (although not yet in all regions), 'open protection centres' have been erected in which a range of community care services is provided to the elderly living in their own homes. In these KAPI centres, medical and social services are provided by a staff of doctors, social workers, visiting nurses, physiotherapists, occupational therapists and home helps. KAPI centres are not very suitable for frail elderly people with a strong need for care. The 250 centres so far created have a total capacity of 135,000 places [10,11].

This formal supply of services is insufficient to cover the entire population of the elderly with the range of needs for care. For this reason, many people have to rely on private solutions. Traditionally the most important solution has been care by family, friends and neighbours. Other options are only feasible to those who are able to pay for them, for instance private nursing homes, foster homes (often run by widows), and hiring a private nurse.

Due to the general shortage of trained nurses, private nurses have usually not been trained. There are also agencies providing nursing and home help care [11].

Capacity of residential service for the elderly in Greece (1988) [10]

	Number of places/beds per 1000 people over 65 years
Old people's homes	3.3
Chronic disease institutes	1.3

2   The organization of home nursing

2.1   Organizations for home nursing

As has been explained earlier, a nationwide comprehensive organization for home nursing is absent in Greece. There are some initiatives in the large cities. These can be summarised as follows:
- Home nursing services provided by State hospitals in Athens (four

working units) and Thessaloniki (one working unit). These services are part of the National Health Service.
- Home nursing services by the Hellenic Red Cross in Athens and Thessaloniki (altogether three or four working units). This is a non-profit private initiative.
- Private commercial nursing services. These are also located in the big cities. The estimated number of agencies is 20, apart from an unknown number of very small initiatives.

The work of these nursing services is to provide curative and preventive care for the chronically and terminally ill. There are no formal working relations between home nursing and the above mentioned KAPI centres.

2.2 Manpower in home nursing services

The next table provides information about the nurses working in the public system in Greek home care. These numbers, once again, illustrate the low level of official home nursing in Greece.

Table 1
Numbers and types of nurses working in home care [*]

Type of nurse	level of education	number [**]	FTEs	% working independ.
Visiting nurse and health visitor	3rd level (higher vocational education)	60-80	60-80	< 10
Assistant nurse	secondary education	120-150	120-1500	n.a.
Auxiliary nurse	no special training	1200-1300	1200-1300	n.a.

---

[*] Since nursing services have a quite incomplete coverage it is not useful to calculate the average number of inhabitants per nurse. Private nurses are not included.

[**] Official manpower data are absent; numbers given and FTEs are based on estimations.

155

2.3 Client population

Owing to a lack of official data, only estimates can be given of the number and type of client that are cared for. Approximately 1 to 1.5% of the Greek population received some kind of home nursing care in 1993. Of them, 60% were male clients and 40% female. An estimate for the year 1993 of the age groups being served is as follows: 40% between 50 and 59; 40% between 60 and 69; 20% over 70 years of age.

2.4 Provision of services

Since home nursing has scarcely developed in Greece in many areas, the service is not available at all. In those areas where home nursing services are provided, mainly in Athens and Thessaloniki, people have no choice as to which organization they approach since the organizations have their own catchment areas which do not overlap.

The first contact between organization and client is usually (80% estimate) initiated by the patient/client or family members. In the remaining 20% of the cases, a hospital or home for the elderly has made the first contact.

There is free access to home nursing services and no referrals are required. General practitioners and other health and social professionals do not seem to play a role in making this first contact.

Patient's needs can be assessed either by a (hospital) physician or by a nurse (health visitor or visiting nurse). If home help services turn out to be necessary, they can also take a decision. The person who did the needs assessment also takes a decision on the type and amount of care to be provided and on the period of time.

Home nurses in Greece usually work in teams from a (public or private) hospital. These teams not only consist of home nurses but also of one or two physicians and one or two persons with secretarial positions.

As regards the provision of home nursing, evidently, all these tasks are also carried out by nurses who are not qualified specifically for them. This is one of the consequences of the severe shortage of adequately trained nurses in Greece. Visiting nurses and health visitors are qualified for all tasks, such as: needs assessment, routine technical nursing, more complicated procedures, patient education, psychosocial activities, and evaluation of care. In practice, all these tasks are also done by assistant nurses. Work for which assistants are qualified, such as hygiene care, are also provided by the less well-qualified auxiliary nurses.

2.5 Problems and recent developments

All home nursing organizations face a lack of financial and manpower capacity resulting in a limitation of the scope of their activities and waiting lists. However these waiting lists seem not to exceed a period of some weeks. Since services are underdeveloped, the population does not rely on them and waiting lists are relatively short. Since it is not expected that more resources will be allocated in a reasonably short term and no other attempts are being made to improve efficiency and quality of services, this situation will not change soon. Home nursing is not a high priority in Greece.

Even without expansion of budgets, much would be gained by better co-operation between different health services and professionals. The system is lacking cohesion. Among General Practitioners, co-operation seems to be absent and in hospitals and home help services too, co-ordination leaves much to be desired. At all levels, the low priority of home care seems to be evident.

3   The organization of home help services

3.1 Organizations for home help services

Available home help services in Greece do not belong to the public health care or social services system. They are provided by voluntary and non-profit organizations and private agencies as follows (the number of operational units are estimated):
- Hellenic Red Cross (two or three units)
- Greek Orthodox Church (25-30 units)
- Private (for-profit) organizations (10-15)

Like home nursing services, only urbanised areas are covered, mainly in Athens and Thessaloniki. Official tasks of the home helps employed by these organizations are cleaning, cooking and shopping for the benefit of elderly and handicapped people.

3.2 Manpower in home help services

The next table provides basic information about the Greek home helps.

Table 2
Numbers and types of home helps working in home care *

Type of nurse	level of education	number **	FTEs
Visiting nurse	1-2 years formal training	45-50	45-50
Auxiliary nurse	6 months formal training	150	100
Auxiliary personnel	1-2 months training	1500	n.a.

Generally speaking, there are no working relations between home help teams and home nursing teams. The visiting nurses and auxiliary nurses mentioned in this table work in different settings from those mentioned in table 2.1. Visiting nurses are in charge of the planning and management of home help care.

3.3   Client population

Statistical information on the clients of home help services is not available. It is estimated that approximately 10,000 inhabitants received these services in 1993, of whom 60% were male and 40% female. Furthermore, it is estimated that 80% lived alone and the remaining 20% with a spouse only. As regards the age distribution: some 20% were in the age category 65-74 years, while 80% were older.

---

* Since home help services only partly cover the country, it is useless to count the number of inhabitants per home help.

** Numbers and FTEs are estimates for 1993.

3.4   Provision of services

If home help services are available at all in a region, the people have no choice as to which organization they approach. There is no overlap in the catchment areas of home help organizations.

In half of the cases, the first contact was made by the client or his/her family. An estimated 30% of the applications were made by a hospital or old people's home. In another 10%, a home nursing service was the intermediary. In the remaining 10% of cases, it was another professional, such as a social worker or physiotherapist.

Anyhow, no referral is needed to be accepted as a client for home help services.

Needs assessment with applicants as well as allocation of services is carried out by visiting nurses and social workers, who can also decide about the possible involvement of home nursing. No standardized assessment forms are used for these procedures.

Home helps operate in teams from the offices of the organizations by which they are employed: the Hellenic Red Cross, the Greek Orthodox Church and private agencies. The teams are made up of one or two visiting nurses and five to seven auxiliary personnel. Occasionally they are working with nurses involved in home nursing care.

A number of possible home help tasks have been specified below. Each task specifies the kind of home help (as mentioned above) involved.

Task	Carried out by:
- Needs assessment (first contact)	Visiting nurse
- Delivery of meals	Auxiliary nurse, Auxiliary personnel
- Cleaning the home	Auxiliary personnel
- Homemaking activities	Auxiliary personnel
- Hygiene and other personal care	Visiting nurse, Auxiliary nurse
- Routine technical nursing procedures	Visiting nurse, Auxiliary nurse
- Moral support / counselling	Visiting nurse, Auxiliary nurse, Auxiliary personnel
- General and family support	Auxiliary nurse, Auxiliary personnel
- Stimulating informal help	Visiting nurse, Auxiliary nurse, Auxiliary personnel

3.5 Problems and recent developments

Problems with home help services are similar to those with home nursing, which means a low priority and lack of resources, scarceness and in many regions, a complete absence of services. Since waiting times do not usually exceed a period of one month, it must be concluded that much need for care is never expressed as a demand and that many frail elderly people rely on various forms of informal care or, if they can afford it, pay for private help. No change is expected in the short term.

For the elderly, in relatively better physical and mental condition and living at home, the KAPI centres for 'open protection' provide a range of services: nursing care, home help services, preventive medicine and health promotion.

4 Relation between home nursing and home help services

The boundaries between home nursing and home help services are not clear cut. The whole range of these services is provided by teams consisting of qualified and unqualified nurses and auxiliaries with different levels of education, training and experience. These teams are employed by and operate from the premises of private non-profit and private for-profit organizations. The disadvantage of this amalgamation is that tasks are carried out by staff who are not qualified to do so.

5 The financing of home nursing care

5.1 Payment and the patient's insurance

The packages of the compulsory health insurance funds do not contain home nursing services. Nor are these services tax funded. Some private insurance schemes cover costs for home nursing care, but only very few people are insured by those schemes (estimated at less than 2% of the population). If home nursing services are available people usually pay considerable amounts 'out-of-pocket'.

Consequently there is no regulation on access or limits on the volume of care to be received by a patient. Only those who get home nursing care refunded need a referral from a physician. Services provided by the KAPI Centres are funded by local authorities and free of charge.

5.2 Funding of the organizations

The way of funding of home nursing organizations is related to the type of organization. Private for-profit agencies are funded by private payments. Private non-profit organizations, like the Hellenic Red Cross and the Orthodox Church, are mainly funded partly from their own resources and from co-payments of their patients. Home nursing from state hospitals is tax-funded.

The total amount of funds available for home nursing services can be broken down to the sources as follows (estimations 1993): 15% from state taxes, 5% from private insurance, 10% from public insurance, 20% out-of-pocket payments, 50% from private organizations.

In general, funding of private home nursing organizations is based on the number of visits and the kind of activities that have been carried out, while the other organizations have a fixed budget depending on the number of inhabitants in the catchment area.

There are no fees or prices fixed by the state; however, there are sometimes voluntary contributions. Fifty percent of all payments from patients are made to private commercial agencies for home nursing.

5.3 Payment of the nurses

All types of nurses working in the home nursing services in Greece are salaried.

The average income of visiting nurses/health visitors is USD 600 per month. Assistant nurses have USD 450 per month and auxiliary nurses USD 400. These incomes are on full-time basis and not related to the number of visits made or the amount of interventions done.

5.4 Problems and recent developments

The level of payment of nurses does not seem to be a problem nowadays. With respect to the funding of organizations, however, scarcity of resources is a continuing problem, for which no solution is foreseen. Provision of services is also hampered by the lack of planning.

6   The financing of home help services

6.1   Payments and client's insurance

Both public health insurance schemes and private schemes have no coverage for home help services. In areas where those services are available clients pay out-of-pocket. For private service the full amount of the costs (USD 5 per hour) has to be paid. The co-payment for services provided by the Hellenic Red Cross and the Orthodox Church is lower. Services by the Red Cross and the Church are partly funded by own resources of these organizations and by voluntary contributions. There are no regulations on access to the services nor on the maximum of services to be received by a client. No referrals by a physician are needed.

6.2   Funding of the organizations

For 1993 it is estimated that 80% of the total budget for home help services came from the Hellenic Red Cross and the Orthodox Church, while 20% have been paid by patients as out-of-pocket payments to commercial private agencies. These private organizations are paid on the basis of the numbers of hours that they have delivered care. The Red Cross and the Orthodox Church have annual budgets.

6.3   Payment of the home helps

All types of home helps have a salary. The average monthly income of a visiting nurse is USD 400. The income of both auxiliary nurses and auxiliary personnel is USD 350 per month. These amounts are all on the basis of a full-time appointment.

6.4   Problems and recent developments

Scarcity of resources, planning problems and lack of co-ordination with other health care and social services are important problems. There are no attempts to reduce them, since home help services do not have a high priority.

Acknowledgement

Both questionnaires on home nursing and on home help services were completed by a team of experts consisting of the following persons:
- John Kyriopoulos (professor of Health Economics, National School of Public Health)
- Despena Sapoutzi (Visiting Assistant Professor, Department of Nursing, University of Athens)
- Vasso Margaritidou (Assistant Professor, Higher Technical Institution)
- Despena Andrioti (Research Fellow, Department of Health Economics, National School of Public Health)
- Mary Gitona (Research Fellow, Department of Health Economics, National School of Public Health)

References

1 BOERMA, W.G.W., F.A.J.M. DE JONG, P.H. MULDER. Health care and general practice across Europe. Utrecht: NIVEL, 1993.
2 OECD HEALTH DATA. Version # 1.5. Paris: OECD, 1993.
3 NIAKIS, D., J. KYRIOPOULOS. Health care resource allocation in Greece before and after NHS Establishment. In: Levy, E., A. Mizrahi, (eds.). From Economic Approach to Health policies. Paris: CREDES-CES, 1993, 85-91.
4 KYRIOPOULOS, J., D. NIAKAS, E. GEORGOUSSI, M. GITONA. Private health consumption in Greece today. In: Chytil, M.K. et al. (eds.). Health Systems; the Challenge of Change. Prague: Omnipress, 1992, 75-78.
5 NIAKAS, D., J. KYRIOPOULOS. Financing health care in Greece and health expenditure. In: Chytil, M.K. et al. (eds.). Health Systems; the Challenge of Change. Prague: Omnipress, 1992, 601-64.
6 KYRIOPOULOS, J., G. TSALIKIS. Public and private imperatives of Greek health policies. Journal of Health Policy; 1993, 26, 105-17.
7 MATSAGANIS, M. Is health insurance in Greece in need of reform. Health Policy and Planning 1991; 6(3):271-81. Oxford University Press.
8 SISSOURAS, A. Backgrounds and developments in health care in Greece and the 1992 perspective. In: Casparie A.F., H.E.G.M. Hermans, J.H.P. Paelinck. Competitive Health Care in Europe, future prospects. Aldershot: Dartmouth, 1990.

9 NIJKAMP, P., A. VOLLERING. Theoretical and empirical developments. In: Pacolet, J., C. Wilderom (eds.). The economics of care for the elderly. Aldershot: Dartmouth, 19..

10 GIAOUTZI, M. Greece. In: Nijkamp P., J. Pacolet, H. Spinnewyn, A. Vollering, C. Wilderom, S. Winters. Services for the elderly in Europe; a cross-national comparative study. Leuven: HIVA/VU, 1991.

11 AMIRA, A. Family care in Greece. In: Jamieson, A, R. Illsley. Contrasting European policies for the care of older people. Aldershot: Avebury, 1990.

8 Home care in Ireland

Wienke G.W. Boerma

1 The setting of home care

1.1 The country

The Republic of Ireland, situated on the 'emerald isle', is the westernmost country of Europe. In 1922 it became independent from The United Kingdom. It is the least densely populated member state of the European Union. Traditionally the country has a relatively low level of economic development, which has been a major reason for many Irish to seek employment abroad. Despite the EU membership since 1973, which has brought significant economic aid, there is still considerable emigration of younger people, mainly to the United Kingdom. Demographic consequences are felt, but not dramatically since birth rates have been relatively high in Ireland.

Wienke G.W. Boerma

Population key figures (1990) [1,2]

Population in mln.	3.5
Inhabitants per sq. km.	50
% Living in urban areas	57
% over 65 years	11.2
% over 75 years	4.4
Births per 1000	15.0
Deaths per 1000	8.9
Life expectancy (men)	72.0
Life expectancy (women)	77.0

1.2   The organization of health care

The health care system is a mixture of public and private schemes. Conditions for access to services vary, depending on level of income. The Minister and the Department of Health are responsible for policy-making in the field of health care. Implementation has been left largely to several agencies. Important in the planning and organization at regional level are the eight Health Boards. In its region, varying in size from 200,000 to over one million inhabitants, a Health Board is responsible for operating the services with respect to community care services, general hospital services and special hospital services.

The division of 'community care services' consists of preventive health services, general practice services and other domiciliary services (e.g. dental care and public health nursing). Parallel to the public system, there is a private sector mainly run by doctors who are also involved in the public system [1].

Secondary care. There are three types of hospitals for acute care. First there are the public hospitals (at the level of the Region, County or District) administered by the Health Boards. These are all directly state-financed. The second type are the Public Voluntary Hospitals, which are largely state-funded. In this heterogenous category there are teaching and non-teaching hospitals, cottage hospitals and special hospitals. The third and smallest category consists of the private hospitals which are funded exclusively by patients' fees. Most hospital doctors also work in the private scheme on a fee-for-service basis. About 10% of the consultants work exclusively in private practice.

Primary care. Community health services include general medical service, community nursing and care for long-term illness, refunding of above-ceiling cost of drugs for category two patients (see 1.3), maternity and infant care, dental, ophthalmic and aural services. Community nursing services, provided by the Health Boards through Public Health Nurses, include: care for acute, chronic and terminally ill people in their homes, care and supervision of the frail elderly and handicapped people, monitoring health of children (until the end of primary school) and ante/postnatal care. In some areas cervical cytology tests are done. The Nursing Board is for registration, undergraduate training and examination (also of midwives) and postgraduate training. Home help services are funded by the Health Boards and provided either directly by the Health Boards or by one of the voluntary organizations for this purpose [1].

Health care figures (1990) [2]

Expenditure

Total expenditure on health		
Absolute per head in ppp$	748	
Percentage of GDP	7.0	
Public expenditure on health		
Absolute per head in ppp$	559	
Percentage of GDP	5.2	

Manpower

Physicians per 1000 pop.	1.5	('88)
GPs per 1000 pop.	n.a	
Qualified nurses per 1000 pop.	6.5	('88)

Hospital care

In-patient care		
Beds per 1000 pop.	6.0	('89)
Admissions per 100 pop.	15.2	('88)
Mean length of stay	8.0	('89)
Acute hospitals		
Beds per 1000 pop.	3.5	
Admissions per 100 pop.	14.9	
Mean length of stay	6.9	
Nursing homes		
Beds per 1000 pop.	4.8	

1.3   Health financing and insurance

The most important source of financing is central taxation (85 to 90%). Secondary sources are contributions from eligible persons and user charges. Two categories of eligibility determine what services have to be paid for and what services one is entitled to without charge. These categories are:

1. Those below a certain income ceiling (approx. IEP 6,300 a year for individuals) and 'unable without undue hardship to arrange GP services themselves' are entitled to the full range of public services without charges: GP services and prescribed medicines, specialist out-patient and hospital services, dental care and ophthalmic care. Some 35% of the population (many pensioners) are covered by this scheme. The 'medical card' which is required for this category is provided by the Health Boards on the basis of a means test.

2. People not belonging to 'category 1' have coverage of specialist out-patient care, hospital services and maternity and infant welfare within the public service. There is no coverage of GP services and the costs of drugs (except those for specific chronic illnesses) are reimbursed only as far as they exceed an amount of IEP 90 per three months. There are also several co-payments.

There is free access, whatever the category, to treatments for infectious diseases, community protection programmes and hospital treatment for certain diseases for children under 16. About 37% of the population, who want to avail themselves of private in-patient care and receive assistance with GP and other out-patient services, have entered the Voluntary Health Insurance scheme. Subscribers can make a choice from a range of 'plans', which provide different coverage for different premiums. Premiums are 'community rated' however, so that the cost does not increase with age.

1.4   Care for the elderly

Resulting from the Working Party on Services for the Elderly, the general policy framework since 1988 stresses the development of community care. Additional resources, e.g. for home help services, were recommended as well as specific individual care packages designed to keep people at home as long as possible. There was some doubt on the efficiency and the effectiveness of the current supply. Informal carers should be better supported [3,4].

The Irish population over 65 usually belong to category 1 and consequently most are entitled to all health care services without charge. This includes home nursing services to frail and elderly people. For those who need more intensive care, however without being institutionalized, there are the public and voluntary facilities, such as home help and day care centres. Organizations for distribution of meals are normally voluntary [5].

Apart from this regular supply there are innovative services, such as community nursing units, day hospitals, initiatives for sheltered housing or making adaptations in homes of the elderly and 'boarding out' (placement in a kind of foster home). People who cannot stay in the community any longer are eligible for residential services, of which there are several types, related to the degree of dependency and need for geriatric or nursing care [6,7].

Informal care networks are becoming more and more important. The informal and voluntary sector have been taken too much for granted and have not been recognized and supported by the authorities. Formal care supply should to a larger extent be supplementary and supportive to informal care. This requires the identification of needs in the population, more information on informal care and co-ordination of informal and formal efforts [6,8].

Important areas of care at home are delivered by voluntary agencies which specialize in caring for specific groups such as terminally ill, mentally handicapped and physically handicapped.

Ireland has been important in the provision of special intramural hospice care for the terminally ill since 1879, when the first Irish hospice was founded by the nuns of the Irish Sisters of Charity. Over the years, the provision of hospice care has spread throughout the country and significant recent developments have been the extension of palliative care by the hospices to the terminally ill at home. Voluntary hospices with the help and financial assistance of the Irish Hospice Foundation are developing home care programmes on a 7 x 24 hours basis. There are also a growing number of day care centres for the terminally ill which supplement the in-patient hospice care services.

Care for the mentally handicapped is another growing area of specialized care at home as care of this category of patient is increasingly transferred from intramural institution to the community. This care is being provided by a mixture of statutory (Health Boards) and voluntary agencies. The Health Boards provide community nurses with specialized training in the area of mental handicap who make home visits (these are different from the regular Public Health Nurse). They also work in special day care centres.

In addition voluntary organizations provide a network of home care services including respite care.

For the physically handicapped there are many specialist organizations who bring their special area of expertise to bear. These include organizations such as The Irish Wheelchair Association, The Multiple Sclerosis Society of Ireland and The Alzheimer Society.

These voluntary organizations network with both the nursing and home help services in the area to bring an appropriate level of support to the client with special needs. They form an essential ingredient of the total package of care at home and provide levels of expertise in their special field which are not available in the public services.

While these organizations do receive a portion of their funding from State grants. They have to raise the bulk of their financial needs through charity fund raising and private subscription.

Capacity of residential services for the elderly in Ireland (1986) [6]

	Number of places/beds per 1000 people over 65 years
Health board geriatric homes	18.9
Long stay district hospitals	4.0
Health board welfare homes	3.9
Approved nursing homes	8.3
Non-approved nursing homes	8.0

2 The organization of home nursing

2.1 Organizations for home nursing

Nursing at community level was first developed by voluntary organizations. Later public health nurses became attached to the offices of the county medical officers of health. These nurses mainly had public health tasks. Since the 1947 Health Act, health authorities have had the opportunity to appoint nurses for community services. This was further developed in the 1950s. By a circular of the Department of Health in 1966, a public health nursing service, which included general domiciliary nursing, became mandatory for individuals and families in each area throughout the country [5].

Nowadays home nursing is provided throughout Ireland by public health nurses employed by statutory Health Boards, which operate in eight geographical regions. Each Health Board is subdivided into Community Care Areas, each with a population of about 100,000 inhabitants. Superintendent public health nurses are responsible for the provision of home nursing services in these Community Care Areas. Public health nurses operate from local health centres throughout each Community Care Area.

2.2   Manpower in home nursing

Most nurses working in the community are public health nurses. They have had a three years training for registered general nursing, followed by training in public health nursing.

In Ireland, 1,550 public health nurses (1,370 FTEs) are employed by the statutory Health Boards. There is therefore one nurse per 2,574 inhabitants. In addition, some Health Boards also employ registered general nurses or state enrolled nurses to provide home care, allowing the public health nurses to carry on with broader functions, for instance for terminally ill or acutely ill or post discharged from hospital. However, their total number is less than 100. And, finally, in recent years home care attendants (about 100) have been introduced, to assist the nursing service by providing personal hygiene care to the elderly sick at home, especially when a patient is discharged early from hospital. These home care attendants have had a short course, but are not qualified as nurses [9].

2.3   Client population

Official figures on users of home nursing services are not available. The following estimate can be made on the basis of two sources for 1993. A survey of over 900 elderly people conducted in that year by The National Council for the Elderly found that 15% of the respondents were receiving visits from PHNs, which is equivalent to about 60,450 elderly people. A 1985 survey of the workload of public health nurses found that 50% of the home nursing component of their work involved care for the elderly sick and geriatric surveillance at home [10]. From these sources, it can be estimated that 15% of persons over 65 years and 2% of those under 65 are receiving home care.

No statistical information is available on the gender of the clients, but clearly most of them are female.

2.4 Provision of services

Normally, potential clients do not have free choice as to which home nursing organization they approach, because there is only one organization in each region and these organizations do not work outside this catchment area. For the small minority of elderly people who are member of the Voluntary Health Insurance Board scheme (VHI) there is an exception. This private scheme provides limited support for up to six weeks per year, of home nursing care. Most elderly people however rely on the mainstream public health nursing service.

The first contact with the home nursing organization is usually made directly by the patient or his/her carer, although sometimes on referral by the GP. No such referral is required, however. Patients or their carers may apply directly to the Health Board for home nursing.

The public health nurse normally makes an initial assessment of the type of care that is needed and arranges consultations or referrals as appropriate. In consultation with a home help organizer it can also be determined that the patient needs home help. Needs assessment forms are usual, but there is no single national standardized form.

In taking decisions upon type and planning of care to be provided, the public health nurse has major responsibilities. Decisions are taken, however, in conjunction with other local workers, such as GP and home help organizer. Social workers are not involved in planning domiciliary care for the elderly.

Most public health nurses operate from a health centre. As regards team work, there are different situations. Traditionally public health nurses worked alone, but with other professionals in the local area, as deemed necessary. More recently - at least in some Health Boards - special teams have been created (usually one per Community Care Area or in a smaller district) focused on elderly people requiring intensive domiciliary care. These teams comprise nurses, physicians, occupational therapists, physiotherapists and care attendants. In these teams, the nurse usually plays a key liaison role, for example with a hospital when a referral is from a hospital source. In other Health Boards district teams have operated as a means of co-ordinating services at local area level.

A number of home nursing tasks have been identified. Public health nurses are qualified to perform all of the following tasks:
- assessment of the need for care
- hygiene and other personal care
- routine technical nursing procedures
- more complicated procedures (e.g. epidural anaesthesia, handling respirator, catheterization)
- patient education
- psychosocial activities
- stimulating informal care

General nurses are generally involve providing personal hygiene care and routine technical nursing and home care attendants only provide hygiene and other personal care. The evaluation of care is usually made by the superintendent public health nurse.

2.5 Problems and recent developments

In 1988 and previously, official reports pointed to shortages in the field of community nursing. Since then the numbers have increased, but the norm of one nurse per 2,616 inhabitants may no longer be appropriate in the light of the changed demographic situation [4]. Real waiting lists, however, do not exist in home nursing. Yet for some treatments there may be delays. In relation to the needs of the patients and clients, all home nursing organizations feel a shortage, though not necessarily a shortage in the available supply of suitable candidates.

As has been stated, there are problems in the co-operation with GPs, home helps and hospitals. Co-ordination at local level is hard to achieve because:
- GPs are independent private practitioners with overlapping catchment areas;
- home help organizations are relatively independent of home nursing services, although they co-operate as far as possible; and
- hospital services are organized and managed under a separate programme within each Health Board.

In addition cut backs in public spending in the late 1980s that resulted in cuts in some services, made co-operation both more difficult and more urgent at the same time. A pilot project initiated by the National Council for the Elderly on Co-ordination of Services at Local Level showed many problems but also some possibilities for better co-operation in the future [8].

Since expansion of resources in health care is not feasible for the time being, according to the Working Party, the aim is to improve efficiency and effectiveness of services with the available means [4]. It is recommended that Health Boards give higher priority to home care by reallocating resources. Liaison nurses should be appointed in all regions in order to improve coordination. Services outside normal office hours need to be extended. Anticipatory care and health promotion deserve more attention in the routines of home nurses. In some districts teams have been introduced to provide intensive domiciliary care for sick elderly people.

3   The organization of home help services

3.1   Organization of home help services

Home assistance services have traditionally been used in an ancillary way to the health services in the care for the aged, sick or infirm people at home. Under the Health Act in 1970 Health Boards were given broad power to make arrangements for this purpose. So, since 1970 regular home help services have been developed in Ireland [5].

There are formal organizations for the delivery of home help services in Ireland, covering the whole country. Home help services are part of the general health services. Statutory funding comes initially from the Department of Health to the eight Health Boards. Under the Health Act 1970, Health Boards are empowered, but not obliged, to provide home help services to people who need it. Services may be provided directly by the Health Board or by voluntary organizations that are funded by a Health Board. Currently about two thirds of the service are provided by Health Boards directly while one third is provided by voluntary organizations.

3.2   Manpower in home help services

The essential unit of organization is the home help organizer who has a specific area to cover. In 1993 there were 73 organizers, each responsible for a local catchment area. These local areas are smaller than the standard subdivisions of the Health Boards, the 32 so-called Community Care Areas. Home help organizers are employed either by the Health Board or by the local voluntary organization. In some Community Care Areas responsibility for the tasks of the home help organizer is taken over by a public health nurse. The services are carried out by home helps, who are mostly part-timers. In 1993, 10,461 home helps (3,026 FTEs) were working in home care. This means one FTE home help per 1,165 inhabitants [10]. Home helps do not have special educational qualifications. Their general suitability for the job is assessed by the home help organizer.

Training of home helps is being increasingly recognised as essential for the service to meet the increased range of home care requirements arising from the shift in emphasis from intramural care to home care that is taking place. Over many years home care organizers have developed special local training courses for their home helps. However, a shortage of resources meant that not all home helps received such training and standards varied form place to place. Arising from the experience of these courses and the need to improve training standards, the National Association of Home Care Organizers (NAHCO) working with the City of Dublin Vocational Education Committee developed a part-time certificate course for home helps in 1993. The courses were funded by special grants from the Departments of Social Welfare and Education. It is planned to make this course available to centres outside the Dublin area in the near future.

3.3   Client population

In 1993, 17,337 clients received home help which is 0.49% of the whole Irish population. Of all clients 83% were 65 years or older and 17% were under the age of 65 [10].

A sample survey in 1993 of 100 rural and 95 urban elderly clients, commissioned by the National Council for the Elderly, showed that 67.7% of the clients were living alone, 17.9% were living with a spouse, 3.1% with spouse and children, and 11.3% with children or other people [10].

3.4   Provision of services

Clients do not have a choice between home help organizations because these are organized on an area basis. A referral from a professional is usual but not obligatory. Information on who refers clients to the home help services is available on elderly clients from the above mentioned survey (see table 1).

Table 1
Percentage of clients noting by whom the first contact was initiated [10]

Initiator	percentage
Client / client system	18.9
Public Health Nurse	43.6
General Practitioner	19.0
Other	10.8
Unknown	7.7

The home help organizer decides how much help a client receives. The issue of whether a client also needs nursing care is decided by the nursing service in conjunction with other professionals, and may include consultations with the home help organizer.

Application forms for the home help service are used, but these vary from one region to another. They typically contain:

- personal details like name, address, age, household composition, proximity of relatives.
- financial details like income, property and whether the client has a medical card or not.
- reason for requiring home help service and assessment of client's needs and duties to be undertaken by the home help.

The assessment is not a standard procedure and there is no system of stated points for entitlement. The assessment is usually a matter of judgement on a variety of factors.

Normally the public health nurse and the home help organizer jointly decide what care needs to be provided. In the case of voluntary organizations in the Eastern Health Board region, this is done by the home help organizer without involving the public health nurse.

Home helps work as soloists and operate from their own homes and are partly chosen on the basis of how near they live to their clients. The home help organizer, who is the one to assess the need for care, usually operates from a local health centre. The usual work of home helps involves cleaning and to some extent housework. The preparation or delivery of meals is usually provided by other organizations, though some home helps also prepare meals. More comprehensive housework, including household management, are sometimes provided to families in crisis, i.e. usually younger clients.

Home helps do provide some basic personal care, such as bathing, using the toilet and other ADL. Home helps are not allowed to carry out nursing tasks such as care of wounds or pressure sores. The study of Lundström and McKeown [10] also showed that moral support is a valued type of help provided by home helps. General support with administrative duties is also commonly provided. The home help organizer, finally, is responsible for monitoring home help standards, but formal evaluation of care is not much in evidence.

3.5   Problems and recent developments

Waiting lists are very unusual in the context of home help service. In some instances, however, clients have reported delays of a month or longer in receiving the service. The delays have been explained by reference to budgetary difficulties. In theory, there should be no delay, and in most regions there is an emergency service to clients who cannot wait until their application is processed.

Shortages of home helps can arise, depending on local factors such as competing employment in tourist areas or in sparsely populated areas. In other areas, particularly urban, there is no shortage. In Ireland home help services rely heavily on a good neighbour ethos, which implies that the client will have some say in the choice of home help and it can be that a home help will not be accepted.

Sometimes there are co-ordination problems with hospitals. In the past, patients might be discharged at weekends without any co-ordination with the home help organizer. This has received considerable attention in recent years, particularly with early discharge from hospitals becoming more common.

There is a potential area of difficulty in relation to the home nursing services, with the introduction by Health Boards of home care attendants. Some home help organizers believe that more attention could be given to developing the home help services to meet this need. They feel the home help services already have insufficient status, are already poorly paid, have insufficient training and rely too heavily on a good neighbour ethos. Yet home helps often perform personal care tasks on a long term basis. The introduction of a more specialized grade with higher pay under another service might serve to reinforce this area of dissatisfaction.

The report "The Years Ahead" which was published in 1988 is still a major policy basis. Several recommendations from this report have not been implemented, although the extent of home help services has been increasing since 1989 [4].

An important issue arises in relation to the discretionary basis of statutory funding to the voluntary home help sector. A White Paper on Voluntary Statutory Partnership is due to be published shortly. The National Council for the Elderly has made recommendations that the funding of voluntary home help services must be put on a firm legal and non-discretionary basis.

4   Relations between home nursing and home help services

The two services are broadly under the community care programme of the Health Boards. However, the home nursing system is much more integrated into the statutory system.

Home nursing and home help services are not uniformly organized in all regions. That is why relations between them are variable. Home help services are all funded by Health Boards, but according to different models. Usually a home help organizer is employed by the Health Board; sometimes this is a special officer and sometimes a public health nurse acts as a home help organizer. In other regions a voluntary agency - funded by the Health Board - provides home help services. Evidently, where the nursing and home help service are part of the Health Board more formal links exist as compared to the last mentioned situation. In many areas there are regular meetings between home help organizers and public health nurses. Ad hoc arrangements are made for the sharing of information and co-operation in relation to individual clients.

5   The financing of home nursing services

5.1   Payment and patient's insurance

Since home nursing is financed completely from general taxation through the Ministry of Health, no public health insurance scheme is applicable. For those not covered by the general scheme, there is the Voluntary Health Insurance, which provides for up to 42 days (IEP 15 a day) home nursing reimbursement. Some 37% of the population have joined the VHI scheme. In the public scheme there are no co-payments or other charges.

Formally there is no maximum limit to the amount of care that a person is entitled to receive. In practice, however, an optimum is found taking into account the limited resources available and local arrangements vary. In 1985 a typical home visit lasted 30-40 minutes in the case of the elderly sick and 20-30 minutes with geriatric surveillance. The duration of home visits to terminally ill patients is relatively long [11].

5.2 Funding of the organizations

As has been mentioned above, home nursing is 100% state tax financed. The allocation of resources for public health nursing is not related directly to the number of the population or the number over 65 years, although this is taken into account.

Health Board regions differ with respect to the proportion of elderly people in the population. In the large Eastern region, for instance, 3.7% of the population are over 75, while this is 6.4% and 6.3% in North-West and West respectively. In practice each Health Board has a different mixture of services, which means that certain regions are better supplied with public health nurses than others. For instance, the Midlands and the East, with nurse ratios of one per 2,390 and one per 2,649 inhabitants respectively, are much better off than the South and South-East, with averages of one per 3,269 and one per 3,143 inhabitants respectively [9].

Since home nursing is under direct statutory control there are no formal criteria that have to be met for financing. No organizations of public health nursing work for-profit. Little is known about the extent of private home nursing care funded by the VHI or funded privately 'out-of-pocket'.

5.3 Payment of the nurses

All types of nurses receive a fixed salary, related to the numbers of hours of their appointment and irrespective of the amount of visits or other services that they carry out.

5.4 Problems and recent developments

There are no evident problems as regards financing of the organizations or payment of the nurses. Level of salaries are negotiated through public service industrial relations procedures.

In general, there is a tension between, on the one hand, policy aims of providing basic nursing care to sick or dependent elderly people at home, which implies an expansion of services, and on the other hand the limited resources available. In this context, we could point to the developments described in section 2.5. Public health nurses, of course, have important responsibilities in relation to the protection of young children, and this is becoming increasingly important and a potential factor in determining the scope for improving services for the elderly.

6 The financing of home help services

6.1 Payment and clients' insurance

Home help services are funded from taxation; neither a public nor a private insurance scheme is applicable.

Out-of-pocket payments are common in relation to home help services. The amount is quite variable. Sometimes the client is asked to pay a contribution matching that of the Health Board. This might be IEP 1.50 per hour for example, but the exact rate varies. Some Health Boards allow weekly client contributions up to IEP 5.00, while others will allow more than this to be paid by the client. Negotiation appears to be commonly practised, with the home help organizer encouraging but not necessarily obliging the client to pay. The above mentioned survey revealed that over 50% of the clients made out-of-pocket payments. Contributions appeared to be more frequent in the case of clients for a service provided by the voluntary sector in an urban community (85%) than a statutory service in a rural area (32%). However, monthly contributions paid by survey respondents were, on average, lower at IEP 5.80 per month in the case of those who paid for the service provided by the voluntary sector, compared with an average of IEP 25.10 among the fewer number who paid for the statutory sector service in a rural area [10]).

In practice, there seems to be a limit on the provision of this service. The number of hours given to clients in the earlier cited survey ranged from one to fifteen hours per week. The break down in table 2 is derived from the study of Lundström and McKeown [10].

Table 2
Percentage distribution of clients by number of hours
received home help a week

Hours per week	percentage
less than 5	34
6 - 10	45
11 - 15	14
16 - 20	4
more than 20	3

The home help services were envisaged as providing for short visits one or more times a week, and these figures show that this is largely the way it operates.

6.2   Funding of the organizations

The proportions of funding from different sources of the home help organizations can hardly be estimated. It is impossible to say what proportion of the budget is paid by clients because methods of collection these contributions are so diverse. Comparing the co-payment amounts of the Lindström and McKeown study with the official figures on public expenditure per client suggest that the clients' contributions are not too far from 10% of the total budget. Considering the limited scope of the study mentioned, this is only a very rough estimation.

Public funding of the home help services takes the form of a fixed budget which is negotiated from year to year, based on assumptions about the number of home help organizers, the estimated number of clients served, historical criteria such as the given pay rates in a given Health Board. These vary greatly for home helps and to a lesser extent for home help organizers. In the light of national policy for the elderly the national budget for the service has been increasing in recent years, from IEP 6.66 million in 1989 to IEP 13.96 million in 1993. This has allowed the number of clients served to increase as well as to some improvements in pay [10].

There are no particular legal criteria for funding or for recognition as a home help organization.

6.3 Payment of home help organizers and home helps

Home help organizers are paid a monthly salary by the Health Board. The average gross income of a full-time employed home help organizer is IEP 1,305 (calculated from the average of midpoints for annual salary scales used in each Health Board; that is 15,667/12 = 1,305). Home helps do not receive a monthly salary, but are paid a fee per hour. The average hourly rate is IEP 2.12. This means that a full-time home help (38 hours a week) receives IEP 350 a month. It should be noted however that home helps only work eleven hours a week on the average, which equals to a monthly income of IEP 101.

6.4 Problems and recent developments

The method of reimbursing home help organizations is sometimes problematic: sometimes voluntary organizations are paid in arrears; there are difficulties arising out of the level and manner of paying home helps and the manner of collecting out-of-pocket contributions from clients.

From time to time issues arise related to the remuneration. For instance, last year an equality officer in the Labour Relations Commission ruled in favour of home helps who sought parity with a male employee of the Health Board in another grade. The ethos of a quasi-voluntary good neighbour scheme is widely shared among home helps and providers. But there is, nevertheless, some anxiety among home helps about their level of remuneration.

There are no new developments in the way of financing the home help services. However, a recently published strategy document from the Department of Health stresses the need to standardize eligibility in relation to health and social services. This would imply improvements in the funding systems for home help services.

Acknowledgement

The questionnaires regarding both home nursing and home help services in Ireland have been completed with the obliging co-operation of Mr. Joe

Larragy of the National Council for the Elderly, Dublin. The text of this chapter heavily relies on his contribution.

References

1 BOERMA, W.G.W., F.A.J.M. DE JONG, P.H. MULDER. Health care and general practice across Europe. Utrecht: NIVEL, 1993.
2 OECD HEALTH DATA. Version # 1.5. Paris: OECD, 1993.
3 O'SHEA, E. Ireland. In: Nijkamp, P. et al. Proceedings of a seminar on national diversity and European trends in services for the elderly. Leuven: HIVA/VU, 1991.
4 WORKING PARTY ON SERVICES FOR THE ELDERLY. The years ahead; a policy for the elderly. Dublin, 1988.
5 HENSEY, B. The Health Services of Ireland. Dublin: Institute of Public Administration, 1988.
6 ROSDORFF, S. Ireland. In: Nijkamp, P. et al. Proceedings of a seminar on national diversity and European trends in services for the elderly. Leuven: HIVA/VU, 1991.
7 BROWNE, M. Innovation and linkage in service provision for elderly people in Ireland. In: Jamieson, A., R. Illsley. Contrasting European policies for the care of older people. Aldershot: Avebury, 1990.
8 BROWNE, M. Co-ordinating services for the elderly at local level: Swimming against the tide. Dublin: National Council for the Elderly, 1992.
9 DEPARTMENT OF HEALTH. Health Statistics 1991. Dublin, Department of Health, 1992.
10 LUNDSTRÖM, F., K. MCKEOWN. Home help services for elderly people in Ireland. Dublin: National Council for the Elderly, 1994, forthcoming.
11 BURKE, T.P. The workload of public health nurses. Dublin: Institute of Community Health Medicine, 1985.

9 Home care in Italy

Jack B.F. Hutten

1 The setting of home care

1.1 The country

In 1957, Italy was one of the founders of the European Economic Community (EEC), the precursor of the European Union (EU).

Characteristic of the postwar political situation is the instability of the governments. Since 1948 the country experienced more than fifty changes of government.

After World War II, the economy showed remarkable development. This progress however could not remove the dichotomy between the rich industrialised north and the poor agrarian south. In the north, unemployment is comparatively low and average incomes are high, meanwhile the south suffers from considerable unemployment [1].

Population key figures (1990) [1,2]

Population in mln.	57.7
Inhabitants per sq. km.	191
% Living in urban areas	69
% over 65 years	15.4
% over 75 years	6.3
Births per 1000	12.7
Deaths per 1000	9.5
Life expectancy (men)	72
Life expectancy (women)	79

1.2 The organization of health care

The National Health Service (the *Servizio Sanitario Nazionale*: SSN) was established in 1978 [3]. The main characteristics of this system are a comprehensive health insurance coverage for the total population, a uniform system of health care provision (all kinds of care are granted by the same institution), a strong distinction between primary and secondary care, decentralization, and democratization [4]. The system is structured by means of indicative regional planning and local managerial control.

In a way five levels in the health care structure are in relevant: the state, the regions, the communities, the local health units and the basic health districts [1]. The state is in charge of the political planning and regulation. The central power is the government, which controls the health regions and reviews (and, if necessary, revokes) regional legislation. Other central health authorities are the National Health Council, which advises the government, and the Ministry of Health which, in turn, is advised by several boards and institutes. The second level concerns the regions. They form the main administrative body of the SSN, and are ultimately responsible for SSN provision. Each of the 20 regions has its own elected council, ruling group (*giunta*) and administrative departments. The regions have a considerable, almost autonomous influence on the provision of social support and health care at local level. As a consequence a large amount of variation exists in the health and social services provided within the 20 regions [3]. Due to this decentralization of public responsibilities, it is difficult to describe these services at a national level.

The regions are divided in local health units, the so-called *Unita Sanitaria Locale* (USL). They are responsible for the daily management of health services. The SSN law originally intended to divide the USLs in smaller divisions, the basic health districts (*distretti*) for the organization primary care. However, due to political and financial reasons only a few USLs have been active in the formation of basic health districts.

Besides the provision of hospital care, (poly)clinics, and the contracting of general practitioners (GPs), the USLs are responsible for health education, occupational health, pharmacy, family advice, child health care, veterinary care, and information services.

Italian primary care is dominated by the GPs because of an excess of doctors and a relative lack of nurses and social workers. GPs usually work single-handed and patients are registered with one single doctor. Patients are referred for specialist examinations by their GP or go directly if fee-paying. Direct access for patients to psychiatric paediatric, obstetrics and gynaecology and ophthalmological out-patient department is allowed without referral from their GPs. Referrals within the SSN can only be made by the GP with whom a patient is registered: mutual referrals between specialists are not allowed.

The country has a large number of hospital facilities. The public hospitals are divided into multi-zone hospitals controlled by the regional authorities, zonal hospitals for which the USLs are responsible, and university institutes. In 1990 the SSN hospital network included 972 hospitals managed by the USLs, eight university clinics linked to the SSN, 40 religious hospitals, and 669 nursing homes [1]. It is legally required that a general hospital contains at least four basic services: general medicine, surgery, obstetrics and gynaecology, and paediatrics.

Like in the United Kingdom important reforms are recently introduced in the Italian NHS. In a number regions, the USLs have been converted into autonomous organizations with an independent legal status [10]. Hospitals and primary health care units are being reformed into independent trusts. The regional health authorities appoint directors for a period of five years and after that period performances will be evaluated and decided whether the contract will be continued. This new system must be introduced in the whole country, but, as with many reforms, the developments differ highly between the regions. The region of Emilia Romagna already works according to the new system, but this is always the first regions to implemented reforms. In general, the northern regions will follow and the south is mostly far behind in the developments.

Parallel to the National Health System, Italy has an extensive private sector. Due to a financial, functional and social crisis, the utilization of private services is increasing rapidly. In some regions 50% of admissions are to private hospitals. The utilization of private health care services varies highly among regions. Private out-patient facilities of specialists are frequently used, especially in large cities [4].

Health care figures (1990) [2]

Expenditure

Total expenditure on health		
Absolute per head in ppp$	1296	
Percentage of GDP	8.1	
Public expenditure on health		
Absolute per head in ppp$	1006	
Percentage of GDP	6.3	

Manpower

Physicians per 1000 pop.	1.3	('89)
GPs per 1000 pop.	n.a	
Qualified nurses per 1000 pop.	4.4	('89)

Hospital care

In-patient care		
Beds per 1000 pop.	7.2	('89)
Admissions per 100 pop.	15.3	('89)
Mean length of stay	11.7	('89)
Acute hospitals		
Beds per 1000 pop.	n.a	
Admissions per 100 pop.	n.a	
Mean length of stay	n.a	
Nursing homes		
Beds per 1000 pop.	n.a	

1.3 Health financing and insurance

The SSN can be used by all inhabitants of Italy. Total expenditure for the health services is determined yearly at central government level through the national budget. Funds are allocated quarterly to the regions. These funds are financed by contributions paid by each independent and/or employed worker, additional quota paid by employers for each of their employees, health taxes paid by independent workers, and the national government which covers the remaining expenses. The original intention that the SSN would change from mainly insurance funding to funding from general taxation has never been fulfilled. Instead the contributions from state income actually fell during the 1980s. In 1991, 40.9% of health care services are funded by social insurance contributions, for 25.7% by tax revenues, and the remaining 33.4% by private health insurance and patient co-payments [4].

Despite the intention of the SSN law to ensure services free at point of use, co-payments are required for some non-hospital services (drugs, diagnostic examinations, therapeutic procedures). However, hospital care and curative treatment is provided free in hospitals, clinics and other establishments within the SSN. A few drugs, which are considered essential, are free of charge, excluding a small fixed fee for each prescription and a percentage of 30% up to 40% for non-essential drugs. For low income groups no charge is made.

The private sector accounts for 20% of total health care expenditure [5]. People can decide not to use public services and go elsewhere (but in any case they have no choice; they subsidize the SSN by paying taxes). The private insurance companies can offer coverage for services supplied by the private sector.

About 65% of the average local health budgets are spent on hospitals. The majority of hospitals are public, mostly directly managed by the USL, but some are contracted. The latter have different financing, compared to the USL hospitals, and are reimbursed by the SSN by a fixed sum per treatment. Since January 1995 a prospective payment system (PPS) has been introduced: remuneration is now based on diagnosis related groups (DRGs). GPs working under the National Health Scheme are paid a fixed capitation fee by the USLs for each patient on their list. Every six months these fees are adapted to possible increases in the cost of living. The capitation fee is differentiated, depending on the patient's age and the GP's years of experience. In addition, the GP receives a reimbursement of practice expenditure, and an amount to cover fees for liability insurance [1].

1.4   Care for the elderly

In 1987, about 13.4% of the Italian population were 65 or older, but it is expected that this percentage will grow to 16.4% in the 1990s [6]. The number of the elderly over 75 is also steadily increasing. The ageing of the Italian population started later than in most of the other European countries such as the United Kingdom, France and Germany [13]. However, the strong acceleration of the process (the development is more rapid and intense), makes Italy one of the European countries with the highest level of ageing nowadays [7].

Care for the elderly is, like health care, mainly the responsibility of the 20 regions. There is no national framework and this leads to large differences in the available services between the regions. However, in all regions a strong trend has been noticed toward improvement of community care services to main the elderly in their own social environment as long as possible [8]. There is also a tendency to increase and improve the residential services for the severely handicapped or the disabled elderly who are not able to care for themselves.

Community services. Most of the care within the community is provided by the informal networks of the elderly: family members, friends and neighbours.

The availability of professional community services differs highly between the regions. A distinction is made between home interventions (*Assistenza domiciliare*) and the day centres for the elderly living in their own homes (*Centri diurni per anziani*). The latter is to be found in a majority of the regions, but the services provided within the centres are not the same. In general, they focus on the promotion of the social integration and participation of the elderly through recreational and cultural activities. Besides, in some regions these centres also provide home help services, rehabilitation, and information or advisory tasks. The home interventions include the home help services and home nursing activities which will be discussed in the next sections.

Residential services. Compared to the other member states of the European Union, the percentage of the elderly living in residential services is rather small: about 2% in 1987 [6]. However, this official data do not include residents of a large number of small private institutes, mostly situated in the larger municipalities. Until recently, most of the services were mainly oriented towards elderly people who can function independently and do not need specific or extended care. There are different types of residential facilities. The *Residenza Servita* are separate flats in a general building which includes some centralized services such as provision of meals, laundry, social and health emergency, and cultural and recreational activities. In general, about one third of the old people's homes are run by private organizations [6].

Some sheltered institutions are available for the more dependent elderly: the *Residenza Protetta* and *Casa Albergo*. The latter is meant for temporary relief to people with contingent needs. Old people with major health problems can be nursed in RSAs *(Residenza Sanitaria Assistenziale)*. Most institutions are rather small: a maximum of 120 residents. The available number of these kinds of services is by no means sufficient. The limited number of beds or places for the (highly) dependent elderly is a main subject of concern.

Capacity of residential services for the elderly in Italy (1987) [6]

	Number of places /beds per 1000 people over 65 years
Old people's homes	22

2 The organization of home nursing

2.1 Organizations for home nursing

It has already been mentioned that decentralization is an important characteristic of the Italian health care system. The 20 regions have almost autonomous power regarding the provision of health care services and social support. Regional planning and local management of the services are emphasized. As a consequence the level of services differs highly between the regions. Also within the regions, there are huge differences in health care facilities and the way they are organized and funded both among the USLs and among the communities. This also applies for the role of private organizations. Another problem is that the Italian language does not differentiate properly between home care in general and home help services. Furthermore, there are no statistical data available covering the whole country. This means that it is very difficult to give a national overview of home care services in Italy.

There are no organizations operating nationally involved in home care. At national level, the government has only recently presented a general framework for home care. At this moment, it is only involved in the financing of special developmental projects with a limited duration of three or four years. The actual implementation of these kinds of services has not yet started. Only recently, since the beginning of the 1990s, did home care become an official policy target for both the Ministry of Health and the

Ministry of Family Affairs [9]. The programme 'total health for the elderly' (*Tutela della Salute degli Anziani*) focuses on the prevention of chronic diseases and handicaps in the elderly and the provision of assistance in the daily living to the elderly when needed. This policy requires new kinds of services in which health care and social services are integrated [10,11].

Home care within the NHS is focused on two different concepts, but they have not (yet) been implemented in the entire country. The first and most important concept is so called integrated home care (ADI, *L'assistenza domiciliare integrata*). This services consists of a combination of health-related activities (nursing, rehabilitation, general practice, and specialist care) and social and welfare services (home help), given to aged or terminally ill patients for a limited period of six months.

The government wants integrated home care as part of the national health service. This means that the USLs are responsible for the actual provision. Consequently, they have to establish so called Geriatric Evaluation Units (UVGs :*Unita di Valutazione Geriatrica*). These multidisciplinary units consists of geriatric physicians, social workers, professional nurses, and GPs. Again, in some parts of the country these teams are already active, while in other parts not even attempts are made to establish them.

A second kind of home care concept which is provided in some parts of Italy, e.g. Turin, Milan and Genoa, on an experimental base, is hospitalization at home (*L'ospedalizzazione a domicilio*). This is a strictly health service aimed to release patients earlier from the hospitals. This kind of home care provision is hospital-based meaning that the same physicians, nurses, and other health professionals who are working in the hospital, provide the same kind of services at home. The accent lays on pure medical care which can be integrated with other kind of support, mostly provided by private (voluntary) organizations. Although, this kind of care is oriented towards elderly patients, an increasing number of the terminally ill make use of this kind of service.

Although a national framework for home care has only recently been developed, in some communities or regions, different kinds of home care services were already established. The first home care services in Italy were established in 1972 by some local authorities in the north, and towards the end of the 1970s, in the centre and south of the country [12]. In the north, local authorities often organized this services without the interference of the regional authorities. In the south it was developed in the context of the establishment of the local health authorities (USLs) as part of the NHS. The range of services varies extremely between the authorities. Sometimes only strict home help services, such as homemaking, laundry and food provision are provided, while other services are extended to home nursing activities as well. It has already been mentioned that local authorities were involved in home care in the past. However, this mainly involved home help services, although some large municipalities have employed nursing personnel within the social services sector. This situation is changing now. However, home care will be delivered by the USLs as suggested in the Law reforming the National Health Service. This law gives the local authorities the opportunity to delegate the provision of home help services to the USLs and also transfer their nursing personnel to them. In e.g. Genoa, the Social Affair Office still supplies home nursing services to the aged, although the financial base has changed: they may no longer employ health personnel because the expenses for health care have been posted to the National Health Fund and it is no longer possible to ensure a turn-over of the costs to the region.

NHS home care is organized by the district health departments (*Servizio per le attività distrettuali*) which are responsible for the actual delivery of health care at the district level.

Besides, these developments in the public sector, there are also a increasing number of private organizations active in home care: both for-profit as non-profit organizations. The most important group are the so called social co-operations (*Cooperativa Sociale*). In the whole of Italy, there are about 2,500 of these kind of organizations but only 600 of them are involved in home care: they provided home nursing care and/or home help services. Furthermore, some charity organizations, mostly for specific categories of patients, provide some home care but it is mainly limited to short social visits; they do not provide medical or nursing help.

Some local authorities or USLs do not provide home care services themselves, but contract these private organizations.

The role of private organizations differs greatly between the regions, e.g. in Lombardi home nursing services are exclusively delivered by private organizations, while in other regions these private organizations do not exist at all.

2.2 Manpower in home nursing services

There is no statistical information available about the nurses working in home care. In general, the professional nurses have had three year's basic training in *hospital* nursing. There is no official national training for the work in the community. However, at the local level there are sometimes specific courses organized, e.g. by the social co-operatives or USLs.

2.3 Client population

Again no statistical information is available. Originally, home care was developed for elderly people. However, since the 1990s, terminally ill patients have also become an important category for home nursing services.

The Ministry of Health estimated that about 140,000 elderly people need to be considered for integrated home care per year [9]. However, this amount is not reached so far because these services are still in an experimental stage and are not implemented throughout the country.

2.4 Provision of services

To describe the ways home care services are actually provided, a distinction must be made between integrated home care, hospital at home (both parts of the public sector), and the home care provided outside these programmes.

Legally, no formal referral by a physicians is required for home care, although in practice GPs and/or hospital physicians are mostly involved in the assessment of needs and actual provision of home care.

According to national legislation for integrated home care, the geriatric evaluation committee's (UVGs) become responsible for the assessment of the needs of the individual patient and the allocation of the resources. These units have to define the specific goals of home care and develop a personal plan of action for each patient. The minimal amount of care the integrated home care services need to provide per patient during one year are legally determined:

- 140 hours of home help services: homemaking activities and personal care;
- 100 hours of nursing care;
- 50 house calls by the GP;
- 50 hours of rehabilitation care;
- 8 medical controls.

This system has already been introduced in the Emilia Romagna region: specific criteria have already been determined and standardized assessment forms developed.

In the 'hospital at home' program, a special team in the hospital decides whether a particular patient is eligible for home care. Accordingly, they use special, mainly medical and social, criteria. The special team is responsible for the total package of care and it includes all kinds of health professionals. One of the professionals visits the patient each day. When the condition of the patient gets worse, the patient can be immediately returned to the hospital.

When home nursing care is organized by the USLs, a district medical officer, mostly a GP, is in charge of the assessment procedure and allocation of care. There are no national guidelines, each department uses its own criteria. Home nursing care provided by the communities is actually organized by a local social worker.

In the private sector, the staff of the social co-operative decide whether home nursing care is needed and to what extent (amount, type and duration). This is mostly done in co-operation with the patients and family members because they, have to pay for the services (see section 5.1). The staff also takes into account the available resources in the organization.

There are fewer differences within the country in respect of functions and tasks of the professional nurses in home care. Medical home care is dominated by physicians. More complicated technical nursing procedures, such as epidural anaesthesia, handling respirator and catheterization, patient education and psychosocial guidance are performed by GPs or hospital specialists. The role of the nurses is limited to personal care (e.g. bathing, dressing, help with going to the toilet) on the one hand and routine technical nursing procedures (injections, dressings, stoma care and bladder washout) on the other. Assessment of needs and the evaluation of the care provided are not the responsibility of nurses.

Generally, nurses work in teams together with other health professionals. Because there is no specific training in community nursing, nurses are not considered to work alone. Nurses can operate from home care premises, hospitals and nursing homes.

2.5 Problems and recent developments

The structure of home care in Italy is quit obscure. Firstly, the decentralized organization of health care and social services causes differences between regions and/or communities. Secondly, national policy regarding home care (national framework) has only recently been established; while these services have already been developed at local levels. This leads to major conflicts about responsibility for home care: the health care sector or the social services of the communities. The Ministry of Health intends to integrate home care within the NHS, but at local level the social services of the communities have often organized home care for a long time. This situation leads to conflicts at the local level which restrict the implementation of the reforms.

Furthermore, the weak position of the nurses in home care is an important point of concern. Their professional status is rather low. There are only some minor courses in specific community nursing tasks and the tasks of nursing working in home care are limited to routine nursing interventions and personal care.

3   The organization of home help services

3.1   Organizations for home help services

Also with regard to the social services, there is an enormous variety between the Italian regions and communities. In some regions, home help services have been long established; while other local authorities, especially in the south, had not even started this kind of services in 1994.

In general, a distinction can be made between the public social system operated by the communities and the home help services provided by a number of the social co-operatives (private sector) already discussed. In this section, we will compare the services of public and private organizations.

More specific and quantitative information is also available for one community: the city of Genoa. This city, situated in the north of Italy, has 659,754 inhabitants of which 20.6% are older than 60 years.

3.2   Manpower in home help services

Home help services are mainly the domain of social workers, home helps and, in some cases special cleaners. Social workers had a three years training at a university. After primary education, home helps receive a number of professional courses during a period of one year (about 600 hours). Cleaning work does not require specific training; only primary education.

National data on the number of home helps are not available. The social services of Genoa employ one FTE social worker per 19,700 inhabitants and one FTE home help per 5,690 inhabitants.

3.3   Client population

Our experts estimated that about 0.1% of the national population received home help services in 1993. The official figure from the city of Genoa was 0.16%: the clients were mainly the elderly (see table 1) living alone (59%).

Table 1
Clients of home help services in Genoa in 1993

Age	percentage
60 years and below	6.6
61-70 years	14.6
71-80 years	31.8
80 years and above	45.4

3.4   Provision of services

All residents can apply for home help services, when they are available in their community. There is free access: no formal referral is required. Consequently, it is estimated that in 70-85% of the cases, the client or her/his family themselves contacts the home care organization first.

Assessment procedures differ among organizations: there are no standardized national guidelines. In most of the social departments of the communities, the social worker is responsible for the assessment procedure. In the social co-operatives, the 'negotiation' between the potential client and the organization is the responsibility of the chief of home care, mostly a social worker or the managerial staff. They discuss the actual needs for home care and the costs. There are of course no other access criteria, other than the financial ability to pay the provided care.

In Genoa, four main subjects are taken into account in the assessment procedure:
- the age of the client: over 60 years or younger in the case of serious health problems limiting the autonomy of the client;
- informal social support: solitude, total or partial incapacity of the family to guarantee assistance and protection;

- insufficient income;
- option of institutionalization or hospitalization.

The first assessment is done by a social worker. The actual decision about the amount, type and duration of home help is done by a special team which consists of the social worker, home helps and a nurse. They do not use a standardized questionnaire. In the assessment interview, a check list is used. The assessment of health condition of the potential client is done by his/her own GP.

Normally, the home helps work in teams. In daily practice, they operate from their own homes or specific service offices. In the case of serious of difficult cases a special team can be established together with a nurse, social worker or even a physician.

The actual daily activities of home helps comprise mainly housework (preparing meals, washing dishes, washing and ironing, and house cleaning). Some organizations employ personnel for cleaning services only. Furthermore, the home helps are involved in hygiene and other personal care (bathing, help with going to the toilet, clothing), moral support (counselling and advice), general and family support (shopping, going for a walk, administrative support), and the encouragement of help and support from family members, neighbours and friends. The home help is not allowed to provide routine technical nursing procedures such as wound care.

The assessment of needs and the evaluation of the care provided are the main tasks of the social workers. They also provide general and moral support and stimulate the social network of the client to help.

3.5 Problems and recent developments

In general, the home help organizations do not have long waiting lists. This, however, does not mean that all demands are met: in the southern regions especially there are communities without any organization in this field.

The main problems are represented by the lack of knowledge of home care services and its functions, poor co-operation and insufficient communication between the social services (home help team) and the health care services (physicians as well as nurses).

As mentioned before, some important reforms are proposed or introduced with regard to the organization of home help. This is a similarity with the reforms of the British system (see chapter 15). Firstly, there is a political tendency to create a so called welfare mix system in stead of a public system.

This means that the local authorities (*comune*) become responsible for all social services, but the management and actual provision of services can also be entrusted to private social organizations. The local authorities do not provide these services themselves any more, but define the access criteria, qualitative and quantitative standards of the services and evaluate the services and its outcome.

Secondly, the idea is to increase the integration of home help and health care services. Consequently, district organizations have to be established which bear responsible for the total population in the determinate zone. Unified assessment procedures for access criteria have to be developed. This means that the home help services are orientated towards a broader group of clients (e.g. the chronically ill and the terminally ill), instead of almost exclusive use by the elderly.

Finally, the Geriatric Evaluation Units (EVGs) will be extended to cover the entire country as a multi-dimensional assessment and evaluation instrument for the provision of all kinds of services, meeting the needs of the elderly in the most effective and efficient way.

4   Relations between home nursing and home help services

The type of relation between home nursing and home help services differs considerably within Italy. Some organizations, public as well as private, provide only one type of home care, while others provide both types. In the latter organizations, joint assessment procedures for home nursing and home help services have been established. Also, in the daily practice, nurses and home helps co-operate.

The integrated home care (ADI) programme requires a functional and operational integration of home help teams (local authority) and medical home teams (USLs). They provide a joint services under specified circumstances. The assessment and evaluation are entrusted to a special committee formed by the home help manager (the social worker employed by the local authority) and the home nursing manager (geriatric doctor employed by the local health authority). Periodic meetings are organized to discuss individual cases.

5 The financing of home nursing services

5.1 Payment and patients' insurance

The way home nursing care is organized has important implications for the patient's insurance and payments. A distinction is made in the developmental experience of regular home care by the USLs (within the health sector); of the communities (within the social sector) and of private organizations (mainly the social co-operatives).

The Minister of Health is only directly involved in the funding of home care in specific developmental experiments. The 'hospital at home' and the 'integrated home care' project receive temporary governmental subsidies. However, after the experimental phase no structural payments are available from the central government. Then, the regions or the USLs decide whether this kind of home care can be continued within their own budgets.

Home care services provided by the USLs themselves or contracted out to private organizations are free of charge for the patients. On the other hand, home care services provided or contracted out by the social services of the communities mostly require co-payments from the patients. The level of co-payment is income-related and varies between the communities because they are determined by the local authorities. In some communities no co-payment is required.

People are not insured for the costs of home care in the private sector. They cover all the costs themselves. Private health insurance schemes mostly include hospital care, but, in general, do not cover home care facilities. There are, however, negotiations between certain social co-operatives and the private health insurance companies on remuneration of home care in the future. The patient or his/her family have to pay a fixed amount per hour of nursing care. Some groups of the severely handicapped receive a state allowance, but this is too small to pay for private nursing services at home.

5.2 Funding of the organizations

Expenditure on home care are part of the global budget of communities (social services) or regions or USLs (health care). Social services are mainly funded by tax revenues (both national and local) and individual co-payments, while health care costs are mainly paid through public and private insurance contributions, general taxation and patients' co-payments. The USLs are for

80% funded on basis of historical expenditures, the other 20% are based on the provided services. They have a large autonomy in spending their budgets. The community also has considerable freedom allocating their financial resources to their different tasks and responsibilities. USLs and communities can spend money to provide home care services themselves meaning that they have to employ their own staff, but a number of them decided to contract out home care to private organizations.

These private organizations, mostly the social co-operatives, do not receive any direct subsidy from the state. They are paid on a fee-for-service base by the patients or their family or the community or USL. A number of these social co-operatives are run on a for-profit basis.

5.3 Payment of the nurses

In the public sector, nurses can be employed by the communities or by the USLs. They all receive a fixed monthly salary independent of the amount of services provided. In the private sector, there is a mixed remuneration system. Mostly, the professional nurses have a fixed basis salary completed by a special fee per working hour.

The salaries in home care are lower than in hospital care. The average income of home care nurses is rated at ITL 1,800,000. There are, however, also differences between the private and public sector.

5.4 Problems and recent developments

A first important problem with regard to the financing of home nursing care in Italy, is the fact that the central government only provides subsidies on an experimental basis. There no structural payments. A number of experimental organizational structures can therefore not be implemented in regular health care facilities.

Secondly, it is often mentioned that the system leads to inequality because some patients do not have to pay for home care, while others have to pay at least a part of the costs themselves.

Because the available amount of home care is considered to be insufficient in a large number of regions and the patients have to pay private home care themselves, the handicapped, chronically ill and terminal ill are more likely be admitted in the hospital because this is free of charge. Maybe, the recent cuttings in the health care budget, especially those of hospitals, will make policy makers aware of the problem that insufficient health services in the community increases the utilization of hospital care.

6. The financing of home help services

6.1 Payment and clients' insurance

There are no public or private insurance schemes covering the costs of home help services.

In general, co-payments by the clients depend upon the financial situation of the users or their families. The level of co-payment differs considerably among region and communities. In some communities, there are no co-payments because services are only provided to the elderly with a low income.

In 1993, a private insurance company, in an agreement with the Ministry of Social Welfare, established the 'Golden Years' insurance which, amongst other things, supplies special home help care for a limited number of days in case of urgent need.

6.2 Funding of organizations

The social services of the local authorities are financed through general tax revenues. The state contribution are distributed among the local authorities by the regions. The amount of subsidy is based on the number of potential users, the actual users, the available personnel and the function of the social services.

It is estimated that about 50% of the costs of home help services (both provided by public as private organizations) are paid by the clients themselves.

In some regions, local authorities contract out the home help services to the private organizations, the social co-operatives. In local negotiations a price per hour is set. Although, there are large differences between communities, an average of ITL 20,000 per hour is charged. The private organizations are reimbursed on the number of hours that home help is delivered and receive no structural funds.

6.3   Payment of the home helps

The employees of the local social services are paid a monthly salary defined by a state law. The average monthly gross income of social workers was ITL 1,600,000 and that of home helps was ITL 1,400,000 in 1993. Cleaning personnel have a monthly salary of ITL 1,100,000.

In the private sector, employees are mostly paid per working hour.

6.4   Problems and recent developments

The most important problem with regard to the financing of home help services is the lack of money. On the one hand the budgets of the local authorities are cut back. As a consequence, they are only able to provide services to the very poor elderly. On the other hand the pensions and allowances of the elderly and handicapped are not adequate to organize home help themselves. This means that a large group of elderly people cannot depend on the formal home help facilities and need to rely completely on informal carers.

Acknowledgement

The following persons and institutes provided the information used to write this chapter:
- Mrs G. Bon Trani, Radar Soc. Coop. A.R.L., Trieste.
- Mrs C. Costanzi, Comune di Genova, Servici Sociali, Genova.
- Dr A. De Benedetti, Cergas, Universita Bocconi, Milano.
- Mrs H. Salini-Keen, Associazione Don Giuseppe Zilli, Milano.
- Centro Studi, Ministero della Sanita, Roma.

References

1 BOERMA, W.G.W., F.A.J.M. DE JONG, P.H. MULDER. Health care and general practice across Europe. Utrecht: NIVEL, 1993.
2 OECD HEALTH DATA. Version # 1.5. Paris: OECD, 1993.
3 KEMENADE, Y.W. VAN. Health care in Europe. The finance and reimbursement systems of 18 European countries. Zoetermeer: Nationale Raad voor de Volksgezondheid, 1993.

4 SCHNEIDER, M., R.K.H. DENNERLEIN, A. KÖSE, L. SCHOLTES. Health care in the EC member states. Health Policy Special Issue. Health Policy; 1992, 1+2, 113-123.

5 VREUGDENHIL, J.C., M. DE BRUINE. Gezondheidszorg in Europa: structuur en financiering van de gezondheidszorg in enkele Europese landen. Rotterdam: EUR, 1992.

6 NIJKAMP, P., J. PACOLET, H. SPINNEWYN, A. VOLLERING, C. WILDEROM, S. WINTERS. Services for the elderly in Europe. A cross-national comparative study. Leuven/Amsterdam: HIV/VU, 1991.

7 BIANCHI, M. Policy for the elderly in Italy: innovation or modernization? In: Everts, A., I. Svetlik (eds.). New welfare mixes in care for the eldery. Eurosocial reports vol 40. Vienna: European Centre for Social Welfare Policy and Research, 1991.

8 PACOLET, J., C. WILDEROM (eds.). The economics of care of the elderly. Aldershot: Avebury, 1991.

9 MINISTERO DELLA SANITA. Servizio centrale della programmazione sanitaria. Piano sanitario nazionale per il triennio 1992-1994. Ministero della Sanita: Roma, September 1991.

10 MINISTERO DELLA SANITA. Il nuovo ordinamento sanitario. Ministero della Sanita: Roma, 1994.

11 ANFOSSI, L., F. BAUSANO, A. BOFFELLI, ET AL. Anziani: bisogni, servizi e progetti. Padova: Centro Studi e Formazione Sociale "Emanuela Zancan", 1994.

12 COSTANZI, C. Home-care services in Italy (with special reference to Genoa). In: Jamieson, A. (eds.). Home care for older people in Europe. Oxford/New York/Tokyo: Oxford University Press, 1991.

13 CONSTANZI, C. Politique sociale en faveur des personnes âgées: tendances et perspectives. Gérontologie et société; 67, 1993, 80-87.

10 Home care in Luxembourg

Peter P. Groenewegen

1   The setting of home care

1.1   The country

Luxembourg is the smallest member state of the European Union with a population of 378,000. It is a constitutional monarchy (the Grand Duchy of Luxembourg). The country has three languages: Letzeburgesch, French and German. French is used officially in public administration, while Letzeburgesch is spoken by native Luxembourgers on their own and German is mainly used in the newspapers.

The developed market economy is based on heavy industries (steel) and international trade and banking. More than 100 banks have branches, and a number of EU institutions are based in Luxembourg [1].

Population key figures (1990) [1,2]

Population in mln.	0.378
Inhabitants per sq. km.	146
% Living in urban areas	84
% over 65 years	13.6
% over 75 years	6.0
Births per 1000	12.9
Deaths per 1000	9.7
Life expectancy (men)	71
Life expectancy (women)	78

1.2 The organization of health care

The structure of the Luxembourgian health care system is based on a highly privatized hospital sector and doctors in independent practice. More than 50% of all hospitals are private and belong to religious communities. The other hospitals are owned by local communities. Despite the major role of private initiative, hospitals, with only a few exceptions, are non-profit. Activities in the hospital sector are subject to government regulation. The Ministry of Health is charged with the organization and planning, the establishment of new facilities and the extension of existing ones. A new hospital plan is being developed by the government. Its main purpose is to reduce the number of beds in hospitals and the number of hospitals participating in the emergency system.

Specialist care may be provided in hospitals or in the specialist's private practice. Many physicians have a part-time arrangement in a hospital and additionally work in their private cabinets. The total number of physicians in 1990 (dentists not included) was 665, or one per 568 inhabitants. Roughly two thirds of them (425) are medical specialists, which means to one per 889 individuals. General hospitals, their number is 20, are usually small. They are classified according to the technical facilities or to the long or short stay character. Of all 3,784 hospital beds (10.3 per 10,000 inhabitants) 60% are in private and 40% in public hospitals. The number of acute beds is 2,560 (ratio 7.0 per 10,000 inhabitants).

Patients are free to choose their hospital. Specialists are accessible without referral, so they are in a competitive relation with general practitioners. General practitioners all work independently in private practice, mostly single handed. Their number is 225, or one GP per 1,680 inhabitants [1].

Peter P. Groenewegen

Tariffs and doctor's fees are centrally negotiated between organizations of physicians and the Union of the Health Insurance funds and subsequently laid down in a collective contract. The establishment of individual practitioners is not regulated. Every medical doctor with appropriate certificates can start a practice and he or she is automatically recognized by the Social Security scheme. As in many sectors of the Luxembourg society, in health care it is difficult to recruit sufficient staff. Many health care workers are of foreign origin. Since remuneration and salaries are good as compared to the surrounding countries and the health care facilities are of a high quality level, this is no problem [1].

Health care figures (1990) [1]

Expenditure

Total expenditure on health	
Absolute per head in ppp$	1392
Percentage of GDP	7.2
Public expenditure on health	
Absolute per head in ppp$	1273
Percentage of GDP	6.6

Manpower

Physicians per 1000 pop.	2.0
GPs per 1000 pop.	n.a
Qualified nurses per 1000 pop.	n.a

Hospital care

In-patient care	
Beds per 1000 pop.	11.8
Admissions per 100 pop.	19.9
Mean length of stay	17.6
Acute hospitals	
Beds per 1000 pop.	7.0
Admissions per 100 pop.	18.4
Mean length of stay	11.0
Nursing homes	
Beds per 1000 pop.	n.a

1.3   Health financing and insurance

The Health Insurance funds play a dominant role in the health insurance system. There are nine of these funds, for several categories of employees, farmers etc., and the whole population, regardless of their income level, is obliged to join their relevant fund. The Health Insurance funds not only grant health care benefits (in kind), but also sickness and death benefits. Insurance contributions for the Social Health Insurance funds are paid equally by employers and employees. The level of the premiums are determined by law and are income dependent. Self-employed people, farmers and voluntarily insured people pay a fixed percentage of their income. Some other groups, like students, chronically ill and invalids, are exempted from paying premiums. The government pays subsidies for them. Certain types of care, like maternity care and long term psychiatric care, do not belong to the benefits of the Health Insurance fund scheme. These services are funded separately by the government. All Health Insurance funds use a restitution payment system, i.e. the patients are reimbursed (after deduction of possible co-payment) after the bill has been paid to the doctor.

For some medical services there are user charges. Main items of co-payment are: out-patient care (5%; for home visits 20%), drugs (variable percentages), dental treatment (5%, unless the insured has a yearly check-up), hospital care (fixed amount per day for lodging). After tariffs for medical services have been centrally negotiated and determined they are binding upon all health care-providers, also in private insurance. The retail prices of drugs are fixed by the government. Alternative medicine has not been recognized by the social insurance scheme. The General Medical Council is reluctant to include it in the nomenclature of the medical services. About 80% of the population have some private health insurance, as a complement to the public scheme.

Private health insurance is supplied by non-profit mutual insurance organizations as well as by commercial companies. They cover certain charges not refunded by Health Insurance funds, such as expensive dental treatment and single room accommodation in hospitals [1].

1.4   Care for the elderly

Residential services. Institutional care for the elderly is provided in old people's homes (*centres intégrés pour personnes âgées* and *maison de retraite*)

and nursing homes (*maisons de soins*). Until 1988 there was a clear difference between the old people's homes (*maison de retraite*) and the nursing homes. The former provided residential care for the valid or semi-valid elderly, while the latter provided - and still provide - residential care to elderly people in need of permanent nursing, medical and paramedical care. For some of the old people's homes - the ten that are run by the Ministry of the Family - the situation has changed. The name has been changed in *centres intégrés pour personnes âgées* and frail elderly do not have to move to nursing homes, but can stay in these *centres*. They provide both residential care to the able-bodied or semi-invalid elderly and nursing, paramedical and medical care to the dependent elderly. Four levels of need are distinguished:
- 1st level: able-bodied elderly who only get occasional help
- 2nd level: semi-invalid elderly who regularly receive some help
- 3rd level: invalided persons who need continuous help
- 4th level: invalided persons who need continuous nursing and (para)-medical care.

The first and second levels correspond with care in old people's homes, whilst the third and fourth level correspond to care in nursing homes. Only people in the first three levels are accepted as new residents, but if people become heavily dependent on nursing and (para)medical care, they do not have to be transferred to a nursing home. The distribution over the three levels is now respectively 28%, 29%, 25% and 18%.

There are no legal or planning requirements to start an old people's home, although practically it is impossible to run one without financial help from the State. Planning requirements are being discussed now. The number of places in *centres intégrés pour personnes âgées* and *maison de retraite* is 2,353 (1993) in 33 homes. Half of them are private, non-profit and originating in religious charity; of the others, ten are organized by the Ministry of the Family (the *centres intégrés*) and seven by municipalities. There is also a total of approximately 1,000 places available in social lodging for the valid elderly and convalescent homes.

There are nine nursing homes with just over 700 beds. They are run by the Ministry of Health (six homes, mainly hospital beds that are now being used for nursing home care) and the city of Luxembourg (two homes) [3,4].

Trends in health care policy for elderly people. The number of nursing home beds is being extended in two ways. Conversion of hospital beds into nursing home beds is still going on and the Ministry of the Family is expanding the capacity of the integrated centres. The change towards integrated centres necessitates increases in staff to residents ratios from a current 1:8 to 1:3.64, based on the distribution of residents over levels, while it used to be 1:15 before 1988.

Still, pressure on care in nursing homes results in waiting lists. This results in persons with long term nursing needs staying in hospitals (and extra costs for the government, because the social health insurance does not pay for hospital stay longer than six months). The pressure on nursing homes is also alleviated by allocating money to dependent elderly persons who are being cared for at home.

As in most health care systems care for the elderly is fragmented and control is divided over different levels (two ministries at government level, municipalities). Initiatives have started by the late eighties to co-ordinate the activities of the Ministry of the Family and the Ministry of Health. At the level of the five regions, centres of care for the aged (Cerpa) have been organized to co-ordinate residential care and different types of ambulatory care [3,4].

A new general insurance for people who become dependent on care by others is being discussed now. This insurance is meant to cover costs of care of elderly people, irrespective of the place where care is given, at home, in a home for the elderly, or in a nursing home or hospital. The idea behind this insurance (*assurance dépendance*) resembles the German *Pflegeversicherung*.

Capacity of residential services for the elderly in Luxembourg (1990) [3]

	Number of places/beds per 1000 people over 65 years
Old people's homes	47.8
Convalescent homes	7.3
Nursing homes	14.5
Centres de logement et d'accueil	12.9

Peter P. Groenewegen

2 The organization of home nursing

2.1 Organizations for home nursing

Home nursing in Luxembourg originated in the activities of religious orders. One of two largest organizations, *Hëllef Doheem* (help at home), developed in 1980 from a joint initiative by a number of religious orders who were increasingly forced to employ lay nurses [3]. The other organization, *Croix-Rouge Luxembourg*, is a more or less independent branch of the Red Cross.

The four smaller organizations originated in the second half of the 1980s; three are non-profit organizations that also provide home help services and a day care centre, and one is an intermunicipal co-operative that only provides home nursing.

All six home nursing organizations are independent non-profit organizations. Services are regionalized, that is only one organization is active in one area, with the exception of the city of Luxembourg where the two large organizations are active. The two largest organizations each have a national organization and regional or local departments. The four small organizations have a contract with the Ministry of Health for the funding of their services; the two large organizations only have a contract for just a few of their local departments, but on the whole they are independent of the Ministry.

2.2 Manpower in home nursing services

Due to the small scale of the country, the nurses working in a local department are one team.

The total number of nurses working in the community is approximately 120. The majority of them work full-time. The number of inhabitants per nurse is approximately 3,150.

All nurses working in the community are state registered nurses. There is no special education for working in the community, nor is there specialization within community nursing.

Apart from the nurses employed by the home nursing organizations there are some self-employed nurses. Their number is unknown, but is supposed to be decreasing.

2.3   Client population

There are no data on characteristics of the clients of home nursing services, in terms of age, gender or impairment. Home nursing services are available to every citizen who needs these services. Elderly persons are the most important group of clients.

2.4   Provision of services

Theoretically people are free to choose the health care-provider they want. In the case of home nursing this freedom is restricted by the fact that - with the exception of the Luxembourg city area - there is only one organization active in each region. People are always free to choose an independent nurse, although their number seems to be diminishing and there is no up-to-date information as to their numbers.

Home nursing services can be divided in specific nursing services, prescribed by the responsible physician, and general nursing services. For this first group of services a referral or prescription by a physician is necessary. For the second group of services people may directly contact the home nursing organization.

The specific services, prescribed by physicians, include technical nursing services such as injections, cleaning and nursing of wounds, catheterizing etc. The general nursing services are personal hygiene services, such as bathing, assistance with the use of medication, psychosocial assistance. The general services may also be provided by home help services. The majority of services of home nursing are prescribed services (in one organization on average three prescribed services are provided to one general service, but with large variation according to region [5]).

As prescribed services are in the majority, the first contact with home nursing is usually initiated by physicians. In these cases there is also no needs assessment by the nursing organization. For the general services, contact is usually initiated by the patient or his/her relatives. The responsible nurse decides how the demands of the patient can be met best. Only in the two smaller organizations that also provide home help services, is everyone who needs help with personal hygiene or other daily activities visited by a specialized nurse (university trained). She assesses the need for help and decides how much help is going to be given. In this case a special form has been developed to assess the extent to which people are able to perform daily activities and to what extent they receive informal help (see section on provision of home help).

The nurses operate from a small clinic or base in each department. Although they all work on their own, the nurses in one department can be said to form a team.

2.5   Problems and recent developments

Thus far there have been no waiting lists for home nursing. The organizations are relatively young and still growing. A shortage of trained personnel is a problem in home nursing, as it is in other parts of health care. Traditionally, a lot of people from outside Luxembourg are employed in the Luxembourg health care system. A specific problem for home nursing is that people have to understand and speak the Letzeburgesch language.

The co-ordination of care for the elderly is on the increase with the organization of regional centres for the aged (Cerpa - *centre régional pour personnes âgées*). The aim of the five Cerpa's is to co-ordinate all the help offered to the elderly by the old people's homes and nursing homes, run by one of two Ministries involved, by the organizations with a contract with the two Ministries and the private and municipal local organizations. Home nursing is, however, officially not involved in the Cerpa's, but some organizations participate in the co-ordinating committees.

3   The organization of home help services

3.1   Organizations for home help services

Home help services were mainly provided by a private, non-profit organization called *Aide Familiale* (family help). This organization was created in 1952 by Caritas, the Roman Catholic charity. The changing function of home help services from assistance to families with small children to assistance to the elderly, was reflected in a change of name in 1982 to *Aide Familiale/Aide Senior* [3].

The larger part of the country is covered by *Aide familiale/Aide senior*. There are three small, non-profit organizations (*service d'aide à domicile a.s.b.l.*). These run an integrated service of home help and home nursing. The services are regionalized with only one organization serving an area.

212

3.2   Manpower in home help services

Home helps are usually employed by the organizations, but to have a flexible supply of labour and to be able to deal with incidental replacements, due to holidays or illness, a number of people, usually older women who re-enter the labour force, work on an hourly basis (36 or 5.5 FTEs in number in 1993). The number of home helps employed by the organizations is 92 (59.3 FTEs) in 1993. This amounts to one FTE home help per 6,400 inhabitants. The total number of productive hours (i.e. hours actually worked, excluding travel time etc.) is approximately 90,000 in 1993 [6].

There are no formal educational requirements for home helps. They receive on-the-job training (for a total of 400 hours) and supervision by a social worker [3].

3.3   Client population

Gradually the emphasis of *Aide Familiale/Aide Senior* has shifted from help to families with young children in case of illness or hospitalization of the mother to help to elderly people. In 1993 approximately one fifth of the activities was directed to families with children and four fifths to elderly people. Four years earlier the proportions were one third and two thirds.

The reasons for help in families with children are presented in table 1.

Table 1
Reasons for home help to families with children in 1993 [6]

Reason	Households number	Percentage
Illness, temporary handicap	58	19
Operation, hospitalisation	82	27
Difficult pregnancy	29	10
Child birth	40	13
Multiple birth	13	4
Social reasons	25	8
Permanent handicap	20	7
Mental reasons, overstrained	20	7
Other reasons	18	6
Total	305	100

Of the elderly home help beneficiaries in 1993, 63% of the households were women living alone, 16% were men living alone, and 21% of the household were couples (1993). This reflects the old age of the clients of *Aide Senior*: more than 80% were over 70 years of age and more than half were 80 years or above. Two fifths of the clients lived in the capital city of Luxembourg [6].

3.4   Provision of services

As in home nursing, theoretically people have free choice of the provider of care. Due to the regional organization of home help for the five Cerpa's, there is, however, no actual choice. Access to home help services is free; no referral is needed. First contact with the organizations is usually made by family or neighbours of the client or by the municipal social service department.

If a request for help is received, the household is visited by the head of the regional service. This is usually an experienced social worker or a specialized nurse *(infirmiere graduée)*. To facilitate needs assessment in these integrated organizations, they recently introduced a form to record the clients' impairments in daily activities on the one hand and the help provided by others on the other. In all organizations, the person who assesses the need for care, also decides how much care will be given.

Home helps are employed by a non-profit organization which co-ordinates the work. The latter has its office in or near an old people's home or a day centre.

The aim of home help services is to allow elderly people to stay at home as long as possible by contributing to their autonomy and integration in the community. The services provided by home helps include help with personal hygiene, laundry, cleaning, cooking, shopping, assistance with administrative formalities, information, transportation to a doctor's office or hospital, and of course social contact. Household work consumed 40% of the hours of help for elderly clients; 30% were used for help with daily activities, and another 30% were used for mixed activities [6].

Through a tele-alarm system people who are living alone can be connected to the home help organization. For help with technical tasks, like helping with administrative forms, special people are sometimes called in.

3.5   Problems and recent developments

Overall, home help and home nursing are relatively small services. There seems to be a large amount of informal care, made possible by the small scale of the country and a strong tradition of helping each other [3]. At the same time, being a relatively new service, people sometimes hesitate to use home help services because of the fees and for fear of stigmatization by their neighbours. Hitherto, there have been no waiting lists for home help services.

4   Relations between home nursing and home help services

On an organizational and policy level both types of care are largely separate, with the exception of the three organizations mentioned in 3.1.

On the operational level of day to day care there is co-operation when necessary and no problems have been mentioned in this field. Help with personal hygiene is provided by home nursing when medical care is needed, and by the home help organizations for the normal everyday situation.

5   The financing of home nursing services

5.1   Payment and patients' insurance

The payment and reimbursement of home nursing services differs according to the kind of service, i.e. prescribed by a physician or general nursing care.

The technical nursing care, prescribed by a physician, is paid for by the patient, but the total amount is reimbursed by the patient's Health Insurance fund. So far there has been no co-payment for technical nursing care. However, the costs of technical nursing services are only reimbursed when they have been provided on a physician's prescription.

For general nursing care there is a social tariff. Patients pay LUF 170 for a major bathing service, LUF 120 for a minor bathing service, and LUF 50 for help to get in and out of bed. Moreover, they pay LUF 70 for travel costs of the nurse. Other services are free. There is no way to have the costs of this general care reimbursed. However, people living at home who need care, receive a monthly government allocation of (in 1994) LUF 13,800. The four small organizations bill the patients up to a maximum of LUF 290 per day

215

(including a big bathing service of LUF 170, help to get out of bed, LUF 50, and travel costs, LUF 70). There is no ceiling to the amount of care provided per day or week, although practically speaking, two visits a day is a maximum.

The general allocation to people who need care and live at home, is given under the following conditions: people have to be over 65, to have lived in Luxembourg for at least ten years during the last fifteen years, to maintain a domicile in Luxembourg, to earn less than 2.5 times the legal minimum income, and to be properly considered as a person who needs help or assistance. The procedure for this allocation is often initiated by the person's general practitioner. The application is then examined by a special committee, the Commission of Inquiries, Information, Orientation and Placement (*Commission d'Enquête, d'Information, d'Orientation et de Placement* or C.I.O.P). The number of people receiving an allocation was 1,536 on the first of January 1994 and is on the increase (in 1990 it was approximately 1,200).

5.2 Funding of the organizations

Funding differs for the two larger, charity based organizations and four small organizations. The two large organizations - *Croix-Rouge and Hëllef Doheem* - receive approximately 70% of their funding from contributions by patients for the services received. The remaining deficit is by and large covered by the charitable funds they raise. Only a very small part is contributed by the government (Ministry of Health), namely for those departments where there is a contract with the Ministry of Health.

The four small organizations also receive the contributions by patients. The percentage contributed by patients differs and depends on the local situation and the stage of development of these rather new organizations. The deficit is paid by the Ministry of Health, based on a contract with the organizations. The budget for these four organizations is based on the results of the past year and an estimate of the results of the current year.

5.3 Payment of the nurses

The nurses are all in salaried service. The two large organizations pay the same salaries as hospitals. The four small organizations use government salary scales and pay lower salaries. The actual salary of an individual nurse depends on age and number of years of service.

5.4 Problems and recent developments

Funding of home nursing is a problem in as far as two of the organizations depend on collection money, incidental gifts and legacies for an important part of their funds.

6 The financing of home help services

6.1 Payment and clients' insurance

Home help is jointly financed by the local and national government. People who receive home help have to pay an income dependent co-payment. Co-payment varies between LUF 50 and LUF 420 per hour; only the actual time spent with the client is counted (not travelling time to the client's home). In 1993 the average amount billed to clients of *Aide Senior* was approximately LUF 330 per hour.

The maximum number of hours of help that people may receive is actually two hours per day. There are exceptions to this rule for people who have just been discharged from hospital or in cases of terminal care.

6.2 Funding of the organizations

The relation between the home help services and the Ministry of the Family is fixed by a convention. The services are financed from three sources: the Ministry of the Family, co-payments by clients, and the municipalities. Theoretically, these three sources each contribute one third. However, based on a law from the end of last century (*loi conc. le domicile de secours*), everything the municipality has to contribute above 20% of the costs, is made up by the state. Hence, in practice the Ministry of the Family contributes between 40 and 50%.

The real costs per hour of providing home help run up to approximately LUF 1,200.

217

Peter P. Groenewegen

6.3   Payment of the home helps

Home helps are in salaried service of the organizations. Apart from that a small number of people work on a hourly basis. In 1993, the gross salary of a starting full-time qualified home help *(aide-senior diplômée)* was LUF 53,063 per month, and the gross salary of a starting full-time unqualified home help *(aide mánager/aide senior)* LUF 47,939 a month.

6.4   Problems and recent developments

The budget increases of the home help organizations depend on the growth percentage allowed by the Ministry of Finance. The share of the total budget for administration of the services is too low. Regional disparities in the amount of services available are too large.

Acknowledgement
Apart from the written sources mentioned below, the information for this section was kindly provided by mr. J. Hansen, mr. F. Bley and ms. L.Deitz *(Croix-Rouge Luxembourgeoise)*, mr. J. Thyes *(Ministère de la Famille et de la Solidarité)* and mr P. Campagna *(Ministère de la Santé)*.

References

1   BOERMA, W.G.W., F.A.J.M. DE JONG, P.H. MULDER. Health care and general practice across Europe. Utrecht: NIVEL, 1993.
2   OECD HEALTH DATA. Version # 1.5. Paris: OECD, 1993.
3   NIJKAMP, P., J. PACOLET, H. SPINNEWYN, A. VOLLERING, C. WILDEROM, S. WINTERS. Services for the elderly in Europe. A cross-national comparative study. Leuven/Amsterdam: HIV/VU, 1991.
4   MINISTÈRE DE LA FAMILLE ET DE LA SOLIDARITÉ. Programme national pour personnes agées. Luxembourg, 1992.
5   CROIX-ROUGE LUXEMBOURGEOISE, Rapport d'activité 1.1.1993 - 31.12.1993.
6   AIDE FAMILIALE-AIDE SENIOR. Rapport d'activité, 1993.

11 Home care in the Netherlands

Ada Kerkstra

1   The setting of home care

1.1   The country

The Netherlands is a small, most densely populated country. Formal head of the state is the queen. Executive powers, however, are with the government. The parliamentary democracy has two chambers; the First Chamber of 75 members is elected for a six year period by the 12 provincial councils, while the Second Chamber (150 members) is directly elected for a period of four years.

Probably due to relative scarcity of living space, extensive regulation is a feature of Dutch society. Despite the high degree of urbanization, no Dutch city has more than one million inhabitants. Parts of the country's extensive welfare system, developed in the 1960s and 1970s, are presently being scrutinized in order to reduce its financial implications [1].

Population key figures (1990) [1,2]

Population in mln.	15.0
Inhabitants per sq. km.	365
% Living in urban areas	89
% over 65 years	12.9
% over 75 years	5.3
Births per 1000	13.2
Deaths per 1000	8.6
Life expectancy (men)	73.8
Life expectancy (women)	80.1

1.2   The organization of health care

The provision of health services in the Netherlands has been structured in four layers. Collective disease prevention, the basic echelon, includes immunization, school health care, mother and child care, and health education. This is organized separately from primary health care (with the exception of mother and child care), also called the first echelon, which is dominated by private initiative. Primary care is provided by individual independent providers and organizations: general practitioners, community nurses, physiotherapists, midwives, pharmacists, home helps and social workers. Generalist primary care is, in most cases, direct accessible. Usually, patients need a referral from their GP to obtain specialist or (acute) hospital care (the second echelon). The third echelon consists of long term care in psychiatric hospitals, convalescent centres and nursing homes.

National policy making and overall financial supervision is the responsibility of the Minister of Health, Welfare and Sports. Since interest groups are strong, in the Netherlands policy making, and even more its implementation, is a process of negotiating and finding consensus or compromise. Planning of hospitals and nursing homes, which are non-profit private initiatives, is a duty of the twelve provinces. The well over 700 municipalities are in charge of public health (the basic echelon).

The need for cost containment and improvement of efficiency in health care has resulted in proposals for a new structure and financing system, that is the government tends to retreat and there is a shift from planning to self regulation, relying on market principles. Some parts of the plans have been implemented while other have been postponed or cancelled [1,3,4,5].

Health care figures (1990) [2]

Expenditure

Total expenditure on health	
Absolute per head in ppp$	1286
Percentage of GDP	8.2
Public expenditure on health	
Absolute per head in ppp$	917
Percentage of GDP	5.8

Manpower

Physicians per 1000 pop.	2.5
GPs per 1000 pop.	0.5
Qualified nurses per 1000 pop.	n.a.

Hospital care

In-patient care	
Beds per 1000 pop.	11.5
Admissions per 100 pop.	10.9
Mean length of stay	34.1*
Acute hospitals	
Beds per 1000 pop.	4.3
Admissions per 100 pop.	10.3
Mean length of stay	11.2
Nursing homes	
Beds per 1000 pop.	3.5

* Includes long-term/permanent stays in nursing homes

1.3   Health financing and insurance

There is a two-tier health insurance system: a public system, run by Health Insurance funds, compulsory for people below a certain income level (about 60% of the Dutch population) and private insurance for the other 40%. In addition there is an health scheme for the entire population. This last scheme, called the General Act on Exceptional Medical Expenses (AWBZ), covers psychiatric hospital care, out-patient mental care, community nursing, home help services and nursing homes. It is financed by tax revenue. As a part of the health care reform, there is a tendency now to increase the scope of this Act.

Health Insurance funds, the financiers of the public scheme, are non-governmental organizations, still working mainly at a regional level (although this is also subject to change). Premiums are deducted from wages and salaries by the employers and paid on a fifty-fifty basis by both employees and employers. The national umbrella organization of the Health Insurance funds, the Health Insurance Fund Council, is an independent multi-party body advising the Minister of Health on coverage and premium levels.

The private scheme is financed by commercial and non-commercial insurance companies. Premiums depend on age, choice of package, optional cost sharing conditions etc. Since a couple of years, more Health Insurance funds and private insurance companies merge.

There were governmental plans to make one tax-financed health insurance system for the whole population, covering 85% of health care costs and leaving 15% to be privately insured. Early in 1992 a first step has been made by bringing pharmaceutical prescriptions under the 'AWBZ' scheme. However, further implementation has recently been postponed [1,4,5].

1.4   Care for the elderly

In the Netherlands a wide variety of care services for the elderly exists: nursing homes, old people's homes, sheltered housing, services flats, respite care provided by nursing homes, mental health advisory services (RIAGG), community nursing, home help services, meals-on-wheels, etc. The cost of these services has grown. Most public money for care for the aged is spent on residential services (about 88%) and less on community services [8,9]. As community services will be discussed later, only the main two other services, nursing homes and the homes for the elderly, are described here.

Nursing homes. Originally, nursing homes offered a cheap alternative to hospitals for convalescent patients or people needing long-term residential care or reactivation. Their main function nowadays is to provide long-term intensive care to the high-need elderly. Over 90% of the patients in nursing homes are above 65 and two thirds are female. The capacity in beds and the number of nursing homes increased sharply from 1970 to the middle of the 1980s, mainly as a result of the encouragement of institutional psycho-geriatric care by the national authorities [7]. In 1988 there were 321 nursing homes with some 50,000 beds. Over half of the available beds were reserved for somatic patients, 46.8% were for psycho-geriatric patients. Between 1988 to 1993 the number of nursing homes did not increase any further (322 nursing homes in 1993); and the number of beds increased by 2,433. However, this increase only involved beds for psycho-geriatric patients [10]. In 1993, 73% of the nursing homes also delivered day care. In total there were 3,749 places for day care available.

A nursing home is often a final residence for elderly people: in 1992 47% of the somatic patients and 82% of the psycho-geriatric patients spent their final days there [10]. However, the role of nursing homes is under discussion. The issues at stake are considerations of costs, privacy, individualization and social integration. Treatment and rehabilitation are being given more emphasis than nursing. The dilemma remains as to whether the focus should be more on medical treatment than on providing an adequate living environment. Although the number of places have stabilized, the range of provisions have become more differentiated. Relatively new provisions are night admissions, weekend and day treatment, respite care, crisis intervention and the consultative task of the nursing home doctor towards homes for the elderly and primary health care staff [7].

Homes for the elderly. In 1960, the number of places for senior citizens in old people's homes were somewhere around 75,000, and practically anyone who applied for residence was accepted. Since 1977, a '7% norm' has been in effect for these homes, meaning that the total number of beds should correspond to 7% of the number of the elderly in a city or province. Nation-wide admission criteria and selection procedures were introduced to ensure that only the high-need elderly would be admitted [7]. As a consequence the number of actual places and the number of residents decreased during the last ten years; in 1983 134,700 people were living in old people's homes (7.8% of the population 65+) and in 1992 128,000 (only 6.5% of the elderly) [10]. About 80% of the residents spend their final years there. Quite often the homes are run by private foundations. In addition, many homes have special accommodation on the premises for self-reliant elderly people who need help occasionally. The number of these so-called *aanleunwoningen* has increased markedly during the past decade. The elderly living in this type of sheltered housing run an independent household, but are able to use certain facilities and services provided by the old people's homes [7]. The original purpose of residential services was to offer an adequate living environment to those among the elderly who can only manage on their own with difficulty. Because of the stricter admission criteria, and also because of the fact that residents are becoming older and therefore require more intensive care, the

Ada Kerkstra

difference between the populations of old people's homes and nursing homes is fading [7,10].

Capacity of residential services for the elderly in the Netherlands (1988) [8]

Number of places/beds per 1000
people of 65 years and over

Nursing homes	27.2
Old people's homes	76.1

2 The organization of home nursing

2.1 Organizations for home nursing

Dutch community nursing care and home help services are organized on two main levels, namely:

National level:	National Association for Home Care
Regional level:	38 Regional Cross Associations
	85 Home help organizations
	31 Home care organizations

The *National Association for Home Care* is an umbrella organization for community nursing and home help services and has four main duties:
1. policy making on the national level;
2. promotion of the interests of its members, i.e. the regional organizations;
3. engaging in collective bargaining with government and insurance companies;
4. provision of services to the Regional Cross Associations, the home care organizations and the home help organizations.

In 1990 the two umbrella organizations for community nursing and home help services were merged into the National Association for Home Care. At this moment this integration is also taking place on the regional level. It is expected that this integration will result in more efficiency in home care and will help to avoid unnecessary overlap between home nursing and home help services. In the middle of 1993, 31 home care organizations had already been integrated, providing both community nursing and home help services. The 38 regional cross associations provide community nursing only and the 85 home help organizations provide home help services only.

Community nurses are employed by the *Regional Cross Associations* or by the integrated *Home Care Organizations*. The regional cross associations consist of a number of so-called basic units. In such a basic unit a chief nursing officer (head nurse), about ten community nurses and two or three auxiliary nurses work in a team. A basic unit is assigned to a defined geographical area (about 35,000 inhabitants). Within this team each individual nurse, or a sub-team of a few nurses and an auxiliary nurse, is assigned to a specific sub-area. Most of the home care organizations have integrated teams in which community nurses and auxiliary nurses and qualified home helps work together. In addition there are separate teams of unqualified home helps who perform mainly household tasks [11,12,13,14,15].

Regional cross associations and home care organizations can be reached 24-hours-a-day and care can be delivered in the evenings, nights and weekends if necessary. Patients are entitled to a maximum amount of nursing care at home: 2.5 hours a day or three visits a day, for an unlimited period of time.

Patients who need more intensive home nursing for a limited period of time, mostly terminal care or patients who are waiting for admission to a nursing home, can make an appeal to additional home care. This additional home care is provided by private organizations or by foundations related to the regional cross associations.

Because the regional cross associations and the home care organizations are the main providers of home nursing in the Netherlands and also because there is no information about the number of private organizations for (intensive) home care, our description of home nursing in the Netherlands focus mainly on the Cross Associations and integrated home care organizations.

2.2 Manpower in home nursing services

There are three types of community nurses employed by the regional cross associations or home care organizations [16,17]:
- *Community nurses (Wijkverpleegkundigen)* who have had either four years of higher vocational training or 3.5 years in-service training in a hospital with another two years of intermediate vocational training.
- *Nurses in the community (Verpleegkundigen in de wijk)* who have had 3.5 years in-service training in a hospital to become a registered nurse but did

225

not have additional training in community nursing.
- Auxiliary community nurses (*Wijkziekenverzorgenden*) who either had two years in-service training in a hospital or nursing home and a six-month course in community nursing or three years intermediate vocational training in nursing.

Community nurses are considered as first level nurses and nurses in the community and auxiliary community nurses as second level nurses. Until 1993 most community nurses worked as generalists; that is they provided nursing care at home as well as preventive mother and child health care in the child health clinic. However, the growing complexity and workload of home nursing affected the viability of working as a generalist. Therefore since 1993 most home care organizations and regional cross associations made separate divisions for home nursing and child health care. As a consequence most community nurses specialized in home nursing or in child health care. Second level nurses are only employed in home nursing.

In January 1993, 6,202 community nurses (4,353 FTEs), 2,017 nurses in the community (503 FTEs) and 2,933 auxiliary community nurses (1,854 FTEs) were employed by the regional cross associations and home care organizations [17]. In fact there are about 2 first level nurses (FTEs) for every second level nurse (FTEs). In 1987 this ratio was 4:1. This means that during the last five years the number of second level nurses increased relatively more than the number of first level nurses. In January 1993 there was one community nurse per 3,500 inhabitants, 30,294 inhabitants per nurse in the community and one auxiliary community nurse per 8,219 inhabitants (FTEs). However, there are regional differences [17].

2.3   Client population

About 5% of the Dutch population receive nursing care at home (5.7% in 1990, 5.8% in 1991 and 5% in 1992) [14,18]. Table 1 shows the age distribution of patients receiving nursing care at home [14,18].

Table 1
Number of patients receiving home nursing care per 100 inhabitants

Age	1990	1991	1992
0-4	40.5	39.4	38.1
5-19	0.4	0.4	0.4
20-39	0.8	0.9	0.8
40-59	1.3	1.1	1.1
60-69	5.5	4.8	4.8
70-79	16.3	15.8	15.1
over 80	38.9	36.5	35.3

The high percentage in the 0 to 4 years of age group is due to the health visits to mothers with babies and young children and is outside the scope of this study. This table shows that mainly the elderly (70 years of age and above) receive home nursing. The number of patients per 100 inhabitants receiving nursing care at home declined during the past five years. However, the average number of home visits per patient increased: from 8.9 in 1985 to 15.4 in 1992 (an increase of 8% every year). Especially, the mean number of home visits to patients of 70 years and above has increased sharply [10]. This means that patients of community nurses have become more care dependent and need more intensive nursing care.

According to a study in 1990, 65% of the patients who received home care were females [15].

2.4   Provision of services

In general, patients do not have a choice as to which home nursing organization they want to approach, because there is only one regional cross association or home care organization in the region. In some places there are local private home nursing organizations patients can turn to. However, the insurance companies only remunerate the costs of supplementary home nursing under certain conditions and not the costs of regular nursing care at home provided by these private organizations. Consequently the patient has to pay most of the cost himself.

Patients can contact the cross associations or home care organizations themselves because no referral is needed. Vorst-Thijssen et al. [15] provide information on initiators of contacts with cross associations (Table 2).

Table 2
Percentage of patients noting by whom the first contact is initiated

Initiator	percentage
Patient self/family	47
General practitioner	17
Home help service	2
Hospital or nursing home	33
Other professional care-providers	7

Most patients appear to initiate the contact themselves, followed by those who are referred by hospitals or nursing homes.

Traditionally, the assessment is carried out by a community nurse (first level nurse), who is also going to provide the nursing care or who delegates the care to a second level nurse. In the regional cross associations this is still the case. However, most home care organizations, delivering home nursing as well as home help services, intend to combine the assessment of patient's need for home help and for nursing care. Within those organizations there is a lot of discussion about who has to pay the assessment visits: a first level community nurse who also provides care, a manager of the home help services, or a member of a special assessment team. The fact is that the health insurance companies are demanding more standardized and objective assessment methods. By now most integrated home care organizations have chosen a special assessment team consisting of a few persons with a nursing background and a few persons with experience in assessing needs for home help services (mostly social workers). The members of the team pay all the assessment visits and they are not involved in direct patient care. This means that in most integrated home care organizations the community nurses are no longer entitled to pay assessment visits.

The assessment forms used during the assessment visits differ from one organization to the other. There is no standardized form that is being used in the whole country. At this moment new assessment forms are being developed suitable for assessing needs for home nursing as well as home help services [13]. At the integrated home care organizations the member of the assessment team also determines that the patient needs home help care. At a regional cross association a community nurse assesses the need for home nursing only. She does not assess the need for home help services.

The same person who does the assessing also decides what type of care the patient is going to receive by what type of nurse (first or second level nurse) and during what period of time. Sometimes the member of the assessment team also makes a nursing care plan, but in most organizations the care plan is made by the nurse who is going to provide the care. Evaluation of the care plan by the community nurse who is delivering the care takes place regularly, but the frequency varies. When the care is provided by an auxiliary nurse, the evaluation is mostly done together with a first level nurse. Community nurses and auxiliary nurses always work together in a team. In the home care organizations they work in a team together also with qualified home helps.

About 7% of the community nurses are attached to a health centre. They work in a team together with general practitioners, social workers, physiotherapists and sometimes home helps.

Community nurses (first level nurses) are qualified to perform all of the following tasks:
- assessment of the need for care
- hygienic and other personal care (e.g. bathing, help with lavatory, help with activities of daily living)
- routine technical nursing procedures (such as injections, dressings, stoma care, bladder washout)
- more complicated technical nursing (e.g. epidural anaesthesia, handling respirator, catheterization)
- patient education
- psychosocial activities
- encouraging help, e.g. from family members, neighbours, friends etc.
- evaluation of care.

Auxiliary nurses (second level nurses) are also qualified to perform most of the tasks mentioned above, except the assessment of the need for care, more complicated technical nursing procedures and the evaluation of care. In addition, auxiliaries more often provide hygiene care and give less often psychosocial support.

2.5   Problems and recent developments

The increase in options for home care technology leads to the question as to what extent the community nurse is qualified to perform medical technical care. The division of tasks and responsibilities between nurses and general practitioners should be made more clear [12].

In many cases the communication between hospitals and regional cross associations or home care organizations could be improved. These problems concern the preparations for discharge and time-continuity between hospital care and home care. Some cross associations try to solve this problem by employing liaison nurses who are based in a hospital and who assess the patients' needs for nursing care at home before the patient is discharged from the hospital. She/he communicates these needs with the cross association in order to bridge the time-gap between discharge from the hospital and aftercare at home.

3   The organization of home help services

3.1   Organizations for home help services

Home help services in the Netherlands are offered by private organizations (foundations), which have a regional function. Together these organizations cover the whole country. As mentioned before, in 1990 the umbrella organizations for community nursing and home help services were merged into the National Association for Home Care. At this moment this integration is also taking place on the regional level. Consequently, Dutch home help services are organized on two main levels:

National level: National Association for Home Care
Regional level: 85 Home help organizations
                         31 Integrated home care organizations

The tasks and duties of the National Association for Home Care have already been described in 2.1. In the middle of 1993, 31 home care organizations had already been integrated, providing both community nursing and home help services. The 85 home help organizations provide home help services only.

Home helps are employed by the home help organizations or by the integrated home care organizations. Most of the home care organizations have integrated teams in which community nurses and auxiliary community nurses and qualified home helps work together. In addition they have separate teams of unqualified home helps, who only carry out household tasks. Traditionally in the most home help organizations (qualified) home helps do not work in teams, they work as soloists.

3.2 *Manpower in home help services*

The home help service is officially defined as help of a domestic and caring nature, occasionally supplemented by help of a personal and supporting nature, offered to all inhabitants of the Netherlands who need at least help of a domestic nature related to illness, recovery, old age, handicap, death, psychosocial, and personal problems that threaten the maintenance of the household. Its objectives are to support families and individuals in need and enable them to live as independently as possible [21].

In home help services, a large variety of workers are employed (see table 3).

Table 3
Staff of the home help services by category in 1990 [22]

	percentage
Management and clerical personnel	6.1
Home-help organizers	4.9
Specialized home carers	1.2
Home carers	13.0
Home helps	73.1
Other	1.7

Within the personnel who actually provide home help care a distinction is made between [23]:
- Specialized home carers (*gespecialiseerde gezinsverzorgenden*) who support households with multiple complex problems.
- Home carers (*gezinsverzorgdenden*) who organize a household and provide also personal care as far as this can not be done by the members of the household.
- Qualified home helps (*gediplomeerd helpenden*) who do the housekeeping and some personal caring tasks as far as they can not be done by the members of the household.

- Unqualified home helps (*ongediplomeerd helpenden*) who are only allowed to do the housework.

In addition to the above mentioned personnel, in 1973 'alpha-help'(*alpha-hulp*) was established as a way of providing cheaper help. This was achieved by allowing people to work as home helps for a maximum of twelve hours a week, which is the limit below which they do not have to pay social security contributions. Alpha-helps have the same tasks as the unqualified home helps, but formally the client is the direct employer of the alpha-help. Alpha-help is therefore formally organized outside the home help organizations. However, most of the organizations operate as an intermediary between the client and the alpha-help [21,23].

A large majority (77%) of the personnel, especially home helps involved in direct care, are unqualified, that is they did not receive any specific education or training. Alpha-helps are also unqualified.

Qualified home helps have had either two years of intermediate vocational training (MDGO-vz) or a two year part-time training (OVDB) one day a week together with practice of at least sixteen hours a week. Qualified home carers have had either three years of intermediate vocational training (MDGO-vz) or two year's part-time training (OVDB) one day a week together with practice of at least sixteen hours a week. Finally, specialized home carers have in addition received specific two year part-time training [24,25].

In 1992, about 109,000 carers/helps (including alpha-helps) were providing home help services. However, most of those people work part-time, because there were only 40,678 FTEs. The capacity of the home help services has not grown since 1988 [10].

3.3 Client population

In 1991, about 300,000 clients received home help services [26]. This accounts for 4% of the Dutch population [27]. In the same year, 80% of the clients were female and 66% of the clients were living alone [28]. Just as with community nursing services, most clients of home help services are elderly people. Moreover, during the last ten years the number of clients above 65 has been increasing (see table 4).

Table 4
Number of clients of home help services during December 1983
and December 1988-1992 by age [10,18]

Age of clients	1983	1988	1989	1990	1991	1992
< 65	48,100	46,000	43,300	42,500	41,410	40,200
65 and older	130,000	141,200	149,300	160,700	168,100	185,800
total	178,100	187,200	192,600	203,200	209,510	226,000

The table also shows a change from helping families to helping chronically ill and elderly people.

3.4   Provision of services

In most regions of the Netherlands there is only one home help or home care organization. Consequently, people formally do not have a choice when they need home help services. Of course, theoretically it is always possible to organize informal care by family members or friends, or to pay a private help for housekeeping, but the last alternative may be much more expensive.

No formal referral is needed, so potential clients can contact the home help services by themselves. There are no national figures available, but a study in the province of Drenthe showed that 77% of the first contacts with the home help organizations were arranged by the client himself or his family, 7% by the general practitioner and 16% by other professional care-providers [29].

Traditionally, the assessment of needs is done by a home help organizer (*leidinggevende gezinsverzorging*): mostly someone with a training in social work, who is not involved in direct patient care. Within the home help organizations this is still the case. As mentioned before, most integrated home care organizations have chosen a special assessment team consisting of a few persons with a nursing background and a few persons with experience in assessing needs for home help services (mostly social workers). The members of the team make all the assessments and they are not involved in direct patient care. Within the integrated home care organizations the members of the assessment team also determine the patient's needs for home nursing care.

All (former) home help organizations use one standardized assessment form the so-called LIER system (*Landelijk Indicatie en Registratie systeem*; National intake and documentary system). This system is used by the home help organizers to assess and allocate the quality and quantity of home help care.

However, within the integrated home care organizations, new assessment forms are being developed suitable for assessing needs for home nursing as well as home help services [13].

After the assessment the care is allocated by the home help organizer. However, because there are waiting lists for home help services the most desirable amount of care can not always be provided and dependent on the urgency of the needs, most clients have to wait a number of weeks or even months before they actually receive the assessed care [11]. Reassessment is made by the home help organizer at least twice a year.

The actual home help care is provided by the different categories of home helps described in section 3.2. The work of the alpha-helps is limited to housework like cleaning the home, washing dishes, washing and ironing. Unqualified home helps are also only allowed to do the housekeeping. Qualified home helps do the housekeeping and some caring tasks as far as they can not be done by the members of the household, like bathing, help with lavatory, and providing general and family support like shopping, take for a walk, administrative support (filling in forms). Qualified home carers provide hygiene and personal care, some homekeeping activities, they organize the household and they support with psychosocial problems. Finally, specialized home carers support households with complex (psychosocial) problems.

A lot of the home helps, especially the unqualified ones, work alone. They usually operate from their own homes. However, a number of the home carers and qualified home helps are involved in so-called home teams [30]. They discuss the client's situation with community nurses, general practitioners, social workers and, although sometimes, with a psychiatrist, a physiotherapist or a pharmacist. In the new integrated home care organizations qualified home helps work in a team with home nurses, and in most of those organizations there are separate teams for unqualified home helps [13].

3.5   Problems and recent developments

Due to shortage of budget and the policy of substitution of hospital care for home care there are long waiting lists for home help services. In December 1992 about 15% of the organizations reported a waiting list for potential clients to be assessed for the need for home help services. The average waiting time between the demand for care by the client and the assessment visit was 12 days. More seriously, however, is the waiting list and waiting time after the assessment visit has been taken place and before the actual care is provided. In December 1992 more than 12,500 clients who were already positively assessed for their need for home help services, were waiting for actual home help care. There were waiting lists for the actual provision of home help services at 82% of the organizations. The average waiting time in 1992 was 45 days (± 6 weeks) for traditional home help services, and 90 days (± 13 weeks) for alpha-help [11].

An other problem is that there is a shortage of home helps and some studies show that the shortages of personnel will be even more greater in the near future [19,31]. Furthermore, research has shown that absenteeism among home helps is extremely high (more than 12% in 1987, and this percentage is only decreasing slowly). Also very high, compared to other professions in health care, is the number of home helps who become incapacitated mostly due to back pain or mental problems: almost 3% every year, compared to 1% of other health care professions. Working with poor quality household-equipment can be physically straining. About half the home helps have had back problems during the last year. Experimental projects are started to reduce absenteeism caused by poor household-equipment [32,33].

4   Relations between home nursing and home help services

The relation and co-operation between the two services varies from region to region because a process of integration of home nursing and home help services is taking place. Consequently, in about 50% of the regions home nursing and home help services are delivered by the same organizations, while in the other regions home nursing and home help services are provided by different organizations. It is expected that before 1996 both services will be integrated in every region of the Netherlands. However, during the integration process a number of problems have to be solved. For instance the division of tasks between home carers, home helps and auxiliary community nurses has to be made more clear, especially regarding the ADL-care, because there is an overlap in the tasks of those care-providers. Furthermore, cultural differences between the services have to be overcome in order for them to work together in an efficient way. Finally, many decisions have to be made about the new organizational form of the integrated organizations.

In summary, developments concerning the (further) integration of home nursing and home help services are and will in the near future be a topic requiring much attention in the organizations for home care. The parties involved continue working on the most effective organizational form for providing help/care to every patient or client.

5   The financing of home nursing services

5.1   Payment and patients' insurance

Since 1980 the regional cross associations (and also home nursing provided by the integrated home care organizations) for about 85% have been funded by a system of public insurance based on the General Act on Exceptional Medical Expenses (AWBZ). Under the provisions of this Act, all residents of the Netherlands are entitled to receive community nursing care, and no prescription from a physician is needed except for medical treatment. The remaining 15% are largely paid by patient's membership fees which vary regionally (average NLG 50 each year per family), because patients have to be (or to become) a member of the regional cross association in order to receive nursing care at home. This annual fee can be regarded as co-payment. The regional cross associations and home care organizations are free to determine the level of the membership fees within certain limits. Cross associations with higher membership fees can provide extra care or service facilities. Based on this General Act on Exceptional Medical Expenses patients are entitled to a maximum of nursing care at home: 2.5 hours a day or three visits a day, for an unlimited period of time (as long as they need help). In addition, loan of nursing equipment like wheelchairs, beds, etc. is free during the first three month. After that period patients have to rent the equipment or to buy the equipment themselves.

Furthermore, there are conditions in which additional home care can be obtained by patients who have a public health insurance, namely when:
- regular community nursing is considered not to be sufficient, for instance in the case of terminal home care.
- additional home care substitutes care in hospital or nursing home.
- the period of time during which additional home care is needed is limited

to a maximum of three months. Only in exceptional cases is a maximum period of six months allowed.
- the total costs of the home care does not exceed NLG 410 a day [34].

The additional home care includes home nursing as well as home help services.

Also nearly all private insurance companies reimburse additional home care, especially when the additional home care substitutes hospital care. However there is a lot of variation in the conditions for reimbursement between the different private insurance companies [10].

5.2 Funding of the organizations

The regional cross associations and home care organizations are non-profit organizations. As mentioned before, since 1980 about 85% of the costs of the community nursing services is financed through a system of public insurance based on the General Act on Exceptional Medical Costs (AWBZ). The organizations receive a fixed budget from AWBZ, based on the number of personnel. They also receive money from membership fees (about 15% of the budget), which of course depends on the number of members.

For a regional cross association (and home care organization) to be eligible for funding by the AWBZ it has to meet certain minimum standards set by the Ministry of Health [35]:
- *Types of care* that should be delivered: (1) nursing activities in the home related to illness, disability, old age; (2) mother and child care, including periodic assessment of the child's health; (3) providing equipment in loan; (4) activities aimed at preventing illness and unhealthy habits.
- *Accessibility*: 24 hours a day, in order to be able to provide care in urgent cases.
- *Manpower in direct patient care*: one community nurse for every 3,450 inhabitants, one auxiliary nurse for every three community nurses, and one head nurse for every nine community nurses and/or auxiliary nurses. This standard, however, has become obsolete.
- *Quality control*: State employed public health inspectors have to be allowed free access at all times.

However, since January 1994, the system of and the conditions for funding are changing. Every individual regional cross association or home care organization has to make an agreement with the insurances companies and Health Insurance funds in the region about the conditions or standards for

funding by the AWBZ. In such a contract the following matters are agreed upon [10]:
- Prerequisites for delivering nursing care to the insured patients;
- procedures concerning refusal or continuation of care;
- right of reimbursement of the care by AWBZ;
- standards of quality of care;
- conditions regarding the registration of personal characteristics of patients;
- supplying information concerning the care provided by the cross association and the manner of control by the insurance company;
- frequency and character of consultations between the parties;
- method of reimbursement;
- procedures in case of disagreement.

In the near future the budget of a regional cross association or home care organization will be no longer based on the number of personnel but on the 'output', ie on the amount of care provided.

5.3 Payment of the nurses

All community nurses and auxiliary community nurses employed by the regional cross associations or home care organizations are paid a fixed monthly salary. In 1993 the gross salaries of community nurses varied between NLG 3205 and NLG 4246 per month. The gross salaries of auxiliary nurses varied between NLG 2827 and NLG 3672 (all on a full-time basis and depending on the number of years of experience and level of education).

Every one or two years, the National Association for Home Care negotiates with the unions about a collective labour agreement, this includes bargaining about the salaries of the nurses. In addition, most cross associations and home care organizations make use of nurses who are not formally employed by them. Those nurses are paid per hour.

5.4 Problems and recent developments

In 1990, the Ministry of Health expected that the integration of home nursing and home help services would lead to an increase in efficiency in home care and in saving NLG 250 million per year. However, recent research has showed that until the year 1997 no savings could be expected from the integration process. From 1998 to 2002 a saving of only NLG 65 million per year has been calculated, and from 2003 onwards a saving of NLG 100 million per year is expected. This implies that less money will be available for direct patient care in home nursing and home help services than was expected [36].

For 1994, the Dutch government reduced the budget for home nursing services by NLG 12 million. However NLG 20 million will be spent in reducing waiting lists and financing the change from care in homes for the elderly to nursing care at home [14].

An important development concerning the financing of home care are experiments, initiated by the Health Insurance Fund Council, in which personal budgets for clients are introduced. With the personal budget clients can buy the care they needed by themselves. The aim of these client based budgets is to give the clients more freedom to choose the care they want. During the experiments, patients who were in need of home care for at least three month were offered the possibility for a personal budget. Forty-five percent of the patients choose for this option. The first results showed that the personal care budgets can be threatening for the home care organizations, because about 25% of the hours of home nursing care and 35% of the hours of home help care needed by the clients were purchased from private nurses or home helps. As a consequence, if the personal budgets are officially offered by the health insurances companies and by the health insurance funds as option for clients in need of home care, then the home care organizations possibly lose a large amount of their budget and as a consequence they have to dismiss a number of their personnel.

6   The financing of home help services

6.1   Payment and clients' insurance

Since 1989 the home help organizations (and also home help services provided by the home care organizations) 90% have been funded by a system of subsidies based on the General Act on Exceptional Medical Expenses (AWBZ). Under the provisions of this Act, all residents of the Netherlands are entitled to receive home help services, and no referral of a physician is needed. However, because there are waiting lists for home help services the most desirable amount of care cannot always be provided and depending on the urgency of the needs most clients have to wait some weeks or even some months before they actually receive the assessed care.

In the Netherlands, a co-payment of NLG 10.00 per hour is required in the costs of home help services. The maximum amount of co-payment per week depends on the client's income and varies between NLG 4.50 and NLG 250.00 per week (rates of co-payment on 1 July 1994). The clients of alpha-helps have to pay the alpha-help directly per hour (NLG 14.60). However, the maximum amount of co-payment is the same as with the more 'traditional' home help services. Therefore every four weeks the organization of home help services reimburses the difference between the actual payment of the clients of alpha-helps and the maximum prescribed co-payment based on the income of the client.

The maximum amount of home help a client is entitled to is four hours a day, for an unlimited period of time (as long as the patient needs care). The amount of alpha-help is limited to twelve hours a week.

6.2   Funding of the organizations

The home help organizations and home care organizations are non-profit organizations. However, there are private for-profit organizations which, among others, provide home help. These organizations compete with the home help organizations and home care organizations. In 1988, there were 31 private organizations for home care in general. Home help was delivered in 6% of the care provided by those private organizations [38,39].

As mentioned above, since 1 January 1989, about 90% of the costs of home help services has been financed through a system of subsidies based on the General Act on Exceptional Medical Expenses (AWBZ).

The organizations receive a fixed budget from the AWBZ based upon the number of inhabitants of the catchment area and the age distribution of the inhabitants. The budget is relatively higher, when many elderly people are living in the catchment area.

Since 1 January 1994, the minimum standards for home help organizations were deregulated. From then, the organizations had to meet only one criterion to be eligible for financing from the AWBZ: an official assessment of the help needed is required, using the LIER-system (as described in section 3.4).

6.3 Payment of the home helps

All types of home helps, except alpha-helps, are paid a monthly salary by the home help organizations. The gross monthly salaries in 1993 were [40]:
- specialized home carers: between NLG 2827 and 3396
- home carers: between NLG 2667 and 3300
- qualified home helps: between NLG 2548 and 2743
- unqualified home helps: between NLG 2386 and 2743

These salaries are based on full-time equivalents and depending on number of years of experience and level of education).

Alpha-helps are directly paid by the clients. They earn the minimum wage of NLG 12.48 per hour.

6.4 Problems and recent developments

As described in section 3.5, due to shortage of budget and the policy of substitution of hospital care for home care there are long waiting lists for home help services. In 1994, the Dutch government reduced the budget for home help services by NLG 23 million. However, NLG 40 million extra will be spent, among others, in reducing waiting lists and financing the change from care in homes for the elderly to nursing care at home [14].

Problems that hinder integration of both services and delegating tasks from home nurses to home helps are the differences in co-payment required for home nursing and home help and the long waiting lists for home help services [11,36]. For instance, for the patient it is much cheaper to receive help with activities of daily living from a home nurse than from a home help.

The new rates of co-payment for home help services went into effect on 1 July 1994. Many clients have protested against them because they consider these rates far to high. As a consequence they decided to receive less help from the home help services.

Because of the expected shortage of home helps in the near future, more people need to be stimulated to work in home help services. An important incentive would be to increase the salary which however, will obviously increase the costs of home help services [31].

References

1 BOERMA, W.G.W., F.A.J.M. DE JONG, P.H. MULDER. Health care and general practice across Europe. Utrecht: NIVEL, 1993.

2 OECD HEALTH DATA. Version # 1.5. Paris: OECD, 1993.

3 NETHERLANDS INSTITUTE OF PRIMARY HEALTH CARE (NIVEL) & NATIONAL HOSPITAL INSTITUTE (NZI). Curatieve zorg in Nederland: feiten, ontwikkelingen en knelpunten. Utrecht: NIVEL/NZI, 1993.

4 SCHNEIDER, M., R.K.H. DENNERLEIN, A. KÖSE, L. SCHOLTES. Health care in the EC Member States. Health Policy Special Issue, Health Policy; 1992, 1 and 2.

5 STG (Steering Group on Future Health Scenarios). Primary care and home care scenarios in the Netherlands, 1990-2005. Houten/Zaventum: Bohn Stafleu Van Loghem, 1993.

6 CBS. Statistical Yearbook 1994. 's-Gravenhage: SDU/uitgeverij, CBS publicaties, 1994.

7 TUNISSEN, C., M. KNAPEN. The national context of social innovation: The Netherlands. In: Kraan, R.J. et al. Care for the Elderly. Significant innovations in three European Countries. Frankfurt am Main: Campus Verlag, 1991.

8 NIJKAMP, P. ET AL. Services for the elderly in Europe. A cross-national comparative study. Leuven/Amsterdam: Hoger Instituut voor de Arbeid/-Vrije Universiteit, 1991.

9 VOLLERING, J.M.C. Care services for the elderly in the Netherlands. Amsterdam: Tinbergen Institute, 1991.

10 VAN DER KWARTEL, A.J.J., D.M.J. DELNOIJ, L.J.R. VANDER-MEULEN, J. HARMSEN. Branche-rapport verpleging en verzorging. Feiten, ontwikkelingen en knelpunten. Utrecht: NZI/NIVEL, 1994.

11 GROENEWEGEN, P.P., A. KERKSTRA, G.A. JANSEN. Wachtlijsten in de thuiszorg. Utrecht: NIVEL, 1993.

12 VERHEIJ, R.A., A. KERKSTRA. International comparative study of community nursing. Aldershot: Avebury, 1992.

13 VERHEIJ, R.H., W.M.C.M. CARIS-VERHALLEN, A. KERKSTRA. Integratie kruiswerk en gezinsverzorging. Utrecht: NIVEL, 1993.

14 MINISTERIE VAN WELZIJN, VOLKSGEZONDHEID & CULTUUR. Financieel overzicht zorg. Rijswijk: Ministerie van WVC, 1994.

15 VORST-THIJSSEN, T., A. V.D. BRINK-MUINEN, A. KERKSTRA. Het werk van wijkverpleegkundigen en wijkziekenverzorgenden in Nederland. Utrecht: NIVEL, 1990.

16 ADRIAANSEN, M., B. VAN DER LAAN. Extramurale gezondheidszorg; functies en taken van de wijkverpleegkundige. Deventer: Van Loghum Slaterus, 1989.

17 HINGSTMAN, L., J. HARMSEN. Beroepen in de extramurale gezondheidszorg (concept). Utrecht: NIVEL, 1994.

18 LANDELIJKE VERENIGING VOOR THUISZORG. Meerjarenraming 'Thuiszorg in Beeld'. Bunnik: LVT, 1993.

19 TITS, M. VAN, H. VERMEULEN. Ontwikkelingen op de arbeidsmarkt(5). TVZ; 1992, 3, 104-107.

20 JANSEN, P.G.M., A. KERKSTRA. Functiedifferentiatie binnen de thuiszorg. Utrecht: NIVEL, 1993.

21 HEUVEL, W. VAN DEN, H. GERRITSEN. Home-care services in the Netherlands. In: Jamieson, A. (ed.). Home care for older people in Europe. A comparison of policies and practices. Oxford: Oxford University Press, 1991.

22 VOG, CFO & AbvaKabo. Functiewaarderingsonderzoek Gezinsverzorging. Rijswijk: 1990.

23 CENTRALE RAAD VOOR DE GEZINSVERZORGING. Handboek Gezinsverzorging. 's Gravenhage: VUGA-boekerij, 1990.

24 GEERLINK-VAN DER GANG, A.M. Beroepenboek in en om de gezondheidszorg. Utrecht: De Tijdstroom, 1993.

25 LANDELIJKE VERENIGING VOOR THUISZORG. Thuiszorg informatiemap voor studie en beroep. Bunnik: LVT, 1992.

26 LANDELIJKE VERENIGING VOOR THUISZORG. Thuiszorg volop in beweging. Jaarverslag 1992. Bunnik: LVT, 1993.

27 CBS. Vademecum gezondheidsstatistiek. Rijswijk: CBS, 1993.

28 VNZ-KLOZ-KPZ-LVT. Onderzoek thuiszorg. April, 1992.

29 KEMPEN, G.I.J.M., TH.P.B.M. SUURMEIJER. Thuiszorg nader bekeken. Groningen: RUG, 1989.

30 HESSELS, E.M.A. Home teams 1988. Utrecht: NIVEL, 1989.

31 TITS, M. VAN, W. GROOT. Zorgen om kruiswerk en verzorging. Tijdschrift voor verpleegkundigen; 1991, 2, 56-59.

32 VEERMAN, T.J. Ziekteverzuim in de gezinsverzorging. Amsterdam/Leiden: NIA, 1989.

33 BEEMSTER, F., R.D. FRIELE. Huishoudelijke materialen, werkomgeving en werkorganisatie in de thuiszorg. Utrecht: NIVEL, 1993.

34 MINISTERIE VAN WVC. Thuiszorg in de jaren '90. Brief van de Staatssecretaris van Welzijn, Volksgezondheid en Cultuur aan de Voorzitter van de Tweede Kamer der Staten-Generaal. Rijkswijk: 16 december 1991.

35 BESLUIT ERKENNINGSNORMEN KRUISORGANISATIES. MGZ; 1981,9,7/8, 52-58.

36 HOMANS, C.F., J.P. GLASER. Evaluatie integratie Kruiswerk en Gezinsverzorging. Enschede: Hoeksma, Homans & Menting, 1993.

37 GROENEWEGEN, P.P., A. KERKSTRA. De omvang van wachtlijsten in de gezinsverzorging en het budgetniveau van de instellingen. Utrecht: NIVEL, 1993.

38 VERHEESEN, H. Ondernemende verpleegkundigen en verzorgenden. TVZ; 1988, 10, 329-332.

39 VISSER, E.T. Van alle markten thuiszorg. Amsterdam: Regioplan, 1989.

40 CAO-gezinsverzorging Juni 1993. Utrecht: De Tijdstroom, 1993.

12 Home care in Portugal

Jack B.F. Hutten

1   The setting of home care

1.1   The country

Portugal is part of the Iberian peninsula. It is a low-density country, the population is mainly concentrated in the coastal areas.

Since 1974, it has been a democratic republic. The president is directly elected for up to two consecutive terms of five years. The assembly of 230 members is also elected directly, but for a period of four years.

Agriculture is still an important factor in the Portuguese economy and industry is dominated by the manufacture of textiles and footwear. Although the economy has benefitted from the membership of the European Union since 1986, the country is still among the poorer ones of the EU [1].

Jack B.F. Hutten

Population key figures (1990) [1,2]

Population in mln.	10.5
Inhabitants per sq. km.	114
% Living in urban areas	34
% over 65 years	13.1
% over 75 years	5.3
Births per 1000	11.8
Deaths per 1000	10.0
Life expectancy (men)	70.9
Life expectancy (women)	77.9

1.2   The organization of health care

The organization of health care is based on the right for health for all inhabitants. The state is the principal provider, employer and financing agency of health care [3,4]. Since 1979, the National Health Service (*Serviço Nacional de Saúde*) has been covering the whole country with a network of hospitals and health centres. However for a number of services, especially primary care diagnostics and certain hospital facilities, this system relies on private health care suppliers [1,3,4,5].

The Ministry of Health is the first responsible. For planning there are five regions and eighteen sub-regions that are responsible for organization and management of primary care and for co-ordination of the National Health Service (NHS). These district authorities, so called regional Health Boards (ARs), are not responsible for individual hospitals which have their own executive bodies [4].

Primary health care, both curative and preventive care, is provided by NHS health centres staffed by general practitioners, public health officers and nurses [1]. In total 355 health centres and 1,876 extensions or health posts are spread all over the country. GPs have a dominant position in health centres. People have free choice of doctor and GPs have a list of at least 1500 patients. Formally, secondary care is only accessible after referral by a GP, but since people show a strong preference for hospital care, they often use the backdoor of the emergency departments [1,4]. In general, health centres are not equipped for carrying out X-rays and laboratory diagnostics. For these procedures patients are referred to private practices.

Hospital care is mainly provided by public hospitals: only 21.2% of the available beds are situated in private hospitals, in 1992. There are two main

246

categories of hospitals in Portugal [4]. Central hospitals provide all forms of specialist care (including high specialized care), while district general hospitals are limited to the usual specialities and provide both in- and out-patient care. There is no competition between the hospitals because their catchment areas are determined by the state.

Additional to the NHS, there are private initiatives in both ambulatory and hospital care. However, their functioning is rather limited and strongly linked to the NHS. They are subject of the rules and regulations of the NHS and are not allowed to compete with the public sector. Physicians who do not work on a basis of exclusive dedication in the NHS, are free to work in private practice.

Half of the usually smaller private hospitals are for-profit and another half non-profit. The last category belongs to *Misericordias*, a national charity organization that used to have many more hospitals before the introduction of the NHS.

Since the end of the 1980s, a trend can be seen towards changes in the NHS. In 1990, a new basic health law was voted by the parliament introducing deregulation, competition between public and private sector and freedom of choice to the patient [4]. There is also discussion about the privatization of health care services. But it is expected that, in the near future, the state will assume a large share of the financing of health care and that the introduction of market mechanisms, as in other European countries, will develop only very slowly in Portugal.

Health care figures (1990) [2]

Expenditure

Total expenditure on health		
Absolute per head in ppp$	554	
Percentage of GDP	6.7	
Public expenditure on health		
Absolute per head in ppp$	341	
Percentage of GDP	4.1	

Manpower

Physicians per 1000 pop.	2.8	
GPs per 1000 pop.	0.6	
Qualified nurses per 1000 pop.	2.8	('89)

Hospital care

In-patient care		
Beds per 100 pop.	4.6	('89)
Admissions per 1000 pop.	10.8	
Mean length of stay	10.8	
Acute hospitals		
Beds per 100 pop.	3.6	
Admissions per 1000 pop.	10.6	
Mean length of stay	8.4	
Nursing homes		
Beds per 1000 pop.	n.a.	

1.3   Health financing and insurance

The total expenditure on the national health service is nationally determined by the parliament. Health services are almost entirely financed through general tax revenues within the established general public budgets. About 5% of the costs are paid by the patients themselves. Co-payments exists for all ambulatory medical services except for services provided by public hospitals. The level of co-payment depends on the kind of care e.g. prescribed drugs, X-ray and other diagnostic procedures, and medical aids.

Some specific drugs are free and several patients (children under twelve, the elderly, pregnant women, the handicapped, the unemployed with a minimum income and several categories of people with chronic and other diseases) have no co-payments for in-patient and out-patient care.

Parallel to the National Health Insurance there are several smaller sub-systems, e.g. for civil servants and personnel of some large companies [1,5]. Under these schemes patients are reimbursed for health care expenses. Private health insurance is a new phenomenon which is still developing: in 1992, about 3.8% of the population had private health insurance [5].

Health care centres maintain their own budgets which are determined by the district health authorities according to historical costs with adjustments for inflation. In the future, these budgets will be related to output. In 1992, the budgets of health centres counted for 46% of the whole NHS budget.

Until 1989, public hospitals were funded by a global budget depending on the size of the catchment area. Since that time, annual global budgets have been specifically computed and are partly based on the sum total costs of different diagnosis related groups (DRGs). Private hospitals are fully paid through a fee-for-service mechanism.

As mentioned before, health centres make use of the diagnostic services of private providers. For this purpose there are contracts, the so called conventions, between the private providers and the NHS. Pre-established prices are the results of negotiations between the policy makers and the representatives of the providers. In practice, the patient pays the bill and this will later be reimbursed (mostly partially) by the NHS. About 26% of the NHS budget are transferred to the private sector.

In the private practices, the professionals are paid on a fee-for-service basis. Within the NHS, all professionals are civil servants with a fixed salary. There are some proposals for an other kind of remuneration system which will be a combination of salary and fee-for-service.

1.4 Care for the elderly

It is expected that by the year 2000, 15.5% of the Portuguese population will be older than 65. This increasing number of the elderly is a result of the improved life expectancy, low fertility rates and the homecoming of large groups of emigrants [6]. These demographic developments have important implications for the provision of care for the elderly.

Care for the elderly was mainly provided by informal carers, especially in the rural areas. The lack of professional carers forced old people to rely on their family and friends. However, due to migration patterns, the participation of family members, friends and neighbours in informal care is decreasing and they are partly being replaced by volunteers on the one hand and professional home helps on the other hand [6].

Social services for the elderly are provided by the regional social security centres, non-profit private institutions for social solidarity (IPSS) and some private for-profit organizations previously licensed by the regional social security centres. The central government, which is responsible for planning, controlling and financing of the services, recently developed a policy regarding the elderly. Since 1988 the National Commission for Ageing Policy has been established, in which the government and private initiators of home care co-operate. The basic political trend is the organization of small facilities in the own environment of the elderly to enable them to stay in their own homes for as long as possible.

Although services have been expanded and new initiatives have been established, Portugal still has an insufficient supply of services for the elderly [6,7]. One of the main problems is the serious lack of a proper tertiary care in nursing homes [8].

Community services. The community services consist of home help services (discussed later), comprehensive day care centres (*centros de dia*) and 'meeting'-centres. These centres are mostly private non-profit institutions and financially supported by the government. The elderly themselves also pay a contribution. Comprehensive day care centres provide practical help (for instance provision of meals and laundry services), as well as psychosocial support and recreation. Meeting-centres only support the development of socio-recreational and cultural activities of the elderly. In the near future, an expansion of home care services for the elderly is expected.

Residential services. There are two types of formal institutions for the elderly. Firstly, there are special flats built around support services (*Residências para Idosos*) for the elderly who are independent and can take care for themselves and their homes. Secondly, old people's homes (*Lares para Idosos*) are established for temporary or permanent attendance of the people of 65 and over whose social, economic and/or health status does not allow them to continue living in their own environment. These old people's homes are mainly designed for the elderly with physical, social and psychological problems who cannot be supported by other types of services. Some of the old people's homes are for-profit privately owned but the quality is controlled by the government. Basically, except in the for-profit institutions, clients pay a monthly contribution of 70% of their income. However, this individual contribution may not exceed the average costs per client in the particular institution.

In 1986, 1.6% of the population of 65 years and above lived in old people's homes and about 1% in service flats [7]. Most of these elderly people lived alone and had a low income. The old people's homes are mostly large-scale, while the service flats have fewer clients.

Capacity of residential services for the elderly in Portugal (1990) [7]

	Number of places/beds per 1000 people over 65 years
Old people's homes	15.6
Service flats	0.1

2   The organization of home nursing

2.1   Organizations for home nursing

Home nursing services are mainly provided by the 355 health centres and 1,876 'extensions' of these centres. These health centres are part of the NHS and have to guarantee home care, also at the more complicated technical nursing level. The only restrictions are the availability of a sufficient number of professionals and means of transport [5]. As mentioned above, health centres operate under the responsibility of the ARs, the district health authorities or administrations which provide the means and determine the global budget of the health centres.

Governmental regulations indicate that each health centre must employ a sufficient number of nurses to provide nursing care, both in the centre as in the community. A ratio of one nurse for every 1,500 inhabitants is the formal guideline.

Besides the health centres, a few private organizations, mostly charity foundations or sometimes insurance companies, provide home care from their own resources [4]. Furthermore in some main cities, hospitals provide home care. In Lisbon for instance, the *Misericordia de Lisboa* also plays a role in home nursing services. Generally, however, the nurses of the NHS are the main providers and this chapter is therefore mainly focused on their position and functioning.

251

2.2   Manpower in home nursing services

In 1992, 5,931 nurses were working in the health care centres. All of them have a full-time job. On the whole, one nurse serves 1,578 inhabitants which is in accordance with the nationally established norm mentioned above. However, one has to keep in mind that there are large differences in the number of nurses available among the regions. The density of nurses is much higher in the coastal areas compared with the inland: the latter is only poorly supplied [5].

Two types of nurse can be distinguished. After a period of twelve years of general education, registered nurses have had a three year training in nursing schools which are connected to the universities. Special public health nurses have completed this basic nursing training with a special course in public health which lasts for eighteen months. None of the nurses work as independent practitioners in the community as in some other European countries.

2.3   Client population

Because home nursing services are part of the regular tasks of the health centres and they have to be provided within their global budgets, detailed information about the patient population is hardly available. According the Ministry of Health about one and a half million home nursing visits were made in 1993. All patient groups are eligible for home visits by a nurse, however, older people are more often visited than younger people.

2.4   Provision of services

The professionals working in the health centres, both physicians and nurses, decide whether home nursing is necessary in a particular case. It is highly unusual that patients apply for home nursing services themselves. Potential patients have no free choice of home nursing services because they have to be listed in a health centre in their region. As a consequence, no formal referral is required.

The health centre professionals are not involved in the assessment of the possible needs for home help services because these activities belong to another organization which is part of the social security scheme. There are no formal national guidelines or criteria for the provision of home nursing services. Therefore, no standardized assessment forms are developed. The assessment of needs and the decisions about the type of care a patient is going to receive and during what period of time are made entirely by the professionals in each health centre separately. In the case of (chronic) illness this is mostly done by the general practitioner; nurses mostly decide about home visits regarding health promotion and preventive activities.

The nurses do not work in specific home care teams. In the community they all work alone, although they operate daily from their health centres.

The tasks and activities provided by registered and public health nurses in home care do not differ substantially. These tasks are strictly limited to technical nursing procedures, patient/health education, psychosocial care, and the support and stimulation of help from informal carers such as family members and neighbours. The technical nursing activities performed in home care are mostly the simple routine interventions like injections, dressings, stoma care, and bladder washout. More complicated or intensive nursing care, like epidural anaesthesia, handling respirator, and catheterization are not performed at home. Patients with severe conditions which require this kind of care have to be admitted to the hospital. In a very small number of cases hospital nurses perform this kind of technical nursing procedure in the community, but this is very uncommon. Furthermore, nurses are not involved in more 'care oriented' tasks. Personal care (helping with activities of daily living: bathing, dressing, helping with lavatory) and domestic care are not part of the nurse's responsibility.

2.5 Problems and recent developments

Discussions about waiting lists are not relevant in the Portuguese system. The health centres are both purchasers of and suppliers of home nursing care. Decisions about the patient's needs and the necessity of home care are always made in the context of the available staff. It is, however, mentioned that the available nursing staff in health centres is not sufficient. Two main reasons are pointed out. Firstly, there is a general shortage of nurses because the nursing schools can train only a very limited number of new nurses each year. Secondly, the payment in hospitals is better than in health centres. So, most of the new nurses will apply for jobs in the hospitals.

There are no concrete plans to change the organization of home nursing activities in the near future. The implementation of home nursing care in the health centres is considered as a efficient solution within the national health service.

Furthermore, there is a tendency for the authorities to focus on the improvement of the quality of home care and extension of the range of nursing interventions that can be provided at home. It is intended that more dependent patients be cared for in the community, reducing hospital care. However, concrete policy measures have not yet developed.

3   The organization of home help services

3.1   *Organizations for home help services*

Care for the elderly and handicapped is mainly provided informally in the context of the family, especially in the rural regions of Portugal. Informal networks are highly developed: about two thirds of the population are involved in the care of the elderly [7]. Professional home help services are provided by public as well as private organizations.

Since 1975, the local authorities have developed professional home help services [9]. These community services are mostly limited to domestic help (*ajuda domiciliaria*).

The public organizations are part of the social services which means that the central government, in particular the State Secretary for Social Security, is mainly responsible at the national level. This State Secretary is part of the Ministry of Employment and Social Security and integrates services organized at three main levels:

- At the national level, the General Directorate for Social Action (*Direcçao-Geral da acçao social*) is a central department in charge of the development, co-ordination, legal framework and the provision of technical support in the total field of social action including home help services.
- The 23 regional social security centres (*Serviço (Sub)-regional de Seguranca Social*) pay benefits and provide social services for children, handicapped and elderly people and for families in less favoured circumstances. They also promote social and community integration and work together with the local authorities (which also provide some social services) and departments in other community areas such as health care, education, housing and employment.
- The local services, supervised by the regional centres, are mainly

254

responsible for attending and informing clients and providing the actual home help services.

The state has been promoting the establishment and development of private organizations for home help services, the so called IPSS (non-profit private social solidarity institutions). They are organized and administered by volunteers and supported by the official social security departments through agreements for technical and financial support. There are 2,465 institutions that provided services for the elderly which can include home help services. One of the biggest are the *Misericórdias* which were discussed earlier.

Furthermore, there is a rapidly increasing number of for-profit organizations in the field of the social services.

3.2   Manpower in home help services

The regional social security centres and the non-profit private organizations for social solidarity employ social workers, nurses and personnel trained for home helping tasks.

There is very little information available about the number of the home helps (*Ajundantés Familiares*). The number of inhabitants per home helps is considered to be very high compared to other European countries.

After primary education the home helps receive a limited specific training which can last from three weeks to three months. This training includes for example information about the ageing process, both the psychosocial and physical development, and practical skills for the daily help and support in the field of personal hygiene and housekeeping.

3.3   Client population

Data available indicate that approximate 16,000 clients receive home help services during one year. It is estimated that about 1.3% of the total Portuguese population received home help services during 1993. The great majority of clients are over 65 years of age.

3.4   Provision of services

Home help services are accessible for all inhabitants, no official referral is required. However, the number of available services is far from sufficient to meet all demands. The clients or their family often contact the organization themselves when they are in need of home help. Besides, professionals in hospitals or social workers often make the first arrangements between the clients and organizations.

The social worker, employed by the home help organizations, first contacts the potential clients and decides whether help is actually needed. She also decides the amount, type and duration of the professional home help the client is going to receive. There are no national standardized assessment forms that can be used to assess the needs for home help. However, within each organization particular forms can be used. The social worker is also responsible for the evaluation of the care that is provided.

The actual home help is provided by the home helps who operate from old people's homes, and day centres. All the home helps, both those of the public as of the private organizations, work in a team which also consists of the social worker, and sometimes a nurse and a physician.

The tasks of the home helps are mostly restricted to domestic help and personal care. All kinds of homemaking activities (e.g. preparing meals, washing dishes, washing, ironing, and cleaning) and general family support such as going for a walk, accompanying the client to the doctor, writing letters, are performed. They are not allowed to provide any medical or nursing activity.

3.5 Problems and recent developments

Most of the organizations that provide home help services have large waiting lists, especially in rural areas and ancient urban areas with many aged in the population. The main reason for these waiting lists is that the number of home helps is far from sufficient to meet all the needs in the population. The governmental policy focuses therefore on an extension of the home help services and the increase of the number of professional helps. The government wants this increase of home helps in private non-profit organizations like the *Misericordias* and not in the public organizations. It is however difficult to induce the private organization to create more services and to recruit home helps because of their low professional status. Accordingly, the governmental measures focus on the extension of subsidies to the private organizations, the training of more home helps and the improvement of their professional status.

Furthermore, some problems are reported about co-operation between home help services on the one hand and other professional care-providers on the other (such as GPs and hospitals). This is caused by the strict distinction between health services and social services.

4 Relations between home nursing and home help services

As mentioned before, a large amount of home care is performed by informal carers, both network members (family, friends, neighbours) and volunteers. The provision of professional home care is divided into two separate organizational structures: the NHS for home nursing care and the social service system and the private institutions of social solidarity for home help services. However, in some districts developments are taking place on more intensive co-operation between the two disciplines, for instance in the city of Lisbon where the *Misericordias da Lisboa* provides both aspects of home care.

Both disciplines in home care have different tasks to perform. Home help services are more developed and spread over the country than home nursing care. So, in only a few situations does the client have the option of both services at the same time.

5 The financing of home nursing services

5.1 Payment and patients' insurance

All inhabitants of Portugal are covered by the national health services. Home nursing care is free, co-payments are not required. As already mentioned, decisions about the need and provision of home care are made entirely by the professionals in the health centres. There are no formal criteria or national regulations about the amount or duration of the care.

5.2 Funding of the organizations

The funding of the health centres is part of the total state budget and therefore financed through the general tax revenues. The actual budget of each health centres is determined by the district health authorities according to historical costs with adjustments for inflation. There are no special funds for the development or improvement of home nursing activities.

5.3   Payment of the nurses

All nurses are employed by the National Health Service. They receive a fixed salary, regardless the services provided. So, nurses are paid for their total work which can include home care. In 1993, the average gross income of registered nurses was PTE 187,900 per month, public health nurse are paid a higher salary, that is PTE 205,400.

5.4   Problems and recent developments

Two minor problems were mentioned. Firstly, the wages of hospital nurses are higher than those of nurses working in health centres. Secondly, nurses are not separately paid for providing home care. But, home visits reflect a higher workload than the regular work in the health centre.

6   The financing of home help services

6.1   Payment and clients' insurance

The public services are part of the system of social services. Social services are financed by the state budget, especially within the social security budget. However, the provided care is not free of charge, co-payments by the clients are required. The percentage of the total costs of the services which clients have to pay themselves is based on the level of their income. There are no formal regulations with regard to the type and duration of the home care. But, due to the limited number of services that are available in the country, the clients can not have them for a unlimited period of time. It is the own decision of the social worker to determine the duration. Her/his decision will of course be based on the available manpower in the organization. In this decision she/he also takes the severity of the needs of the clients into account. Generally, dependent people receive help more hours a day than other clients.

Nowadays, the private insurance companies start to work in their area, but this is only weakly developed.

6.2   Funding of organizations

The budgets of the organizations, both public as well as private non-profit organizations, consists of governmental subsidies and co-payments by the clients. The Ministry of Employment and Social Security provides a financial contribution. The budget of each organization is based on the number of clients and the types of services delivered.

The private non-profit organizations for social solidarity (IPSS) have to meet certain functional and organizational criteria to become financed by the government. To be recognized as IPSS, they have to pursue specific objectives in the field of social action in order to be registered by the General Directorate for Social Action.

6.3   Payment of the home helps

All professional home helps are employed by the public and private non-profit organizations. They are payed a fixed salary a month. The latter have special regulations regarding payment levels which are lower than those of the public organizations.

One of the ways of promoting volunteer participation in the field of social action is to enable volunteers to enrol themselves in the so called voluntary social insurance scheme. A special branch of this scheme is meant for persons working in IPSS without monthly payment. They are entitled to old age or invalidity pensions.

6.4   Problems and recent developments

No specific problems are reported concerning the reimbursement system of home help organizations or the salary of home help aides.

Acknowledgement
The information about home nursing services was provided by Dra Helena Pontes Carreira, Ministry of Health, Department of research and planning, Lisbon. Dra Maria Joaquina Madeira of the General Directorate for Social Action, Lisbon completed the questionnaire on home help services.

References

1   BOERMA, W.G.W., F.A.J.M. DE JONG, P.H. MULDER. Health care and general practice across Europe. Utrecht: NIVEL, 1993.

2   OECD HEALTH DATA. Version # 1.5. Paris: OECD, 1993.

3   CORREIA DE CAMPOS, A., J.M. CALDEIRA DA SILVA, C. COSTA. Market elements and new developments for competition in the health care system in Portugal. In: Casparie, A.F., H.E.G.M. Hermans, J.H.P. Paelinck. Competitive health care in Europe: future prospects. Aldershot: Dartmouth, 1990.

4   KEMENADE, Y.W. VAN. Health care in Europe. The finance and reimbursement systems of 18 European countries. Zoetermeer: Nationale Raad voor de Volksgezondheid, 1993.

5   SCHNEIDER, M., RK-H. DENNERLEIN, A. KÖSE, L. SCHOLTES. Health care in the EC member states. Health Policy Special Issue. Health Policy; 1992, 1+2, 113-123.

6   PACOLET, J., C. WILDEROM. (eds). The economics of care of the elderly. Aldershot: Avebury, 1991.

7   NIJKAMP, P., J. PACOLET, H. SPINNEWYN, A. VOLLERING, C. WILDEROM, S. WINTERS. Services for the elderly in Europe. A cross-national comparative study. Leuven/Amsterdam: HIV/VU, 1991.

8   CALDEIRA DA SILVA, J.M. Aspects of the health-care system in Portugal. Acta Hospitalia; 1991, 1 (special issue), 95-102.

9   NAZARETH, J.M. Portugal. In: Nijkamp, P. et al. Proceedings of a seminar on national diversity and european trends in services for the elderly. Leuven: HIVA, 1991.

13 Home care in Spain

Diana M.J. Delnoij

1   The setting of home care

1.1   The country

Of the two countries that form the Iberian peninsula, Spain is the largest.
Compared with the rest of Europe, Spain is a vast, mountainous, low-density
country, with a relatively young population [1]. It has been a parliamentary
monarchy since 1978, with two chambers of parliament (the *Cortes*) elected
every four years. Spain is a semi-federal state, consisting of seventeen
communities that enjoy a considerable amount of autonomy. Yet, the state is
still centralist-oriented and the health system is no exception to that rule [1].

Until the 1960s, Spain had little developed industry except in Catalonia, the
Basque country and the Madrid environs. Since then, however, industry
(including tourism) has developed rapidly and between 1960 and 1980 Spain
was one of the fastest growing economies in the industrialized world. Despite
EU-membership in 1986, economic growth has slowed down, resulting in
quite high unemployment rates [2,3].

Diana M.J. Delnoij

Population key figures (1990) [3,4]

Population in mln.	39.4
Inhabitants per sq. km.	78
% Living in urban areas	78
% over 65 years	13.7
% over 75 years	5.6
Births per 1000	9.9
Deaths per 1000	8.7
Life expectancy (men)	74
Life expectancy (women)	80

1.2   The organization of health care

The main body in Spanish health care is the Ministry of Health and Consumer Affairs, which is in charge of defining the national health policy. Since 1986, when the General Health Law (*Ley General de Sanidad*) passed parliament, Spain has been in a process of establishing a National Health Service (*Sistema Nacional de la Salud*). The NHS is run within the social security system. Three institutes operate the social security system:
- The National Institute of Social Security (INSS), responsible for financial services (e.g. supplementary benefit, support grants, pensions).
- The National Institute of Social Services (INSERSO), in charge of social services ancillary to those of the social security (e.g. home help services, and other services for the disabled, the aged).
- The National Institute of Health (INSALUD) [2,5], in charge of running the social security health services.

The aim is that finally each of Spain's seventeen Autonomous Communities will be responsible for managing its own health service [5]. As yet, health competences have been completely transferred to the so-called 'historic communities': the Basque Country, Catalonia, Andalucia, Galicia, Pais Valenciano, and the Balearic islands. These communities now control 35% of all non pension Government spending [5]. In the rest of the country, the NHS is operated through INSALUD.

The 1986 General Health Law further decrees that within the Autonomous Communities, health services are planned around geographical units: the so-called Health Areas, catering for a population somewhere between 200,000 and 250,000. Finally, each Health Area is subdivided into Basic Health Zones: territorial units for primary health care, in which the health centres are to operate. In health centres, staff should be grouped in cross-disciplinary medical teams, denominated primary health care teams [5].

In parts of the country where health care is provided through INSALUD, public establishments are run by INSALUD itself, or INSALUD has contracted private physicians and non-profit hospitals [3]. Ambulatory physician services are usually provided in INSALUD practices, the so-called *consultorios* or *ambulatorios*, in which a minimum staff of a GP, a nurse and a paediatrician is employed. Many *ambulatorios* also employ specialists without hospital privileges [6].

The provision of primary health care is changing from an old pattern, in which GPs would work in clinics for two hours a day, to the new system of above mentioned primary health care teams. In these teams, GPs and nurses provide care for six hours a day [7].

GPs working in the new primary health care teams are usually salaried, GPs in the traditional *ambulatorios* are paid by capitation, based on the number of 'insurance'-cards held. The average number of cards held by GPs varies from 700 to 1,300. However, insurance coverage extends to financially dependent spouses, children under 26, brothers and sisters under 18, close relatives in an ascendant line and their spouses, and exceptionally people adopted into the family [2]. As a result, as many as five or more members of a household or family may be 'attached' to one insurance card, so that the real population at risk per GP may well vary from 1,300 to 3,500 for the same income and nominal list [6].

In order to visit a specialist, a referral by a GP or paediatrician is required. In the *ambulatorios* a complex three-tier referral system exists: the specialists without hospital privileges, who work in the health centres, for the first line of referral for GPs. If patients should be seen by a hospital-based physician, they are referred a second time by the ambulatory care specialist [6]. Hospital treatment is frequently possible only after a waiting period; in Madrid [8] and other big cities waiting time can exceed one year. INSALUD runs 147 of its own hospitals that together account for a third of total bed capacity in Spain. These hospitals are funded by means of global budgets by local health authorities or provinces. Doctors working in hospitals are usually paid a fixed salary [2].

Diana M.J. Delnoij

Health care figures (1990) [4]

Expenditure
Total expenditure on health
  Absolute per head in ppp$ 774
  Percentage of GDP   6.6
Public expenditure on health
  Absolute per head in ppp$ 623
  Percentage of GDP   5.3

Manpower
Physicians per 1000 pop.   3.8
GPs per 1000 pop.   n.a
Qualified nurses per 1000 pop.   4.1

Hospital care
In-patient care
  Beds per 1000 pop.   4.3   ('89)
  Admissions per 100 pop.   9.8   ('89)
  Mean length of stay   12.2   ('89)
Acute hospitals
  Beds per 1000 pop.   3.5   ('89)
  Admissions per 100 pop.   9.6   ('89)
  Mean length of stay   9.6   ('89)
Nursing homes
  Beds per 1000 pop.   1.0   ('88)

1.3   Health financing and insurance

Spanish health insurance originated in a more comprehensive social security which was created in 1942 to cover, among other things, health care expenses of workers earning an income below a certain level. Since then its coverage has been increased up to 99% of the population.

The NHS, therefore, practically covers the whole Spanish population with the exception of certain self-employed persons and the majority of civil servants, who are members of special private health insurance schemes. In 1989, some 24% of the total population had taken out additional private health insurance, covering the costs of private ambulatory and hospital care [9]. The percentage of people with private insurance differs across regions; it is the highest in Catalonia [2]. Private insurance companies are free to fix prices and premiums, which are risk-based and individual.

As a NHS, the Spanish health care system is now largely financed through general taxation (approximately 80%). The percentage of funding from general taxation has gradually increased and as the NHS further evolves, the share of public funding will become even greater [10]. Specific social security contributions still amount to about 20% of total revenue [3]. These premiums are paid as a percentage of the income and they are divided between employer and employee.

Benefits under the NHS include outpatient treatment, hospital care, provision of drugs, ambulance services, and dental extractions [2]. Ambulatory medical services and care provided in public hospitals are free of charges to the consumer. For drugs a co-insurance rate of 40% is in effect (except for pensioners).

1.4   Care for the elderly

In Spain, the old age pensions are low, but to a certain extent they are compensated by other benefits, such as free travel, old age pensioners holidays during the low season (October to May), low price meals, and subsidized home care [11]. Pensioners, the disabled and the mentally ill are entitled to free home care [2]. The policy with regard to the elderly is determined at three levels in Spain: (1) the national government gives an outline by means of their social security policy; (2) regional programmes contain community integration programmes, rural environment programmes and mental health programmes; and (3), at the local level policy concerning the elderly is mainly developed in big cities [11]. Currently, town councils are the driving force behind the development of domestic services for the elderly as an alternative to institutionalisation [12].

Because of Spain's relatively young population, care for the elderly became a policy issue later than in most European countries. In 1973, a new social security law was passed, based on an ambitious plan to build old people's homes [13]. Currently, however, the emphasis is on increasing community services for the elderly. The main problem in the care for the elderly is how to co-ordinate the different policies (developing community services and at the same time increase the capacity of old people's homes). Striving for co-ordination, the Ministry of Social Affairs has launched the so-called gerontological plan, in which it is outlined that in the year 2000 the total number of residential places should double, unless a growth of community services enables a less dramatic growth [12].

Residential services. As a result of the development of old people's homes (*residencias de tercera edad*), the institutionalization of the population over 65 has increased. Partly due to a shortage of residential places, however, the vast majority of the elderly (98% in 1985) do not use residential services. Yet more than 40% of people over 65 are partially or totally handicapped [11] and hence in need of some type of home care.

Community services. Though professional help is becoming increasingly important in the Spanish care for the elderly, still the family is the main carer for the elderly. As far as professional help is concerned, the two most common community services for the elderly are clubs (*hogares*) and the home help system (*ayuda a domicilio*). The former are very popular day centres with recreational, medical and integration facilities of which there were some 1,800 in 1988. The latter, the home help system, is in many aspects new in Spain. Home help services are provided mainly in big cities and they are mostly organized by public authorities.

Capacity of residential services for the elderly in Spain (1985) [11]

	Number of places/beds per 1000 people over 65 years
Old people's homes	19

2 The organization of home nursing

2.1 Organizations for home nursing

Home nursing is provided within the Spanish primary health care system, which now covers approximately 65% of the total Spanish population. The organizational structure of home nursing is thus similar to the organizational structure of the total health care system:

National level:	INSALUD, six historic communities (the Basque Country, Catalonia, Andalucia, Galicia, Pais Valenciano, Balearic islands)
Regional level:	Health Areas (covering a population of 200,000-250,000)
Local level:	Basic Health Zones, in which health centres operate that employ primary health care teams (GPs, nurses, social workers).

Different programmes for home nursing may coexist within the Autonomous Communities. For example, in Catalonia home nursing is delivered by the *Programa de Atención Domiciliària, Equipos de Soporto (PADES)* and by the primary health care teams, the so-called *Equipos de Atención Primaria (EAP)*. In general, in the Autonomous Communities home nursing is provided by the primary health care teams (EAP) and by home nursing organizations (APD/Zona).

2.2   Manpower in home nursing

In Spain, all nurses receive a three-year in-service training at a university, resulting in a bachelor's degree. There is no specialty training for nurses in primary care, therefore the difference between primary care nurses and hospital nurses is not well defined.

In December 1993, some 17,500 nurses worked in primary care, devoting approximately 0.9% of their total activities to home care. The number of inhabitants per full-time nurse varies greatly, from about 300 to about 2,200. In Catalonia, the estimated average is 1,750 inhabitants per nurse, in the Basque Country the average is somewhat higher: about 2,000 inhabitants per nurse. Nurses do not work in independent practices as they are employed by the government.

2.3   Client population

Official figures on the number of clients of home nursing are not available. According to estimations, about 8% of the national population received some kind of home nursing in 1993. Figures on the age-sex distribution of home nursing clients are not available for the whole country. In the Basque Country all in all 354,974 home visits were made for a total population of 1,093,712. The majority of visited clients were over 50 years old. In the Area of Zaragoza (region of Aragón), a predominantly rural area, nurses realized 107,957 home visits in 1993. According to official data, in Zaragoza about 35% of the total population used some form of home nursing care in 1993.

2.4   Provision of services

In general, clients do not have free choice as to which home nursing organization they approach. Though in different parts of the country,

Diana M.J. Delnoij

different programmes can exist for home nursing, in the end all programmes form a part of the governmental organization. However, sometimes patients can turn to private home nursing organizations.

Contact between a primary care nurse and a patient is usually initiated by a GP or by the patient himself or his family. Contact can also be initiated by the home help service or the hospital.

Normally, patients have free access to home nursing services. No referral is needed, but patients need a specific document, which is signed by a physician, in order to receive special assistance or drug administration.

In order to assess a patient's need for nursing care, standardized assessment forms are used. Assessment takes place during a first visit (a so-called *Visita domiciliaria de valoración*). The assessment procedure is described, for example, for the *Programa d'Atenció Domiciliàra (PAD)* and for the home nursing provided by the primary health care teams (EAP) that co-exists in Catalonia. During a first visit to a patient, a doctor and his/her nurse determine the course of treatment: the frequency of home visits to the patient, the type of therapy and other specific procedures provided, and the treatment goals. The team also evaluates the need to contact the social work department. In order to assess the needs of the patient, standardized control and evaluation forms are used (*ficha de control y evaluación*) that include information on, e.g. patient's morbidity and handicaps (degree of autonomy in activities of daily living), informal care provided to the patient, patient's economic situation, living conditions and so on [14]. The primary health care teams (EAP) in Catalonia use similar criteria in assessing patients' needs: degree of autonomy in carrying out activities of daily living, mental health status, health problems, basic needs of the patient and his/her family, social support, living conditions, and individual characteristics of the patient [15]. In other parts of the country, similar protocols are used in assessing patients' needs. In the region of influence of INSALUD, assessment is carried out by members of the multidisciplinary team consisting of a physician, a nurse and a social worker. Attention is given to both medical, as well as functional and psychosocial problems of a patient. The nurse also pays attention to patients' needs as regards nutrition, hygiene, cognitive behaviour, stress, activities, mobility and so on [16].

In general, the same person/team who does the assessment also decides what type of nursing care the patient is going to receive and during what period of time. Care is then provided by primary care nurses operating from a health centre. Primary care nurses always work in team together with GPs and social workers. Sometimes home helps work with them as well.

Because of their university training, (primary care) nurses are qualified to perform all of the following tasks:
- assessment of the need for care;
- hygiene and other personal care (e.g. bathing, help with lavatory, help with activities of daily living);
- routine technical nursing procedures (such as injections, dressings, stoma care, bladder washout);
- more complicated technical nursing (e.g. epidural anaesthesia, handling respirator, catheterization);
- patient education;
- psychosocial activities;
- encouraging help, e.g. from family members, neighbours, friends etc.;
- home help care (e.g. preparing food and drinks, washing clothes, dishes, shopping etc);
- evaluation of care.

In home care, of course, not all of these tasks are regularly performed by nurses. In Catalonia, for example, hygiene and other personal care, psychosocial activities, home help care and complicated technical nursing procedures do not take place in home nursing care. Elsewhere too, home help care is not provided by nurses working for INSALUD: this is the responsibility of the social services represented by INSERSO and municipalities, and certain private organizations. In the Basque country too, home help is not provided by nurses: this is the domain of home help organizations of the *Bienestar Social*. In general, complicated technical nursing procedures are not carried out in home nursing care either.

2.5   Problems and recent developments

There are no waiting lists for home nursing in Spain, nor is there a shortage of nurses working in home care. The Catalonian Ministry of Health, however, indicates that the primary health care teams providing home care have as yet only been introduced in about 50% of Catalonia, and that the nurses working in the teams devote little time to nursing patients at home. The main objective of INSALUD for 1994 is to increase the provision of home care services so that this type of assistance may cover 15% of the population over

65 years of age.

Problems in the co-operation between home nurses and other professional care-providers exist mainly in the relation with hospitals, but problems of co-ordination sometimes also occur in the relation with GPs (Basque country) or home helps (Basque Country, Catalonia, region of influence of INSALUD). The communication between hospitals and primary health care centres could be improved. Therefore, programmes and protocols are being developed, e.g. for patients who are discharged from public hospitals and who need home care. The co-operation between hospitals and the primary health care teams will continue to be the focus of attention in Spain. Since April 1994, for example, public hospitals in the region provide primary health care teams with a list of discharged patients, who are then contacted by a nurse in order to make an appointment for a home visit. In the Basque country, too, several programmes are developed and implemented in order to improve the co-ordination within the public health sector and between the health sector and social services. For example, a programme is being implemented in order to ensure continuity of care between hospitals and primary care. Both in the Basque Country as well as in Catalonia, 'framework programmes' for home care are developed: the *Programa marco de atencion domiciliaria* (Basque Country) and the *Programa marc d'atenció a domicili - ATDOM -* (Catalonia). The general trend in home care and home help services is towards *visita domiciliaria* (home visits) and *cuidados paliativos* (palliative treatment). Many educational programmes are directed to these kind of activities, and efforts are being made to develop these aspects.

3   The organization of home help services

3.1   Organizations for home help services

Home help services are part of the social services in Spain. Two types of organization can be distinguished:
1 Intermediary governmental organizations:
   - On the national level the Ministry of Social Affairs, working through INSERSO.
     INSERSO, as a central organization on the national level, conducts necessary studies, co-operates with local authorities and on occasion with private organizations for the provision of home help services,

provides additional home help services in some provinces, processes individual complaints and monitors the activities of the providing organizations, especially in case they do not employ qualified personnel.
- On the regional level Autonomous Communities operating through the Councils of Social Wellbeing (*Consejerías de Bienestar Social*). Of the seventeen Autonomous Communities, ten still fall under the influence of INSERSO: Aragon, Asturias, the Balearic islands, Cantabria, Castilla-La Mancha, Castilla y Leon, Extremadura, La Rioja, Madrid, and Murcia. These Autonomous Communities, in their role of financing organizations, frequently collaborate with the local authorities.
- On the local level 858 municipalities and communities (the *Ayuntamientos, Mancomunidades* and *Diputaciones*). Local authorities contract providers of home help services. Small municipalities contract individual home helps, whereas larger municipalities delegate the provision of services to private organizations.
2 Providing organizations (generally of a private nature), that are contracted by municipal authorities for the direct provision of home help services to beneficiaries. In some cases, home help is provided directly by employees of the governmental organizations.

3.2   Manpower in home help services

Two types of professionals work in home help services: social workers and home helps. Social workers have a three-year university training and hold a bachelor's degree. In order to be a home help only primary education is required.

Data on manpower are available for the area of influence of INSERSO (*Zona de influencia del INSERSO*). This area includes the ten Autonomous Communities listed above. In this area, about 750 social workers (562 FTEs) are involved in the provision of home help services. This adds to an average of one social worker per 26,986 inhabitants. Apart from that, an estimated number of 6,000 home helps (3,000 FTEs) contribute to the provision of services, which constitutes an estimated average of 5,055 inhabitants per home help.

3.3   Client population

In the ten Autonomous Communities that fall under the influence of INSERSO, 0.18% of the population (27,228 beneficiaries) received official home help services in 1993. Of these beneficiaries in 1993, 61% were male, 39% were female. The majority (63.7%) were over 75 years old, 26.3% were between 65 and 74 years old, and the remaining 9.9% were younger than 65.

In Bizkaia (a region in the Basque Country), 3.2% of citizens over 64 received home help services in 1993. As in the rest of Spain, the majority of clients are over 65 in the Basque Country: in the region of Gipuzkoa 2,771 clients received home help services, 2,329 (84%) of whom were over 65. In the region of Alava too, 84% of the clients were 65; 66% were over 75; 65.8% were female; 17.2% lived alone; 22.2% lived with a spouse only; 23.9% lived with a spouse and others; and 36.7% lived with others.

3.4   Provision of services

The actual provision of services takes place on the local level. Potential patients do not have free choice as to which home help organization they can turn to, since there is only one home help organization in each municipality. In general, about 90% of the patients contact the home help organization themselves; in 10% of the cases, the first contact is initiated by other professional care-providers, such as social workers. These figures are estimations. No referral is needed: patients have free access to home help services.

The assessment of a patient's needs is done by the social worker of the area. In the area of influence of INSERSO, a standardized form is used to assess the need for home help services. Standardized forms are used also in Autonomous Communities such as the Basque Country. The INSERSO form consists of four chapters. A patient's need is expressed in points. For example, for activities of daily living the social worker can rate a patient from completely dependent on others (5 points per activity) to completely self-reliant (0 points). The four chapters on the form are:
- a client's self-reliance in activities of daily living (10 items: maximally 50 points)
- a client's social and family situation (maximally 30 points)
- a client's financial situation relative to the minimum wage (maximally 40 points)

- other factors (including mental and physical health status, maximally 20 points).

Basque assessment forms too take into account patients' social, physical, psychological, and economic situation, though the exact lay-out of forms may differ across regions.

On the basis of the number of points a patient has been assigned on the items concerning daily living, and social and family situation, the number of hours is determined that home help services are provided. Patients with over 30 points on 'dependency in activities of daily living' and 25 or more points on 'social and family situation' receive a maximum of 52 hours of home help services a month. Patients with 20 points or less on 'dependency in activities of daily living' and ten points or less on 'social and family situation' receive a maximum of 20 hours (and a minimum of twelve hours) of home help services a month.

In Spain, home helps operate from a home help services building, and all home helps working for official organizations, work in teams co-ordinated by a social worker. From the Basque Country, however, it was reported that in some small municipalities (where only one or two social workers are employed) home helps work more or less on a solo-basis. Teams do not include health care professionals.

Apart from co-ordination of the teams, *social workers* take care of the following tasks:
- assessment of the need for care;
- moral support, e.g. in the form of counselling and advice;
- encouraging help from family members, neighbours, friends etc., and
- evaluation of care.

Home helps provide the actual home help services, such as:
- delivery of meals
- cleaning services
- homemaking activities (e.g. preparing meals, washing dishes, washing, ironing etc.)
- hygiene and other personal care (e.g. bathing, help with lavatory and activities of daily living)
- general and family support (e.g. shopping, administrative support).

3.5   Problems and recent developments

Due to budgetary limitations, the main problem of home help organizations is the existence of waiting lists. Practically all organizations for home help services have waiting lists, though there are no data on how many weeks clients have to wait. Attempts to reduce the waiting lists consists of:
- an increased financial effort on behalf of the public administration and the users of home help services;
- better management of home help services, in order to maximize agility.

A second problem is the shortage of home helps mainly in rural areas. This shortage is caused by a general trend of young people migrating from rural to urban areas, a lower cultural level in rural areas, and the relatively low professional status of the occupation of home help.

An important future development is the planned delegation of INSERSO's authority to the remaining ten Autonomous Communities that fall under the jurisdiction of the central institute. This decentralisation is scheduled for 1995. Autonomous Communities will gain legislative and executive power in the field of social services such as home help.

4   Relations between home nursing and home help services

In most of Spain, home nursing and home help services are provided by separate organizations. Home nursing belongs to the health care sector provided by INSALUD or the Autonomous Communities, home help is part of the social services provided by INSERSO or Municipal Councils (the *Ayuntamientos*). In the Autonomous Communities of Catalonia and the Basque Country, there are few contacts and little co-operation between the two types of services. In the Basque Country, home nurses and social workers discuss the situation of specific patients, but this does not take place on a regular or formal basis.

In general, a link between home nursing and home help services is offered by the activities of social workers, e.g. in primary health care teams. The co-operation that does exist, depends on good personal relationships between workers in health care and home help services.

Collaboration between the two types of services is being initiated on an experimental basis. In some regions, there are integrated home care organizations providing both home nursing and home help services. This is the case, for example, in Asturias. There, home nurses and home helps take part in the same team. In the integrated teams, nurses and home helps discuss mutual patients during regular meetings.

5 The financing of home nursing

5.1 Payment and patients' insurance

The financing of home nursing is part of the Spanish National Health Service, therefore, practically the whole Spanish population is covered for the costs of nursing care at home. There are no co-payments and patients have free access to the service. The National Health Service is financed for about 80% out of general taxation. Private insurance for home nursing does not exist.

5.2 Funding of the organizations

Funds for home nursing are included in funds allocated to primary health care by either INSALUD or the Autonomous Communities. There is no separate budget for the provision of home nursing care.

5.3 Payment of the nurses

Nurses are employed by the government and receive their salaries from public administration. Their salaries are based on the number of inhabitants that their primary health care team works for, and the population density and dispersion. They may also receive incentives depending on patient's location, night care etc. On average a nurse earns about ESP 122,000. Including incentives and extras bases on population parameters, their salary may add to some ESP 230,000.

5.4 Problems and recent developments

A specific problem which was mentioned for the region of Zaragoza, but which may well exist in other regions, is that the nurses payment within a team does not differ according to the age of the population cared for. This also leads to marked differences in the payment of nurses and physicians (who do receive payment differentiated according to patient's age). The solution to this problem has been to individualize the payment of nurses and to introduce financial incentives.

6 The financing of home help services

6.1 Payment and clients insurance

As a part of the social services in Spain, the costs of home help services are covered by public insurance. There is one scheme for all inhabitants. Private insurance for home help services does not exist.

Normally, clients have to make an income-related contribution to the costs of home help services. Municipalities use a progressive scale in order to determine income-related co-payments. Outside the zone of influence of INSERSO, a client's income is also an important determinant of out-of-pocket payment. E.g. in Bizkaia (Basque Country), out-of-pocket payments depend on a client's income, the total hours of help received during a certain period of time, the number of household members that have received help. The minimum contribution for clients is ESP 265 per month.

There is a ceiling to the amount of care that clients are entitled to. The maximum is two hours per day up to 52 hours per month. The amount of care that a client receives is determined on the basis of his/her needs (compare section 3.4). The criteria established for allocating home help services to clients are less strict in special circumstances. For a limited period of time, patients in specific circumstances may receive more care than would be assigned to them strictly on the basis of the criteria, provided that the maximum of 52 hours per month is not exceeded.

6.2 Funding of the organizations

In the zone of influence of INSERSO, home help organizations are 90% funded by social welfare administrations. The remaining 10% are financed by clients' out-of-pocket payments. In the Basque Country, these percentages differ from one region to another: e.g. in Gipuzkoa clients' out-of-pocket payments amount to only 5% of the total budget, in Bizkaia to about 7%, and in Alava to 10-27%.

Under INSERSO, the budget allocated to home help organizations is based on the number of hours of care delivered. Outside the zone of influence of

INSERSO other arrangements may be in effect: e.g. in based in the number of inhabitants over 65 (a method used in some areas in the Basque Country).

In general, home help services are provided by non-profit organizations. However, a small percentage of the organizations (estimated at about 2%) works for-profit.

6.3 Payment of the home helps

Two types of professionals work in the provision of home help services. Social workers are salaried employees. Their average monthly income is about ESP 160,000. Home helps are paid according to a mix of a salary and a fee for every hour worked. Their average monthly salary is estimated to be ESP 80,000. A home help's salary, as well as the profession's social status, is low because 'home help' is no officially recognized profession for which special qualifications are required.

6.4 Problems and recent developments

In the near future, INSERSO's authority in the field of home help services will be delegated to the remaining ten Autonomous Communities that fall under the jurisdiction of the central institute (compare section 3.5). In the near future, the central funds available for home help service (about ESP 4,500 million) will also be handed over to the Autonomous Communities.

Acknowledgement
The information presented in this chapter was provided by the following persons and institutions:
Teresa Moreno Casbas, Ministerio de Sanidad y Consumo, Subdireccion General de Difusion de la Investigación y Formación, Madrid - co-ordination team
Neus Maymon Pijuan, Coordinadora del Programa de Atencion Domiciliaria de l'ABS centre Hospitalet de Llobregat, Barcelona
Carmen Lacasa Plana, Servicio Catalan de Salud, Barcelona
Mª Concepción Martin Arribas, Subdirectora de Enfermería Area 5, Madrid
Carmen Granda Menedez, Subdirectora de Enfermería Area 11, Madrid
Mariangeles Custey Male, Directora de Enfermería Area 2, Madrid
Isabel Garcia Mejido, Servicio Vasco de Salud

Diana M.J. Delnoij

Ina Jordan Gil, Dirección de Atención Primaria Area 7, Zaragoza
Jose Luis Vigil-Escalera Quintanal, Centro de Salud, Laviana, Asturias
Maite Santamaria Zarain, Responsable del Trabajo Social en los Servicios de
Asistencia Primaria y Comunitaria, Servicio Vasco de Salud
Miguel Gil Motalbo, Instituto Nacional de Servicios Sociales (INSERSO),
Madrid

References

1   DE MIGUEL, J.M., M.F. GUILLÉN. The health system in Spain. In:
    Field, M.G. (ed.). Success and crisis in Nntional health systems: A
    comparative approach. Routledge, New York-London, 1989, 128-164.
2   HEALTH POLICY. Spain. Health Policy; 20 (1992), nr. 1+2, 220-
    227.
3   BOERMA, W.G.W., F.A.J.M. DE JONG, P.H. MULDER. Health
    care and general practice across Europe. Utrecht: NIVEL, 1993.
4   OECD HEALTH DATA. Version # 1.5. Paris: OECD, 1993.
5   MINISTERIO DE SANIDAD Y CONSUMO. The Spanish health
    system: high lights. Ministerio de Sanidad y Consumo, Secretaría
    General Técnica, Publicaciones, Documentación y Biblioteca, Madrid,
    1989.
6   HART, J.T. Primary medical care in Spain. British Journal of General
    Practice; 40 (1990), 255-258.
7   RODRIGUEZ, M. The health care system in Spain, competition and
    other issues after 1992. In: Casparie, A.F., H.E.G.M. Hermans, J.H.P.
    Paelinck. Competitive health care in Europe, future prospects.
    Erasmus Universiteit Rotterdam, Dartmouth, 1990, 345-360.
8   KEMENADE, Y.W. VAN. Health care in Europe. The finance and
    reimbursement systems of 18 European countries. Zoetermeer:
    Nationale Raad voor de Volksgezondheid, 1993.
9   SCHNEIDER, M., P. BIENE-DIETRICH, M. GABANYI, M.
    HUBER, A. KÖSE, L. SCHOLTES, J.H. SOMMER. Gesundheits-
    systeme im internationalen Vergleich, Ausgabe 1992. Augsburg:
    BASYS, 1993.

10   IBERN, P. Trends and evolution of the Spanish health care system: Combining financing and delivery of services. In: Casparie, A.F., H.E.G.M. Hermans, J.H.P. Paelinck. Competitive health care in Europe, future prospects. Erasmus Universiteit Rotterdam, Dartmouth, 1990, 361-373.

11   NIJKAMP, P., J. PACOLET, H. SPINNEWYN, A. VOLLERING, C. WILDEROM, S. WINTERS. Services for the elderly in Europe, a cross-national comparative study. Leuven: VU Amsterdam / KU Leuven, 1991.

12   PACOLET, J., C. WILDEROM (eds.). The economics of care of the elderly. Avebury, Aldershot-Brookfield, 1991.

13   CABRERO, G.R. Spain. In: Nijkamp, P., J. Pacolet, H. Spinnewyn, A. Vollering, C. Wilderom, S. Winters (eds.). Proceedings of a seminar on national diversity and European trends in services for the elderly. Leuven, 1991, pp. 33-35.

14   MAYMÓ, I PIJUÁN, N., A. RIBAS, I BATTLORI, E. JUNCADELLA, I GARCÍA. Programa .d'Atenció Domicilièra. Salut Catalunya; 5 (1991), 2, 85-90.

15   DIVISIÓ D'ATENCIÓ PRIMÀRIA I HOSPITALÀRIA SERVEI CATALÀ DE LA SALUT. Programa marc d'atenció a domicili - ATDOM -, Gener, 1994.

16   DIRECCIÓN ATENCIÓ PRIMARIA AREA 3. - Zaragoza, Protocolo de Atención Domicialiaria.

14 Home care in Sweden

Jack B.F. Hutten

1   The setting of home care

1.1   The country

Sweden is one of the three new member states which entered the European Union in January 1995. It is a constitutional monarchy, but the king has a ceremonial function only and no real political power. The one chamber parliament (*Riksdag*) consists of 349 representatives who are chosen for a period of four years. There are contemporary elections for the parliament, the 23 county councils (*Landstinget*) and 288 municipal councils (*Kommuner*). During the last decades, the decision-making process is decentralized. Especially in the field of health care, education and social services the role of the municipal councils has increased.

In general, living standards are quite high. For many years, Sweden has been one of the most comprehensive welfare states in the world. This has been, of course, coupled with a high level of taxation. Recently, the worse economic situation has forced the government to cut down public expenditures by reducing the financial support of county councils and municipalities.

Population key figures (1990) [1,2]

Population in mln.	8.6
Inhabitants per sq. km.	19
% Living in urban areas	84
% over 65 years	17.7
% over 75 years	8.1
Births per 1000	14.4
Deaths per 1000	11.0
Life expectancy (men)	74.8
Life expectancy (women)	80.4

1.2 The organization of health care

Health care in Sweden is mainly organized and provided by public bodies. The health care system is dominated by the provincial governments, the so called county councils. The Health and Medical Services Act of 1982 guarantees equal access for all health care services to the entire population. The 23 county councils and three large municipalities (Göteborg, Malmö and the island of Gotland) organize and provide health care within the central guidelines established by the Ministry of Health and Social Affairs. About 80% of the county councils' activities are devoted to medical and health care services [3]. In general, they are in charge of the total range of health care delivery; from public and preventive care to specialist and hospital care [4]. The Federation of County Councils negotiates with the national government on political and financial subjects and with the trade unions on salaries and working conditions of health care personnel [1,3].

Since the beginning of the 1990s, important reforms are proposed and abolished. The main reasons for these reforms are the efficiency problem (especially the long waiting lists for surgical treatments and accessibility of the primary health care centres) and the call for a free choice for consumers in health care. The basic idea is comparable with the health care reforms in the United Kingdom: an internal market requires a split between purchasers and providers of care [5].

There are three important reform acts which came into force recently. The *Guarantee of Care reform* (1992) legally guarantees a maximum waiting time of three months for twelve medical procedures such as coronary artery disease surgery, hip-joint replacement, gallstone surgery and hearing aid tests. The *Care of the Elderly reform* of 1992 moved the responsibility for nursing

281

homes from the county councils to the municipal councils as a part of the Social Services Act. Besides, it became possible that the county councils hand over the responsibility for home nursing services to the municipalities. In about 50% of counties this situation was established, at the end of 1994. This means that the municipalities become fully responsible for the total long-term care of elderly and disabled people. One of the measures of the *Family Doctor Reform* of 1994 was the free establishment of (private) physicians. It was decided that they did not need a contract with the county councils any more to be remunerated. However, this regulation changed again in January 1995.

Furthermore, like in other Scandinavian countries, Sweden is developing a so called personal doctor system. The emphasis on personal care must increase the role of the GP in primary care. In August 1994, about 75% of the population have been listed to a personal doctor of their choice [6].

It must be mentioned that the stage of the implementation of these reforms differs considerably among the county councils. Furthermore, Sweden has a new Social-Democratic government, since the autumn of 1994. It is most likely they will reverse at least some parts of the reforms. As mentioned, since January 1995, physicians have no longer been allowed to start a private practice without a contract with the county councils.

Swedish health care is mainly hospital-oriented: hospitals and specialists are directly accessible which means that no formal referral is required. There are three categories of general hospitals [1,7]. Highly specialized clinical care is provided in six regional (teaching) hospitals. In every county, there is one central county hospital for a comprehensive range of specialist care. District county hospitals are only involved in basic specialist care such as internal medicine, surgery and radiology. All hospitals have outpatient departments. Most people seeking out-patient care directly apply to these departments.

A private sector is still weakly developed in Sweden. However, recent political developments have increased working in private practices.

In the last two decades, the government and county councils have seriously tried to stimulate primary care. A network of multidisciplinary primary health care centres and nursing homes now covers the whole country. The centres employ GPs, sometimes specialists, district nurses, and paramedical personnel such as physiotherapists. Furthermore, there are private physicians working in primary health care.

Health care figures (1990) [2]

Expenditure

Total expenditure on health		
Absolute per head in ppp$	1455	
Percentage of GDP	8.6	
Public expenditure on health		
Absolute per head in ppp$	1161	
Percentage of GDP	6.9	

Manpower

Physicians per 1000 pop.	2.9	
GPs per 1000 pop.	0.4	('91)
Qualified nurses per 1000 pop.	9.8	

Hospital care

In-patient care*	
Beds per 1000 pop.	12.4
Admissions per 100 pop.	19.5
Mean length of stay	18.0
Acute hospitals	
Beds per 1000 pop.	3.9
Admissions per 100 pop.	16.3
Mean length of stay	6.6
Nursing homes	
Beds per 1000 pop.	5.4

*   Figures of total in-patient care include long-term care in hospitals and nursing homes.

1.3   Health financing and insurance

Almost 90% of the Swedish health care expenditures are financed through taxation and social insurance premiums paid by the employers. The largest part (70% of the total) is raised by the county councils, mainly through income taxes. The national government pays the county councils general and tax equalization grants [3]. The Federation of County Councils negotiates with the Ministry of Health and Social Affairs about the level and allocation of these central funds. Nowadays allocation among the different counties is based on the number of inhabitants and some social-economic criteria (e.g. the economic situation). The county council itself decides how to spend the grant: only a small part is earmarked for health promotion and preventive health services.

Within the counties, resources are allocated to hospitals and primary health care centres through a system of fixed budgets. Recently, some county councils have started to use a Diagnosis Related Groups (DRG) - system for hospital reimbursement. The introduction of a personal doctor system also requires new forms of remuneration. The main part of the budgets of primary health care centres is paid as capitation fee, weighted for the age of the patients, and the remaining part includes patients fees.

Physicians work in hospitals on basis of a fixed salary; only a few of them also operate a private practice. Private practitioners are reimbursed by 'fee-for-service'- payments. A contract with the county council is required for remuneration.

All inhabitants are entitled to a broad package of services. Co-payments are required for out-patient medical care (including home nursing care), dental care (on average 60% of the costs), and pharmaceutics (50% of the costs). A maximum amount of co-payment per person is legally established [7]. In 1994, it was SEK 1,600 a year. The whole of these kinds of co-payments cover about 10% of the health care expenditures [3].

The medical treatment and nursing care in hospitals are free of charge. However, the patients pay a small daily fee for 'hotel services' such as meals. This fee is not included in the co-payment system mentioned above.

1.4   Care for the elderly

Sweden is the EU member state with the largest proportion of elderly people in the population: almost 18% are over 65 [8-10]. Furthermore, the average life expectancy is the highest in the world. The group of very old people especially (above 80) is rapidly increasing: since 1980 this group grew by 31% [8]. There is also a trend for a growing number of elderly people to live alone. It is expected that these developments will lead to a higher demand for old-age care and services.

Care for the Swedish elderly is mainly provided by the public sector and, as a consequence, is mainly funded by taxation. The role of private organizations is still negligible. However, in the future it may be possible that private initiatives are integrated within the publicly financed and controlled system. In general, Sweden has a high level of services available for the elderly. Despite the large variation in public services among geographic areas, research show that there are only small local differences in unmet needs [8].

According to the 1982 Social Services Act, all inhabitants have the right to receive social services at all stages of life, regardless their income. In general, old-age policy promotes the independence of older people through the provision of general pensions and specific allowances (e.g. for housing).

Municipalities are responsible for a wide range of services for the elderly such as housing, social welfare, home help and long-term medical treatment in nursing homes [9,10]. The latter since the introduction of the Care of the Elderly reform in 1992. Before this reform, long-term medical treatment was the responsibility of the county councils. Previous to the 1992 reform, state subsidies to municipalities were earmarked to specific services, such as home care services, and were based on the number of personnel and the amount of services delivered. Nowadays the subsidies are given in a lump sum related to the number of elderly people in the municipality, the number of people with early retirement, the number of elderly people living alone, and the degree of urbanization. The municipalities can decide themselves how to allocate these resources [10].

Besides formal or professional care, informal carers are also involved in care for the elderly: certain studies showed that they account for almost two thirds of all care provided within the community [8]. Some municipalities put up special support schemes for caring family members. The social security system allows 30 days of paid leave to care someone 'near'. This scheme is mainly used to care for terminal patients who want to stay in their own homes [8].

Community services Swedish old-age policy increasingly focuses on community services provided by municipal councils. The decline of the role of institutional care must be compensated by alternative services in the community. Besides home help and home nursing services which will be discussed later, many kind of services are organized: e.g. food services in district day centres, meals-on-wheels, alarm systems, transport services, and more specific services such as snow clearance in the winter [8-10]. About 80% of the municipalities run district day centres for all pensioners. These centres have mainly a social function: maintaining social contacts with hobby programs, gymnastics and excursions. Nowadays, they are increasingly being transformed into rehabilitation centres.

Residential services Originally care for the elderly in Sweden was dominated by institutional care. Until the 1980s, the number of places in old people's homes and long-term care institutions (mostly nursing homes) grew remarkably. However, over a period of 10-15 years many old people's homes have been closed or replaced by service houses (*sheltered accommodation*) [9].

The total number of places available in institutional care has not changed since the 1980s, although the number of the elderly have increased enormously. As a consequence the percentage of the elderly living in special institutions has dropped and a large number of the elderly kept living in their own environment. Nowadays, about 7% of the people over 65 and 25% of the people over 80 are living in institutions or special housing facilities for the elderly. In 1991, there were about 106,000 places (flats or beds) available in the whole country. In addition old people's homes, nursing homes and service houses, more intensively sheltered houses are being built for the demented elderly. About 2% of the elderly live in service apartments owned and managed by the municipality [8]. These sheltered accommodations contain 20 to 100 housing units. The services provided in these apartments are comparable to the home help services for people living in ordinary houses.

Nursing homes are intended for people with chronic illnesses and physical and/mental disabilities in need of a great amount of nursing care. Furthermore, so called geriatric departments, mostly linked with hospitals, are involved in rehabilitation and relief care.

The facilities are mainly funded by the municipal councils. The monthly personal fees charged by old people's homes differ between regions. Some have income-related fees, others fixed amounts. There is no specific state regulation.

As mentioned before, the administration of nursing homes is being transferred from the county councils to the municipalities. They are also financially responsible for patients in hospital once medical treatment is completed to reduce the number of "bed blockers".

Capacity of residential services for the elderly in Sweden (1991)

	Number of places/beds per 1000 people over 65 years
Old people's homes	22
Nursing homes	20
Service houses	27
Intensive sheltered houses	3

2 The organization of home nursing

2.1 Organizations for home nursing

There are two important reasons why it is difficult to describe the current situation of home nursing in Sweden. Firstly, as described in the previous sections, Sweden is still in a process of reforming health care and social services. As a consequence, the situation differs among areas. In about half of the municipalities, home nursing activities are the responsibility of the municipal councils, while in the other half, the county councils still provide these services. The organizational structures can therefore differ. It must be stressed that less than half of the population receive home nursing care from the municipalities. Smaller municipalities in particular take over responsibility. Secondly, the assistants involved in *home care* can provide home nursing as well as home help tasks.

Home nursing is a part of the Swedish welfare system. It is almost totally provided by public organization; there are hardly any private organizations active in this field. It must be mentioned that there are no organizations which exclusively provide home nursing care. When county councils are responsible, home nursing is mostly organized by the primary health care centres (*vårdcentral*). There are, however, also about ten hospitals in Sweden that provide nursing care at home. When the municipalities are involved, home nursing care is part of the social services (general care for the elderly and disabled). In this situation, the actual provision of care is mostly organized within home help services organizations, old people's homes or day centres.

2.2 Manpower in home nursing services

Two types of professional care-givers can be distinguished in home nursing. The first level of competence is that of the registered nurse. They have had higher education for a period of three years. There is also an additional training in community nursing for one year but, in general, this special training is not formally required for work as home nurse. Secondly, there are, as we shall call them, *home care* assistants. Originally, there were two different kinds of assistants: nursing assistants and social service assistants (home helps). However, for practical reasons and the increasing level of education in both professions, their actual tasks look increasingly alike and no

287

distinction is made any more. The home care assistants are trained at upper secondary school for a period of three years.

Official figures on manpower in home nursing care are impossible to determine. County councils do not provide these kinds of figures because home nursing is part of the total package of services of the primary care centres. The nurses or assistants employed in these centres are also involved in other tasks of these centres. In 1991, the county councils employed almost 5,000 FTEs community nurses [11]. It is estimated that about 6,000 registered nurses (4,500 FTEs) were working in home nursing care, in 1993*.

Only combined figures with social service assistants are available for nursing assistants: a total of 144,400 assistants (98,800 FTEs) were employed in 1993. One has to keep in mind that about 80% of their working time are spent on home help activities in stead of home nursing care.

2.3   Client population

The percentage of the national population that has received any kind of home nursing care during one year is unknown. No statistics or empirical data are available about the clients of home nursing services for the same reasons as mentioned above. There are some general figures about the clients of home care provided by the municipalities. But the problem is that no distinction can be made between home nursing and home help services. Because it is assumed that the later form the largest part, these figures are discussed in section 3.3.

Figures about the home nursing care provided under the responsibility of the county councils are missing completely. The only figure that was published recently was that about 40,000 clients received both home help and home nursing services in November 1993 [12].

2.4   Provision of services

A consequence of the public system is that patients do not have any choice of whom to approach for home nursing care. The national government determines the legislations and the municipalities or county councils have the

---

* These figures are calculations by our respondents and do not include the nurses working in the primary health care centres (county councils).

total responsibility for the actual provision of care. There is no internal market with different (private) providers.

It is estimated that more than a half of the home nursing patients (55%) are referred by hospitals. Other initiators are GPs, home help services and the patient or his/her family. Formally, there are no legal regulations about the access to home nursing care. But in some places a referral may be required because of local legislation.

After the first contact with the organization, an assessment of the specific needs of the patient is performed. When the care is the responsibility of the county councils this is done by a registered nurse or a physician working in the primary health care centre. In this situation, needs for home help care are not involved in the assessment. It is, however, possible that nurse or physician contacts the home help organization. When the home nursing care is provided by the municipalities, the assessment is the responsibility of the home help administrator of the social service department. The decision is made within the framework of the Social Services Act. The home help administrator mostly assesses the total need for home care: both home nursing and home help needs. No official standardized assessment forms are used, but there might be a standardized checklist especially developed in the organization.

The same person responsible for the assessment, usually decides upon the type of care the patient is going to receive, for what period of time and the expected goals of the care provided.

Home nurses can operate from different places: primary health care centres or, although marginally, hospitals (county councils), home nursing premises, day centres, old people's homes and home help services buildings (municipalities). Sometimes nurses work alone, but usually they work in a team which can have various compositions. Nursing assistants, social service assistants, physiotherapists and occupational therapists can e.g. be part of the team. The exact composition of the teams differs between regions.

The daily work of the home nurse mainly consists of more complicated technical nursing procedures (such as pain relief, complicated wound care, handling respirator and catheterization) and counselling (health education, discussion and advising on psychosocial problems, and stimulating help from the social network of the patient). When she/he works in a primary health care centre, she is responsible for the whole care process and evaluates the care provided to a patient. To have a better impression of the work of these home nurses, one has to keep in mind that physicians hardly provide any home visits in Sweden which indicates an extra workload. Furthermore, it must be mentioned that registered nurses also see patients in the health care centre (only when county councils are responsible).

Personal care (bathing, help with lavatory and support of other activities of daily living) and routine technical nursing procedures (injections, dressings, stoma care) are done by the nursing and social services assistants. They are also involved in home help tasks which will be in section 3.4.

2.5 Problems and recent developments

The main development is that the municipalities are taking over the responsibility of home nursing services from the county councils. This must be seen in the light of the central goal to promote home care in general. A major problem is, however, that the responsibilities of hospitals and home care organizations are not well established. In the field of rehabilitation especially this leads to problematic situations. A lack of continuity and communication between the care-providers is reported in some parts of Sweden.

There are no waiting lists in the whole country and there is a sufficient amount of home nursing staff available.

3 The organization of home help services

3.1 Organizations for home help services

According to the Social Services Act, all Swedish municipalities provide home help services (*hemtjänst*) for elderly and disabled people [10]. This is the responsibility of the municipal social service departments. Home help can be provided in the client's own home as well as in special housing services such as old people's homes, service houses and group dwellings. There are a few municipalities who contract out home care services to private non-profit organizations.

3.2 Manpower in home help services

The home help administrators are in charge of the actual provision of home help services. In the entire country, about 6,500 home help administrators work (5,900 FTEs) who have had a three years higher training [12].

Home helps are municipal employees who assist elderly and disabled people in their daily lives when needed [10]. As mentioned in section 2.2 this can be both nursing assistants or social services assistants. For reasons of simplicity, we will call them home care assistants. They receive three years training (upper secondary school). In 1994, a total of 144,400 assistants (98,800 FTEs) work in home care (home nursing and home help services) [12]. It is interesting that the municipalities do not employ people with less training for cleaning services only, as in many other countries. Most workers involved in home care have at least three years training, nowadays, which seems to be a rather high standard.

3.3   Client population

In 1993, about 2.5% of the total Swedish population received home help services from the municipalities [13]. In the population older than 64 years this was 14%, and 34% of the people aged 80 years or more [11]. Almost 80% of the clients were living alone and 67% of the clients were female. Of course, the elderly were the largest group of clients (89%). In this group, people over 74 were the main users (74% of the total).

A majority received only limited help for a few hours a week. A registration in November 1993 showed that 38% received less than nine hours per month; only 4% received help for 120 hours or more [13].

3.4   Provision of services

As with for home nursing services, there is no competition in the field of home help services. Everyone has to approach the municipality to apply for home help. In some areas there are some private organizations active but they play only a minor role. It is, however, possible that the elderly or disabled organize support in homemaking activities privately.

In most cases the client or his/her family is the initiator to apply for home help services (85% as estimated). An official referral is not required.

The home help administrators of the municipal social services firstly contact the potential clients to assess the specific needs. As mentioned, they also can determine the need of home nursing services, when they are performed by the municipalities. Again, no official standardized assessment forms are used, but all municipalities have their own assessment system. The home help administrators decide what type of help the client is going to receive and the number of hours per week. They are also involved in the actual care providing process: mostly in counselling and advice, both to the client as well to the family members. Therefore, they are responsible for the total care provided and have to evaluated it.

All *home care* assistants operate from home help services buildings and work in teams. They are involved in a broad range of homemaking activities such as preparing meals, washing dishes, washing and ironing, and cleaning. Also personal care (hygienic care, bathing, clothing) is part of their daily activities. As mentioned, they also perform routine technical nursing tasks (injections, dressings, stoma care), mostly formally supervised by a home nurse. When necessary, help is available during the evening, at night and during the weekends.

3.5   Problems and recent developments

No waiting lists or shortage of personnel in home help services are reported. The main problem in the organization mentioned is the fact that in half of the municipalities the county councils are still responsible for home nursing services. As a consequence, in these areas, neither aspect of home care is geared for the other which leads to competence and communication problems. This situation will have a negative influence on the care provided.

4   Relations between home nursing and home help services

It is mentioned before that the way home nurses and home helps co-operate differs largely between regions. Recently, the central government provided special funding to encourage co-operation and communication between health and social services, especially in the field of rehabilitation. The Care for the Elderly Reform is an important step towards further integration of social and health care for elderly people. When the municipalities are in charge of both services, more integrated home care is provided because one organization is responsible for the total care for the elderly and disabled. In some regions therefore home helps and home nurses work together in special teams. They discuss shared patients and are more able to tune in their tasks.

5 The financing of home nursing services

5.1 Payment and patients' insurance

The cost of home nursing care are part of the public health care scheme or the public social services. There are no private insurance companies offering special coverage in this field.

With regards to co-payment again a distinction must be made between home nursing care provided by county councils (health care) and by the municipalities (social services). In the first situation, patient's fee for home nursing care is a part of the co-payment scheme which is described in section 1.3 (with a maximum amount of SEK 1,600 a year in 1994). However, one has to remember that this also includes other kinds of primary health care and pharmaceutics. The exact amount charged per home nursing visits can differ between the regions. It is estimated that the average is about SEK 50. The fees are not income-related. The municipalities providing home care can operate different co-payment systems for home nursing activities. Sometimes, they are included in the total home care fees which will be discussed in section 6.1.

In the county councils, the amount of care needed is decided by the registered nurse or physician involved. In the municipalities this is done by the home help administrator. In both situations, no maximum amount of care or limited duration are officially determined.

5.2 Funding of the organizations

In the county councils, the funding of home nursing care is an integrated part of the total health care budget. As a consequence, it is mainly paid from general tax revenues. When primary health care centres provide home nursing services, they receive a yearly fixed budget based on their catchment area. This budget includes all kind of care: there are no earmarked payments for home nursing care. However, in areas where GPs have capitation payments, home nursing is financed by extra earmarked money.

When municipalities are responsible, the funding of home nursing activities is part of the whole grant provided by the central government and the municipal tax revenues. This means that the municipalities are free to decide how to allocate the central governmental grant among their different responsibilities such as e.g. education, sport facilities and social services.

Furthermore, these municipalities are allowed to increase their local taxes which is compensated by a reduction of the county council taxes. Because home nursing services are part of the social service system, no specific distinction can be made.

5.3   Payment of the nurses

All nurses working in home care are civil servants employed by the municipalities or county councils. They all have a fixed salary. The average monthly income in 1993 was SEK 14,800 for the registered nurses and about SEK 12,000 for the *home care* assistants.

5.4   Problems and recent developments

There is a need for more money and more efficiency in the provision of care, if the Swedish authorities are willing to maintain the recent standards of care. There is an increasing group of very old people who are in need of nursing care. The shift from hospital to home care indicates that more money must become available to provide these services.

6   The financing of home help services

6.1   Payment and clients' insurance

The provision of home help services is part of the extended Swedish social welfare system. This means that all people, regardless of their income, can apply for home help services provided by the municipalities. All clients have to pay a fee, but the level of co-payments varies largely between the municipalities. Most of the municipalities use an income-related system, but this is not common everywhere in the country. It is estimated that, on average, people pay about SEK 600 a month for home help services. The individual amount of co-payment is, besides income, also depending on the number of hours of care.

There is no official maximum amount of care determined. The home help organizers decide, within the framework of the Social Service Act, about the kind of work that is required, of course restricted by the resources of the municipalities.

6.2   Funding of organizations

Home help is mainly financed by the municipal councils through local taxation (75%). Furthermore, the central government contributes 17% of the total income of the municipal councils. For many years the central government promoted the expansion of home help services by providing a grant earmarked for this purpose. However, since 1991 they have received a global grant which can be spent on different programmes.

As mentioned, there are a few municipalities which contract *home care* services out to private non-profit organizations. It is estimated that this counts for about 4% of the total expenditure on home care services.

6.3   Payment of the home helps

All home helps are employed by the social services of the municipalities. The majority receive a fixed salary. The average monthly income of home help administrators was SEK 14,700 and *home care* assistants earned, on average, SEK 12,000 a month in 1993.

6.4   Problems and recent developments

No specific problems regarding the financing of home help services are reported.

Acknowledgement
This information in this chapter is mainly provided by Kerstin Einevik-Bäckstrand and Rut Hedvall, Swedish Institute for Health Services Development (SPRI), and Ylva Behr of the Swedish Association of Local Authorities, both situated in Stockholm.

References

1 BOERMA W.G.W., F.A.J.M. DE JONG, P.H. MULDER. Health care and general practice across Europe. Utrecht: NIVEL, 1993.
2 OECD HEALTH DATA. Version # 1.5. Paris: OECD, 1993.

3 BERLEEN, G., C. REHNBERG, G. WENNSTRÖM. The reform of health care in Sweden. Stockholm: SPRI rapport 339, 1994.

4 VREUGDENHIL, J.C., M. DE BRUINE. Gezondheidszorg in Europa: structuur en financiering van de gezondheidszorg in enkele Europeses landen. Rotterdam: BMG, 1992.

5 COMMITTEE ON FUNDING AND ORGANISATION OF HEALTH SERVICES AND MEDICAL CARE (HSU 2000). Three models for health care reforms in Sweden. Stockholm: Ministry of Health and Social Affairs, 1993.

6 ANELL, A., P. SVARVAR, M. SVENSSON. Husläkare i offentlig och privat regi: En studie om producent och konkurrensneutralitet. Lund: IHE working paper, 1994:7.

7 KEMENADE, Y.W. VAN. Health care in Europe. The finance and reimbursement systems of 18 European countries. Zoetermeer: Nationale Raad voor de Volksgezondheid, 1993.

8 SUNDSTRÖM, G., M. THORSLUND. Caring for the frail elderly in Sweden. In: Olson, L.K. (eds.). The graying of the world: who will care for the frail elderly? New York/London/Norwood: The Haworth Press, 1994.

9 THORSLUND, M. Home care in Sweden: past and future trends. In: Evers, A., G.H. van der Zanden (eds.). Better care for dependent people living at home: meeting the new agenda in services for the elderly. Bunnik: LSOB/NIG, 1993.

10 HEDIN, B. Growing old in Sweden. Stockholm: The Swedish Institute and the National Board of Health and Welfare, 1993.

11 THE SWEDISH INSTITUTE. The care of the elderly in Sweden. Fact Sheets on Sweden, August 1994.

12 STATISTISKA CENTRALBYRÅN (SCB). Social hemhjälp och hemsjukvård den 31 december 1993 samt social hemhjälp november 1993. Statistiska meddelanden, 18-7-1994.

13 STATISTISKA CENTRALBYRÅN (SCB). Personal inom den kommunala äldre- och handikappomsorgen 1993. Statistiska meddelanden, 16-6-1994.

15 Home care in the United Kingdom

Jack B.F. Hutten

1 The setting of home care

1.1 The country

The United Kingdom is a constitutional monarchy consisting of three countries (England, Wales and Scotland) and a province (Northern Ireland) which have a considerable degree of autonomy in areas such as education, health, housing and social policy [1].

The Queen is the Head of State but the executive power lies with the Prime Minister. There is a two chamber parliament. The lower chamber (The House of Commons), is elected by universal suffrage whereas the upper chamber (The House of Lords), is non-elected but has only limited powers.

The country used to be highly industrialized, but nowadays, service industries are becoming more important.

The United Kingdom entered the European Community in 1973, some years after its first application. Fear of loss of sovereignty still dominates the attitude of many British people towards the European Union [2].

Jack B.F. Hutten

Population key figures (1990) [2,3]

Population in mln.	57.2
Inhabitants per sq. km.	234
% Living in urban areas	89
% over 65 years	15.8
% over 75 years	7.0
Births per 1000	13.8
Deaths per 1000	11.2
Life expectancy (men)	73.2
Life expectancy (women)	78.8

1.2 The organization of health care

Since 1948, health care has been provided by the National Health Service (NHS). The Department of Health is responsible for the broad arrangements and general policy regarding health, assessment of needs, the definition of priorities, and the allocation of resources.

Until April 1991, the management of the NHS was mainly organized at two levels [2,4,5]. Firstly, there were fourteen Regional Health Authorities (RHAs) which managed health care provision in their own region. Secondly, these RHAs were (in England) divided into the 193 District Health Authorities (DHAs). District Health Authorities were involved in the provision of hospital care, community nursing services and primary medical care. Providers of hospital care and community nursing care were employed by DHAs. In Wales, Scotland and Northern Ireland the organization was only slightly different. Since April 1994, the fourteen RHAs are replaced by eight so called Regional Executive Offices. However, community nursing is still the responsibility of the District Health Authorities but their number has been reduced in favour of the so called NHS Community Trusts.

Traditionally general practitioners have a central position in the British health care system. Almost the entire population is registered with a general practice. Furthermore, except in an emergency, patients do not have direct access to the hospital. The GP is the gatekeeper which means that the patients need a formal referral if specialist or hospital care is required. General practitioners are independent contractors to the NHS, through the Family Health Services Authorities (FHSA) [2].

Parallel to the NHS, there is a private sector which is small in primary care but significant in secondary care and currently increasing, especially in the richer south [6]. The private sector accounts for about 10% of the total health care expenditures [7].

Since the mid 1980s, the position and functioning of the NHS has been subject of a lot of discussion. Critics concentrate on the financial situation of the NHS, the cost-effectiveness of the services, the long waiting lists for hospital care, the limited influence of patients on the care provided, and the strong dependency of health professionals and organizations on the political decisions of government and parliament [4].

As a reaction, the so called white paper 'Working for patients' was published in 1989 [8]. This policy paper contains a large number of proposals to radically reform the NHS. The central idea is the formation of an internal market introducing competition and market mechanisms (structured incentives) in the provision of health care [9]. A market structure requires a separation between demand or purchase and supply. In the new situation, the DHAs have been reformed and now purchases services for the people in their district. Hospitals and their staff, community nursing organizations and other care agency are the providers and can compete with each other. The position of the GPs is equivocal: on the one hand they are the independent providers of primary health care, but on the other hand some of them, the so called fundholders, are the purchasers of health care for their own patients (see section 1.3.). Owing to the reform of the British health care system, there is now a considerable variety in the health services between the localities and this makes it more difficult to describe the British system at a national level.

Jack B.F. Hutten

Health care figures (1990) [2]

Expenditure
Total expenditure on health
Absolute per head in ppp$ 988
Percentage of GDP   6.2
Public expenditure on health
Absolute per head in ppp$ 825
Percentage of GDP   5.2

Manpower
Physicians per 1000 pop.   1.4
GPs per 1000 pop.   0.6
Qualified nurses per 1000 pop.   4.3   ('88)

Hospital care
In-patient care
Beds per 1000 pop.   6.4   ('89)
Admissions per 100 pop.   15.9   ('88)
Mean length of stay   14.5
Acute hospitals
Beds per 1000 pop.   2.8   ('86)
Admissions per 100 pop.   12.9   ('86)
Mean length of stay   7.8   ('86)
Nursing homes
Beds per 1000 pop.   1.4   ('88)

1.3   Health financing and insurance

All inhabitants of the United Kingdom are offered free medical care by the NHS, irrespective of income and contribution paid [7]. Co-payments are required for e.g. drugs, visual aids, and dental care. Certain patient groups, for instance children, pregnant women, the elderly and persons with certain chronic illness, are excluded from co-payments.

The NHS is mainly funded by general taxation, completed by social premiums of employers and employees (National Insurance), co-payments by patients, and reimbursements from private health insurances [2,5,7,9]. The premiums of the National Insurance are divided into four classes based on position (salaried workers or self-employed) and the income-level. Only 10% of the premiums of the National Insurance are spent on health care, the remaining part cover other social services.

As mentioned before, a number of radical reforms with regard to the financing of health care have recently been implemented. In April 1991, the National Health Service and Community Care Act came into force [10]. Two major changes in health financing are the introduction of independent hospital trusts and the introduction of fundholding general practice units. NHS hospital trusts are operating independently from the DHAs. The DHAs contract the hospitals and make specific arrangements about prices and levels of quality. The hospitals are capable of providing services to a wider range of purchasers and can generate funds in new ways e.g. dispose of assets such as land and borrow money [2]. In April 1995, all hospitals have to become trusts; in 1992 about 160 hospital were already transformed [9].

Furthermore, the Act allows GPs to become fundholders on a voluntary basis. GP fundholders are free to negotiate contracts for diagnostic facilities, hospital consultant services and community services such as district nursing and chiropody within their assigned budget [2]. Prescribing costs are also included in the budget. GP budgets are presently based on previous spending but it is intended that eventually be determined by list size and relevant characteristics of the practice population. Services for patients of non-fundholding GPs are purchased on their behalf by the DHAs. There is some concern that the scheme might lead to a 'two-tier' service, in which the advantages gained for the patients of fundholding practices are achieved at the expense of patients in other practice. In April 1992, more than 500 fundholding general practices were already established in the United Kingdom [9].

1.4   Care for the elderly

The percentage of elderly people in the population of the United Kingdom is expected to grow rapidly, an increase of 6% of people over 65 between 1986 and 2000 is estimated [11]. The provision of care and support of the elderly has always been a mixture of state, commercial, voluntary and family sources, but over time the importance of these resources has changed [12]. The National Health Service and Community Care Act leads to fundamental changes in the delivery of care and support of the elderly [13].

The central aim of the national government regarding the elderly is to maintain people in their own homes as long as possible [14]. The national government is responsible for the legislation of all services and for the funds, health service and grants to municipalities. Before the National Health

Service and Community Act became effective, the local authorities provided (personal) social services and housing facilities. Now, the split between purchaser and providers is also made in social services [15]. Moreover, a shift from public to private initiatives is recently seen. The withdrawing of the state from direct provision of welfare services has led to a changing and uncertain situation in the field of care for the elderly [12].

Community services. Besides home care services (home nursing and home help services) which will be discussed in the next section, a number of other community services are available for the elderly in the United Kingdom, such as meals-on-wheels, day centres, community psychiatric nursing, health visiting, and social work. Most of the services are provided by health or local authorities.

Residential services. In 1986, only 4% of the population over 65 lived permanently in one of the residential services' [11]. Firstly, there are old people's homes which are managed by both local authorities as well as private organizations. A second kind of service is sheltered housing, that is housing accommodations with special supervision by resident or peripatetic wardens. For the elderly with severe (mental) handicaps or impairments, beds are available in nursing homes, geriatric and psychiatric hospitals. It is estimated that about 70% of the expenditure on residential services are paid by the government and 30% by the elderly themselves [11].

In recent years, there has been a decrease in reliance on hospital beds, which is only partly compensated for by the growth in the number of places in other residential services. There is a shift from old people's homes in the public sector to homes which are privately run. An increase of places in private old people's homes with more than 300% is reported between 1976 and 1986, while the number of places in public old people's homes kept constant in the same period of time [12]. This development was caused by a liberalization of the reimbursement system in favour of private home owners. However, these regulations have changed again and no further increase of private old people's homes is expected in the near future.

One of the important policy measures of the 1990 National Health Service and Community Care Act is a change in the payment of the residential services. The care element of the social security income support for nursing and residential home care was in the old system directly paid to the people through a means-test. Now it is paid to the local authorities which means that potential new applicants need to approach these authorities for support. As a consequence publicly funded places in nursing homes are no longer available without the agreement of the local social services, unless paid for by the health service or the individuals themselves [13].

Capacity of residential services for the elderly in the United Kingdom (1986) [11]

	Number of places/beds per 1000 people over 65 years
Old people's homes	51.2
Sheltered housing	n.a.
Nursing homes	10.2
Geriatric hospitals	14.1

2 The organization of home nursing

2.1 Organizations for home nursing

Community nursing is a part of the National Health Service and, as stated above, the NHS system is going through a period of significant change.

At national level, the Ministry of Health has overall responsibility. Since April 1994, eight Regional Executive Offices are situated at the regional level instead of the fourteen RHAs.

However, community nursing is still the responsibility of the District Health Authorities or NHS Community Trusts. There were 192 DHAs, but their number has been reduced in favour of the NHS Community Trusts. Most of the remaining DHAs have a community unit within which community nursing is located. Each trust or community unit is usually subdivided into geographical local units for the purpose of management. These units have a manager who may or may not be a nurse (e.g. a district nurse or a health visitor) .

In addition, fundholding GPs may purchase nursing services from the community trusts or community units of the DHAs. Mostly GPs employ practice nurses but they are more involved in health promotion and screening activities and to a lesser extent in the nursing of ill people at home.

Furthermore, there are also private nursing agencies in the United Kingdom, but there is hardly any statistical information available about them.

303

In 1990, there were at least 500 commercial home care organizations caring for an estimated 45,000 people [16]. It must be noted that the nursing care provided by these agencies often differs from the nursing care of the public organizations. The majority of the work of the private nurses contains personal care such as bathing, dressing, and putting a patient back into bed. These private agencies are mostly used by the rich and in some districts, the NHS community trusts are utilizing the private agencies for staff.

Finally, the increasing role of the voluntary sector in home nursing activities must be mentioned. One of the major providers of home care outside the NHS is the Marie Curie Cancer care. This charity organization provides home care to terminally ill people; mostly cancer patient, although the proportion of AIDS patients is rapidly growing. The organization is based in London but has regional offices all over the United Kingdom. Sometimes the district authorities call in the support of the voluntary sector when specific care can not be provided by community nurses.

2.2   Manpower in home nursing services

The nurses working in home care in the United Kingdom can be divided into four levels of expertise. The highest level are the registered district nurses (RDNs). They have had a three year hospital-based training followed by a nine month training for community nursing (District nursing certificate). The second level are the so called RGNs (registered general nurses) working in the community. They have had three years basic nursing training in a hospital, but no district nursing certificate. Enrolled district nurses, who received a two year training, are the third level of expertise. Although a number of them are still working in the community, enrolled district nurses are not trained any longer. Finally, there are nursing auxiliaries or health care assistants who only receive on the job training which requires no formal qualifications. However, recently, a new range of vocational qualifications is being introduced within the framework of the National Council for Vocational Qualifications.

The clinical grading structure for nursing staff, which was introduced in 1988, distinguishes nine grades (A through I). Each grade has its own task profile and required qualification.

In 1992, 11,010 (9,650 FTEs) district nurses, 2,830 (2,110 FTEs) registered general nurses, 4,060 (3,310 FTEs) enrolled nurses and 6,000 (3,490 FTEs) unqualified nursing auxiliaries were employed by the DHAs in England [22].

The NHS reforms will have important impacts on the number of nurses employed by the DHAs. It is expected that a large number community nurses will be employed by the community trusts or fundholding general practices.

Most of the nurses are employed by the public organizations: the community units of the DHAs and NHS community trusts.

2.3   Client population

In 1992-93, 2.4 million first contacts were reported which is an indication of the number of different people who received home nursing care in England (Ministry of Health, 1994). The majority were over 65. About 10% of the elderly between 65 and 74, 23% of the group between 75 and 84 and even 42% of the people aged 85 and older were cared for by home nurses. On the whole, about 37.5 million face to face contacts between community nurses and these patients were registered; about 86% were located at the patient's home. Furthermore, 6% of the contacts took place in residential accommodations because some of them do not employ nurses themselves.

2.4   Provision of services

The actual provision of home nursing services is the responsibility of NHS community trusts, the community units of the original DHAs or the GP fundholders. In most cases requiring home nursing care, health professionals such as GPs, hospital or nursing home staff will contact the community nursing service manager. Practically there are no alternative organizations for patients to choose between. There is a possibility for rich people to purchase private nursing services, but this is not very common.

After the first contact, an assessment visit takes place by the team leader, usually a G-grade district nurse. This assessment of the patient's needs and the decision about the amount, type and duration of the required care is mostly a personal and subjective judgement of the nurse. Within some local teams, standardized assessment forms may be used, but there is no national form available for the whole country. The nurse does not determine the needs for home help care. However, she/he can decide that home help is needed and make a referral to the home help services, but the actual need is usually reassessed by the home help agency. The evaluation of the care provided is also the responsibility of the team leader.

In most health authorities or trusts, nurses work in a team. There is a distinction between primary health care teams and nursing teams. The latter consists of a team leader, qualified district nurse(s), staff nurse and enrolled nurse(s) or nursing assistant(s). Primary health care teams are multi-disciplinary teams: besides district nurses, GPs, practice nurses, social workers, health visitors and e.g. midwives can participate in these kind of teams.

Most district nurses operate from health centres or home nursing premises, though this does not mean that nurses work from health centres on a daily basis. Also the nurse's own home may be considered as work base, especially in rural areas. Furthermore, nurses operate from local hospitals, and many are attached to GP practices.

The tasks of district nurses and nursing assistants differ. The G-grade district nurses are mainly involved in the process of (re)assessment, evaluation and co-ordination of care. They have a minor role in the provision of actual nursing procedures. All other types of nurses and assistants provide hygienic and other personal care such as bathing, help with going to the toilet, and assistance with other activities of daily living. Also the stimulation of help from the social network (family members, neighbours and friends) is part of the work of all types of nurses and assistants. Routine technical nursing procedures (e.g. injections, dressings, stoma care and bladder washout) are performed by district nurses. In addition, G and H grade district nurses and specialist nurses, like MacMillan nurses for cancer patients, are also involved in more complicated nursing procedures such as epidural anaesthesia, handling respirators and catheterization. Patient education and the provision of psychosocial care are also elements of the work of district nurses and specialist nurses.

2.5 Problems and recent developments

Recent developments have already been discussed. Because the United Kingdom is in a period of significant change, it is very difficult to make general statements about community nursing in the United Kingdom. There is now a great deal of variability between different authorities. The entire health service has been re-organized since the National Health Service and Community act. The main change is the purchaser-provider split: DHAs purchase health care and hospitals, community units and GPs provide it. Some GPs have become fundholders which means that they purchase hospital and community nursing services on behalf of their patients. Many hospitals and community units have become NHS trusts. This means that they are financially independent and actually operate as any other business.

Furthermore, there has been a major policy shift towards private health care. Hence the community nursing services have been re-structured. This means reducing the number of qualified district nurses and replacing them with other grades e.g. RGNs or care assistant/nursing auxiliaries. G-grade district nurses then become team leaders and hence managers of a team. An observed problem is that too many hours of their working time has to be spent on this function and that less time is available for actual home care.

There is no shortage of district nurses. The number of students entering district nurse courses, however, showed a decrease of 6.5% between 1985/86 and 1989/90 [1].

3 The organization of home help services

3.1 Organizations for home help services

There are formal organizations providing home help services in the United Kingdom. The public home help services are part of the social services, but there are also a number of private home help agencies, especially in wealthier areas [15]. However, the National Health Service and Community Care Act which became into full effect in April 1993, has also important implications for the way in which social services are delivered. Before that date, the public home help services were run by Local Authority Social Services Departments and, because of the lack of formal national regulations for the provision of home help services, there was a large variation regarding the actual provision and organization of the services between the 116 local authorities involved.

As in health care, a reduction of institutional social care in favour of a mixed economy of care has become the main policy goal [12]. The role of local social services authorities must change from being the provider of a range of services into the purchasing agency role. This means that the social services departments will have to assess the needs of individual clients, arrange individual tailored services to meet those needs, and commission the services as appropriate where possible. More and more, privately managed organizations will be called in to provide social services. Local authorities are required to spend 85% of their budgets on independent providers. This means that in an increasing number of local authorities the home help service has been privatized and the staff now work for independent providers who have to negotiate contracts with Local Authority Social Services Department for the provision of home help services.

3.2   Manpower in home help services

The actual provision of the services is done by home helps. As a result of the changes outlined above the designation of home helps (care attendants, home carers, care assistants) differs between local authorities. Also the content of their work varies and has become the subject of contract negotiations.

Generally, the training of the workers is minimal, containing a simple introductory course, accompanying an existing home help, and sometimes participation in a series of in-service courses on particular aspects of caring and safety [17]. There is no formal legislation with regard to training and there is a large variation between local authorities [15].

A detailed report of the staff of Local Authority Social Services Departments gives information about the number of the home helps in England [18]. The section Domiciliary service staff contains six divisions which accounts for a total of 57,593.1 FTEs. This total number includes home care organizers as well as home helps. The latter group are the actual providers of care in the homes of the clients. In 1993, English local authorities employed 82,940 home helps (50,743.5 FTEs). More than 90% of them are part-time workers. So, this means that there is one FTE official home help available for every 1,100 inhabitants.

The figures presented include only the home helps employed by the public organizations in England. It is, however, also common that domiciliary help is supplied on an individual basis and that the home helps are paid directly by the client. Furthermore, there is also an increase in private organizations delivering home help services, on a for-profit as well as non-profit or voluntary basis [19]. Major providers are the Crossroads Care Attendant Schemes (CCAs), established in 1974. This voluntary organizations intend to provide home-based care to relieve informal carers and to enable disabled and elderly people to stay in the community.

3.3   Client population

The 1985 General Household Survey reported that 9% of people aged 65 and over who lived in private households were receiving formal home help.

As regards those over 75, this percentage was even higher namely 25% [15]. Home help services were mostly provided to the elderly living alone. Only 10% of the clients were younger than 65; 68% were people over 75. One fourth of the clients lived with other people such as spouses and children.

It is estimated that private domiciliary individual help and care may serve twice as many retired people as the home help services organized by local authorities [19]. The growth of private organizations is inadequately documented, but e.g. the CCAs provided 1.5 million care hours to 15,000 families in 1991 [19].

3.4   Provision of services

Under the new legislation there is growing choice for the clients and a decreasing role for direct public provision. There is no recent empirical information about referral patterns, but historically 70% of the clients of local authority home help services are referred by the primary health care teams or hospitals and the remainder are largely self-referrals. However, a formal referral is not required.

Before the National Health Service and Community Care Act came into force, the needs of the potential clients were assessed by home help organizers employed by the social services departments. There were a number of senior home help organizers covering a geographical sub-area of the authority and each senior had one or more organizers assisting them. The decision about the allocation of services in numbers of hours was also made by the home help organizers.

Under the new legislation all referrals received an assessment by a local authority social worker, now often called a care manager. The new act has separated the tasks of assessment and provision so the home help organizers now play only a subsidiary role in assessment.

The decision as to the number of hours is decided by the purchaser. For those with low incomes and with high needs this will be the care managers; in other cases, the number of hours will largely depend on the amount of money the clients are willing to pay. There are no national indications or norms, therefore the policy differs between the authorities.

As mentioned before, the organization of the actual delivery of home help services differs between the local authorities. Home helps can e.g. operate from different places. Examples can be found of home helps operating from their own homes, health centres, nursing homes or home help services buildings. Also regarding the question whether they work in teams or alone, no national pattern can be seen, though solo work is by far the most common.

There is a large variation among the authorities regarding the specific tasks of home helps. No national task profile exists by which different kinds of home helps do different tasks. Recently, a shift has been made from domestic to personal care. The statutory home help service has been re-defined in many authorities as 'home care' and the job descriptions of home helps re-written to emphasise provision of care rather than domestic help [19].

Home helps are mostly involved in the following activities: homemaking activities (preparing meals, washing dishes, washing an ironing, cleaning), hygiene and other personal care (bathing, help with activities of daily living) and giving general and family support (shopping, take for a walk, administrative support). Simple routine nursing procedures, moral support, and encouraging help from the social network are not the responsibility of the home helps.

3.5   Problems and recent developments

Recent developments have already been discussed as part of the changes of the British system since April 1991. The public welfare services responsible for the care of the elderly are going through a period of uncertainty, even crisis. This makes it difficult for people in need to get the required care and leads to large differences between authorities.

The Audit Commission for Local Authorities and the NHS in England and Wales has identified some major problems in establishing the role of the local authorities in the new system [13]. Firstly, resistance of the social services departments is expected. The focus of community care shifts from the service provision to the service user. This presents a challenge to the traditional role and structures of the departments; established power structures and vested interests will be undermined. Secondly, the current system for policy making and operations in the local authorities seem to be inadequate for the new role. The needs within the community have to be defined and measured and new methods of priority or target setting and budget allocation need to be tested. The third main problem mentioned by the audit commission was the lack of co-operation between all agencies involved in community care, especially between the key agencies of social services and health care.

An important problem regarding the content of home care is that only the minority of dependent old people in the community with no source of family care get intensive state support from local social services. Even then the level of available provision is low related to the needs and therefore most people in this situation will finally enter residential care [20].

Another problem mentioned is the weak co-ordination and collaboration between formal and informal carers: where one is present, the other tends to withdraw [12].

Formal waiting lists for home help services, often a problem in other member states of the European Union, are rare in the United Kingdom. People either get care if the Local Authority or themselves are prepared to pay for it. Otherwise it is refused until further application.

4   Relations between home nursing and home help services

One of the major conditions for the new approach in home care is an extended co-operation between home nursing and home help services. The new legislation requires e.g. consultation between social services and health agencies [15]. Where more than one agency is involved in arranging for care to be delivered, the service delivery should be co-ordinated so that the users and carers experience a 'seamless' service.

In the public system, separate organizations exist for the provision of home nursing care on the one hand and home help services on the other hand. In the private sector, there are organizations which provide both home nursing and home help services.

The amount of co-operation between the organizations and their workers differs considerably between the regions. Few regions have a joint assessment procedure, in others pilot schemes of working in one team are tested, while in other regions no form of co-operation between these two kind of services exists.

There are mainly problems in the co-operation between home help services and home nursing services, especially regarding the blurring of roles between the home helps and auxiliary nurses. A possible solution is the introduction of the so called care manager to manage the care, from a variety of sources, for each individual. The care manager under the new legislation is supposed to co-ordinate the care. Evidence so far is that they have little influence over the supply of community nursing.

5 The financing of home nursing services

5.1 Payment and patients' insurance

As mentioned before, the NHS covers the whole population of the United Kingdom. About 15% of the population have an additional private health insurance [7], but usually this does not cover home nursing services. Public community nursing services are fully funded by the central government from general taxation. No co-payments are required.

In the United Kingdom, there are no national or other regulations stating the maximum amount of care a patient is entitled to receive. This fully depends on the assessment of needs by the team leader and the availability of nurses and care assistants in the team. In some areas care is guaranteed for 24 hours a day.

5.2 Funding of the organizations

The total amount of money available for public home nursing organizations comes from state taxes. Before the NHS reforms, the DHAs received a budget depending on the number of inhabitants and the demography of the population. Now services are purchased by fundholding GPs and DHAs. The funding of home nursing organizations, the so called NHS community trusts, is based on the services that they deliver to the patients of the GPs or the DHAs. The community units of the DHAs work with fixed budgets based on a so called case-load profile of the region.

The policy to discharge patients earlier from the hospitals has led to an increasing utilization of high tech nursing procedures in the community. However, this kind of care is very expensive and can not be paid from the general budget. Therefore the home nursing organizations have to negotiate with the local authorities for extra money to provide high tech care for each patient separately.

5.3 Payment of the nurses

District nurses as well as nursing auxiliaries are payed a fixed salary by the DHA, the NHS community trusts or GP fundholders. Since 1984, the salaries of nurses has been determined by an independent Pay Review Body appointed by the Prime Minister. NHS community trusts are able to set local pay, but so far only 2% have done so [21]. The level of payment of the nurses is related to the clinical grading system. Scales A to C are reserved for care assistants. In 1993, the wages of this category workers were between GBP 7,105 (start of scale A) and GBP 11,350 (end of scale C), gross a year. Qualified nurses start on grade D. A newly qualified staff nurse earned GBP 10,980, G-grade district nurses (often team leaders) earned between GBP 16,445 and GBP 19,030.

5.4   Problems and recent developments

The NHS reforms have consequences for the way home nursing activities are financed in the United Kingdom. The introduction of NHS community trusts on the one hand and the changing role of the local authorities and the introduction of GP fundholders on the other hand, indicate the allocation of the available money will take place through market mechanisms.

There are still a number of uncertainties and problems which have to be solved. For instance, there is the question as to whether fundholding GPs are allowed to purchase home nursing care outside their own district.

With regarding to the payment of the nurses, two sources of dissatisfaction can be noted. First, with the introduction of the clinical grading structure, in 1988, thousands of nurses felt they were wrongly graded and have been using the established appeals process to gain a fair grade ever since. A second problem is that the employers (local authorities, NHS community trusts) are often offering a lower clinical grade to the nurses than could be determined on the basis of their qualifications and actual tasks performed.

6   The financing of home help services

6.1   Payment and clients' insurance

Home help services are not covered by the social security system but are paid for and occasionally provided by local authorities only to a minority of people who pass through needs- and means-tests. These tests vary largely between the authorities.

Private health insurance almost always rules out home care of more than a few weeks. A few insurance companies are experimenting with the introduction of long-term care insurance but the premiums are too high to attract many consumers. They remain very rare.

The arrangements about co-payments for the home help services vary among the authorities because there are no national guidelines. A distinction is made between four types of arrangements [15]:

1. free service (no co-payment by clients);
2. flat-rate charge (each client pays the same amount regardless of the available means);
3. two-tier system whereby those on supplementary benefit (or equivalent income) receive free service or pay less than the other clients);
4. payment according to means (a means-tested sliding scale is used to determine the amount of co-payment).

In this unsettled period there is huge variety in the amounts paid.

The allocation of home help services is the responsibility of the authorities. In theory 1 to 1.5 hours are minimally provided per week. Maximum allocations are more likely to be subject to stricter guidelines. Some authorities set clear limits of hours while others operate a principle of providing whatever service is required to keep an individual in their own home [15]. The average hours home help services in the United Kingdom was 3.3 per week in 1986/87. This pattern of one to two hours a week is part of what the new system is designed to change. The aim is to target scarce hours more generously on those who need them (at the expense of those of lesser need who must now find and pay for their own care).

Finally, attention must be paid to the so called Attendance Allowance. This benefit is paid to people who need constant attention and help. Eligibility depends upon a doctor's assessment of the need of the client. His/her income is not taken into account [12]. People receiving this benefit are free to pay it to the carers they prefer: a relative, friend, neighbour or (commercial) care agency. The public social services have encouraged their clients to apply for the allowance and, later, charge them for the services they receive. In this way the costs of the care do not burden the budget of the local authorities.

6.2 Funding of organizations

The formal home help organizations are funded for 80% by general taxation. Recently, the out-of-pocket payments increased close to 20%.

As already described, the new system largely involves local authorities buying blocks of hours of home help from private agencies. The number of hours bought and provided varies enormously across the country.

It is estimated that in this transition period some 50% of home help agencies are exclusively for-profit while the remainder are voluntary or still run by local authorities.

6.3   Payment of the home helps

The whole system for contracting out of service provision is currently in flux with all sorts of models apparent. There are differences between the authorities but in general, home helps are paid per hour, mainly on a casual basis, with limited opportunities for a guaranteed number of hours per week.

There is no national salary scale for the remuneration of home helps as it exists for home nurses. However, there is a national salary structure for local authority manual workers including home helps. Under this agreement home helps were eligible for a gross weekly salary of GBP 159.99 in 1993. This is generally interpreted by local authorities as the minimum rate.

6.4   Problems and recent developments

The most relevant new developments have already been discussed in the previous sections. A changing situation leads to uncertainty and differences between local authorities and individual people or clients.

One of the major policy goals in the United Kingdom is the introduction of market mechanisms in the provision of health and social welfare. This development requires a clear distinction between purchasers and providers. Moreover, purchasers need money to buy cure, care, support and help from the providers. Two possible strategies can be followed. On the one hand local authorities or other public agencies can operate as the purchasers on behalf of the patients or clients. However, this may be insufficient to create and maintain a market. To enter the market and survive, organizations may be dependent upon individual purchasers using private income or benefits to add to the low and uncertain payment by social services departments. These payments can be low and uncertain because of possible competition between the organizations [19]. A second option is that money will be transferred to the people themselves e.g. by care-related benefits. However, a difficulty of this option is that the complex care system makes knowledge and expertise necessary to translate the available money into the provision of care.

Jack B.F. Hutten

Acknowledgement

The questionnaire about home help services was completed by John Baldock (Senior Lecturer in Social Policy, University of Kent, Canterbury). Prof. Karen Luker (Department of Nursing, University of Liverpool) and Mrs Sue Thomas (community health adviser, Royal College of Nursing, Department of Policy and Practice, London) provided most of the information about the home nursing services.

References

1 VERHEIJ, R.A., A. KERKSTRA. International comparative study of community nursing. Aldershot: Avebury, 1992.
2 BOERMA, W.G.W., F.A.J.M. DE JONG, P.H. MULDER. Health care and general practice across Europe. Utrecht: NIVEL, 1993.
3 OECD HEALTH DATA. Version # 1.5. Paris: OECD, 1993.
4 MAYNARD, A. Whither the national health service? In: Casparie, A.F., H.E.G.M. Hermans, J.H.P Paelinck (eds.). Competitive health care in Europe: future prospects. Aldershot: Dartmouth, 1990.
5 VREUGDENHIL, J.C., M. DE. BRUINE. Gezondheidszorg in Europa: structuur en financiering van de gezondheidszorg in enkele Europeses landen. Rotterdam: EUR, 1992.
6 MCCARTHY, M., ST. GEORGE D. Prospects in health care for the United Kingdom. In: Casparie, A.F., H.E.G.M. Hermans, J.H.P Paelinck (eds.). Competitive health care in Europe: future prospects. Aldershot: Dartmouth, 1990.
7 SCHNEIDER, M., RK-H. DENNERLEIN, A. KÖSE, L. SCHOLTES. Health care in the EC member states. Health Policy Special Issue. Health Policy; 1992, 1+2, 113-123.
8 HER MAJESTY'S STATIONERY OFFICE. Working for patients. London: january 31, 1989.
9 KEMENADE, Y.W. VAN. Health care in Europe. The finance and reimbursement systems of 18 European countries. Zoetermeer: Nationale Raad voor de Volksgezondheid, 1993.
10 DEPARTMENT OF HEALTH. The national health service and community care bill. London: Department of Health, 1989.

11 NIJKAMP, P., J. PACOLET, H. SPINNEWYN, A. VOLLERING, C. WILDEROM, S. WINTERS. Services for the elderly in Europe. A cross-national comparative study. Leuven/Amsterdam: HIV/VU, 1991.

12 BALDOCK, J. The welfare mix and the elderly in Britain. In: Everts, A., I. Svetlik (eds.). New welfare mixes in care for the elderly. Eurosocial reports vol 40. Vienna: European Centre for Social Welfare Policy and Research, 1991.

13 The Audit Commission for Local Authorities and the National Health Service in England and Wales. The community revolution: personal social services and community care......

14 PACOLET, J., C. WILDEROM (eds.). The economics of care of the elderly. Aldershot: Avebury, 1991.

15 LAWSON, R., B. DAVIES, A. BEBBINGTON. The home-help service in England and Wales. In: Jamieson, A. (eds.). Home care for older people in Europe. Oxford/New York/Tokyo: Oxford University Press, 1991.

16 FIELDING, N. Home cares guiding force. Community Care; 808, 1990, 14-15.

17 DEXTER, M., W. HARBERT. The home help service. London: Tavistock, 1983.

18 DEPARTMENT OF HEALTH. Staff of local authority social services at 30 September 1993. London: Department of Health, Statistics Division, 1993.

19 LEAT, D., C. UNGERSON. Creating care at the boundaries: issues in the supply and management of domiciliary care. Canterbury: University of Kent, Department of social policy, 1991.

20 BEBBINGTON, A., H. CHARNLEY. Community care for the elderly: rhetoric or reality. British Journal of Social Work; 20, 1990, 409-432.

21 ROYAL COLLEGE OF NURSING. Nursing pay. RCN factsheet 6, London: October, 1993.

22 NHS EXECUTIVE HEADQUATERS, LEEDS. Personal communication, October, 1994.

Appendix 1

List of participating experts

The following experts provided information on behalf of this study:

Belgium   Mr L. Geys, Head Nursing Department, National
               Federation of the White-Yellow Cross organizations,
               Brussels.
               Mr G. Hedebouw, Project leader Home Care and Care for
               the Elderly, HIVA (Higher Institute of Labour Studies),
               Catholic University of Leuven, Leuven.
Austria   Mrs R. Ertl, Dachverband wiener pflege- und social dienste,
               Wien.
               Mr Mag. P. Jakadofsky, Dachverband wiener pflege- und
               social dienste, Wien.
Denmark   Mr P. Sanderhof, Ministry of Social Affairs, Copenhagen.
               Mrs L. Holländer, Copenhagen Community.
Finland   Mrs A. Noro, researcher, STAKES, Helsinki.
France   Mrs C. Niclausse, CASSPA, Soissons.
               Prof J.C. Henrard, Université René Descartes, Laboratoire
               Santé et Veilleissement, Paris.
Germany   Mrs D. Wagner, Arbeiterwohlfahrt Bundesverband, Bonn.
Greece   Prof J. Kyriopoulos, professor of Health Economics,
               National School of Public Health, Athens.

Mr V. Margaritidou, Assistant Professor, Higher Technical Institution, Athens.

Mrs D. Andrioti, Research Fellow, Department of Health Economics, National School of Public Health, Athens.

Mrs M. Gitona, Research Fellow, Department of Health Economics, National School of Public Health, Athens.

Ireland Mr J. Larragy, the National Council for the Elderly, Dublin.

Italy Mrs G. Bon Trani, Radar Soc. Coop. A.R.L., Trieste.

Mrs C. Costanzi, Comune di Genova, Servici Sociali, Genova.

Dr A. De Benedetti, Cergas, Universita Bocconi, Milano.

Mrs H. Salini-Keen, Associazione Don Giuseppe Zilli, Milano.

Luxembourg Mr J. Hansen, Mr F. Bley and Mrs L. Deitz, Croix-Rouge Luxembourgeoise, Luxembourg.

Mr J. Thyes, Ministère de la Famille et de la Solidarité, Luxembourg.

Mr P. Campagna, Ministère de la Santé, Luxembourg.

Netherlands Dr A. Kerkstra, NIVEL foundation, Utrecht.

Portugal Drª H. Pontes Carreira, Ministry of Health, Department of research and planning, Lisbon.

Drª M. Joaquina Madeira of the General Directorate for Social Action, Lisbon.

Spain Mrs T. Moreno Casbas, Ministerio de Sanidad y Consumo, Subdireccion General de Difusion de la Investigación y Formación, Madrid.

Mrs N. Maymon Pijuan, Coordinadora del Programa de Atencion Domiciliaria de l'ABS centre Hospitalet de Llobregat, Barcelona.

Mrs C. Lacasa Plana, Servicio Catalan de Salud, Barcelona.

Mr M. Arribas, Subdirectora de Enfermería Area 5, Madrid.

Mrs C. Granda Menedez, Subdirectora de Enfermería Area 11, Madrid.

Mrs M. Custey Male, Directora de Enfermería Area 2, Madrid.

Mrs I. Garcia Mejido, Servicio Vasco de Salud.

Mrs I. Jordan Gil, Dirección de Atención Primaria Area 7, Zaragoza.

Appendix 1

Mrs J. Luis Vigil-Escalera Quintanal, Centro de Salud, Laviana, Asturias

Mrs M. Santamaria Zarain, Responsable del Trabajo Social en los Servicios de Asistencia Primaria y Comunitaria, Servicio Vasco de Salud.

Mr M. Gil Motalbo, Instituto Nacional de Servicios Sociales (INSERSO), Madrid.

Sweden   Mrs Y. Behr, Swedish Association of local authorities, Stockholm.

Mrs K. Einevik-Bäckstrand, SPRI, Stockholm.

Mrs R. Hedvall, SPRI, Stockholm.

United Kingdom Mr J. Baldock, Senior Lecturer in Social Policy, University of Kent, Canterbury.

Prof K. Luker, Department of Nursing, University of Liverpool.

Mrs S. Thomas, Community health adviser, Royal College of Nursing, Department of Policy and Practice, London.